European Economies

a comparative study

See also.

Andrew BOLTHO (1942) The European Economy
Growth & Crisis. Oxford University Press.

European Economies

a comparative study

Edited by Drs Frans J L Somers
Groningen Business School,
Hanse Polytechnic, Groningen

Contributors
Professor Rudi Kurz
Professor Milagros García Crespo
Professor Arantza Mendizábal
Dr Marisol Esteban
Kirk Thomson
Professor Andrea Fineschi
Dr Ian Stone

Pitman Publishing
128 Long Acre, London WC2E 9AN

A Division of Longman Group UK Limited

First published 1991
Reprinted 1992
© Milagros García Crespo, Andrea Fineschi, Rudi Kurz,
Frans Somers, Ian Stone, Kirk Thomson, 1991

British Library Cataloguing in Publication Data

European economies: a comparative study.
  I. Somers, Frans J.L.
  330.94

ISBN 0 273 03636 X

Printed in Great Britain by Dotesios Ltd, Trowbridge, Wiltshire

Contents

Part C: International comparisons

Part D: Statistical annexe

Preface

This book is concerned with the individual economies of the five major countries of the European Community (EC): Germany, France, the United Kingdom, Italy and Spain. These countries are by far the largest in terms of Gross Domestic Product, area and population in the EC.

Since the war Western Europe has experienced a strong trend towards economic and political integration. The European Community, founded in 1957 by six countries, nowadays comprises twelve members. Within the EC the progress towards integration has been accelerated by the adoption of the Single European Act at the end of 1985, which sets the route for the achievement of a European Single Market before the end of 1992. The final goal of the Act is the foundation of a European Economic and Political Union, mainly based on the principles of a free market economy (*see* part A in this book).

Although Western Europe is moving towards being an economic entity, many differences will remain between individual countries in the Community in terms of economic structure, national policies, labour market, industry, trade patterns, etc.; not to mention distinctions in mentalities, tastes and cultures.

This book is intended to provide a basic understanding, within a limited space, of the economies of the major countries of the Community. It focuses on long-term developments and underlying trends rather than on short-term economic surveys. In this respect it differs greatly from the existing publications from international organisations like the OECD. Special attention is paid to the strengths and weaknesses of each economy, its dominant industries, trade patterns and future perspectives within the emerging common market (part B).

In section C comparisons are made between the countries involved. Differences and similarities in the fields of government involvement, output and growth, productivity and competitiveness and the financial system are mentioned and possible fields of specialisation are identified.

The book concludes with a uniform Statistical Annexe with harmonised data, mainly based on Eurostat and OECD sources (part D). In other parts of this book, referrals to tables in this Annexe are frequently made (prefixed with a D).

At the end of the country chapters in part B the reader will find lists of information sources where additional information on the country concerned can be found (other publications, statistical institutions, government and private agencies).

The book thus serves as an accessible introductory text, giving the reader a basic grasp of the economic structure of the major European countries, as well as a source of information for further investigations. In this sense, it can be used to 'guide' study of the economies of the main EC countries.

The book is aimed at students in business schools, polytechnics and universities. It can be used for business environment studies, EC courses, course offerings focusing on economic policies, preparation for studies abroad.

This publication is the result of a considerable exercise in international co-operation. The chapters on the individual countries are exclusively prepared by contributors living in that particular country: Professor Rudi Kurz from Germany, Professor Andrea Fineschi from Italy, Dr Ian Stone from the UK, Kirk Thomson and Rachel Condon from France and Professor Milagros García Crespo, Dr Marisol Esteban and Professor Arantza Mendizábal from Spain.

The editing, introductory chapter and chapter on international comparisons was done by someone from a 'neutral' country: the Netherlands.

Most of the participants in this project are working for institutions co-operating in international programmes with Hanse Polytechnic Groningen, having its seat in that country.

In total citizens from six EC member states were involved in this project. It did not turn out to be a barrier to a very fruitful co-operation and intensive and interesting discussions.

Frans Somers
Groningen, The Netherlands
January 1991

Contributors

Frans Somers (*Editor*) is Lecturer in Economics at the Hanse Polytechnic, Groningen, The Netherlands, and is also manager of International Projects and International Liaison Officer at that institution. Since graduating in 1973, he has worked mainly in the field of higher education and has so far published four books; one on political economy (1980), two on macroeconomics (1988 and 1990) and one on government policy (1900). From 1988 to 1990 he was Editor-in-Chief of an economics magazine intended for business students and lecturers.

Professor Rudi Kurz worked for ten years as a research fellow and as Deputy Managing Director at the Institute for Applied Economic Research Tübingen (IAW). He prepared studies and specialist reports for the German Federal Ministry of Commerce and for the Commission of the European Community during that time. He has undertaken research and has given lectures in the United States and was guest scholar at the Brookings Institution, Washington DC. He has been Professor of Economics at the Pforzheim Business School (FHW) and consultant to the IAW since 1988.

Milagros García Crespo is Professor of Applied Economics at the University of the Basque Country. She was Head of the Faculty of Economics in Bilbao from 1982 to 1987. Her interests in European issues led her to set up in 1983 a European Documentation Centre at the same University. She established and maintained links with European academic institutions (Kingston Polytechnic in London, Université de Grenoble). From 1987 to 1989 she was Councillor of Economy to the Basque Government. In 1989 she was appointed First President of the Public Accounts Court of the Basque Country, a post that she currently holds. She is the author of many books and articles on economic policy, the Spanish economy and European issues.

Arantza Mendizábal is Professor in Economics in the Faculty of Economics and Business Administration of the University of the Basque Country in Bilbao where she has been Rector of the University. She has considerable experience on economic policy issues and has written widely on the economy of the Basque Country. She is currently a member of the Central Parliament in Madrid.

Marisol Esteban is a Lecturer in Urban and Regional Economics at the Faculty of Economics and Business Administration of the University of the Basque Country in Bilbao, where she has also lectured on Contemporary Spanish Economy. Her special fields of interest include land and housing markets and policies, labour markets and regional economic development. She has published articles on these topics and has done consultancy work for the Basque administration.

Kirk Thomson studied at the London School of Economics, the Free University of Berlin and at the Sorbonne. He is now Director of Studies at the Ecole des Practiciens du Commerce International in Paris, where he also lectures in Economics and on aspects of the European Community.

Andrea Fineschi is 'professore straordinario' of poltical economy at the University of Messina after previously teaching in the universities of Siena and Florence. His special fields of interest include aspects of economic theory of the classical economists and problems of the Italian economy.

Dr Ian Stone is a Senior Lecturer in Economics and Head of the Newcastle Economic Research Unit at the University of Northumbria & Newcastle. He has previously held lecturing posts at the Victoria University of Wellington (New Zealand) and the University of Newcastle upon Tyne. His earlier research and publications were in the field of Third World development. Since the early 1980s his research interests have been directed towards aspects of industrial and regional economics in a UK context, and he has recently completed a major study on inward investment and labour markets for the government's Employment Department.

Part A

Introduction

1 The European Community

Drs Frans Somers

1.1 Introduction

Since the signing of the Treaty of Rome in 1957 the European integration has made significant progress. It is intended that the internal market will be completed before the end of 1992 and there are serious plans for achieving an economic and monetary union before the end of the millennium. Does this mean that it is no longer necessary to study the existing national economies? Certainly not.

In the first place there are still substantial differences between these countries in terms of economic performance as well as in government policies. Possibly they will be reduced in the future; economic convergence and policy harmonisation are prerequisites for further integration.

Apart from the variations in performance and policies there are considerable distinctions in economic structure between the Member States. Every country has its own industrial structure and business traditions, reflecting historical circumstances, comparative advantage, government decisions, geographical conditions and chance. Even a successful integration does not necessarily mean that these categories of differences will disappear; some features may be reinforced. Integration can lead to more specialisation, because it is to be hoped that full exposure to international competition will result in a better allocation of factors of production. This reallocation may be realised on the basis of existing industry patterns, comparative advantage, development of new trade relations, etc.

In this book we will examine the economies of the five major countries of the European Community: Germany, Italy, the United Kingdom, France and Spain. Within the Community, they are by far the most important in terms of Gross Domestic Product (GDP) and population. Together they accounted in 1990 (including East Germany) for 87% of the total Community GDP and for 84% of its population. France,

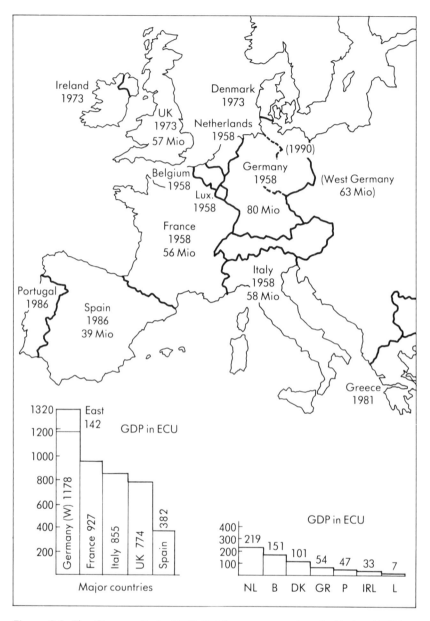

Figure 1.1 The Community in 1990. GDP at current prices in Mrds of ECU (European Commission estimates); Total GDP EC = 4870 Mrd ECU; East Germany (former GDR) rough estimate; Population in millions (indicated on map); Total population EC (including East Germany) 345 Mio.
Source: European Commission, European Economy, DEC. 1990

Italy and (the Federal Republic of) Germany have been Members from the start in 1958; the UK entered, after a long period of reluctance in 1973 and Spain joined only in 1986 after the disappearance of the undemocratic Franco regime. In Figure 1.1 some data on the five major EC countries are presented, to facilitate comparison of the main features.

This introductory chapter will start with a discussion of the European integration process: its origins, aims, progress and policies involved. The next subject will be the size and relative strength and importance of the European Community as an entity. The chapter ends with a brief discussion of the main economic indicators of the five economies concerned.

Within this framework, the national economies will be studied in more detail in the other parts of the book. Special attention will be paid to their institutional and historical background, industrial structure, trade patterns, strong and weak points and problems and prospects within a future united Europe.

1.2 The European integration

1.2.1 *The origins of the European integration process*

After the Second World War there was a very strong impetus in Europe towards international co-operation. Several reasons contributed to this attitude. First of all there were economic considerations. The war left Europe with immense physical destruction, loss of capital goods and an impoverished population. In order to revitalise the European economy the United States introduced the Marshall Plan in 1948 (by means of the Foreign Assistance Act). The plan was intended to provide Europe with sufficient funds and goods to carry out the necessary recovery programmes. The US aid was granted on a *European* rather than on a *national* basis. A special international institution, the Organisation for European Economic Co-operation (OEEC), was created to distribute the aid among the member countries and to co-ordinate the assistance programmes. Within the framework of the plan, separate measures were taken to intensify the intra-European trade.

The OEEC, however, was not abolished after the termination of the Marshall Plan in 1950. It continued to promote the liberalisation of international trade and economic co-operation. In 1961 it transformed itself into the Organisation of Economic Co-operation and Development (OECD), an organisation eligible for all developed industrial countries in the Western World.

A second driving force behind the European integration was the

Soviet threat and the beginning of the Cold War. By the end of the 1940s the division of Europe into a Western part and a Soviet-dominated sphere became apparent, after Soviet-inspired Communist take-overs in Romania (1945), Bulgaria (1946), Hungary, Poland (1947) and Czechoslovakia (1948). In response to this development a range of organisations was established, e.g. the West European Union (WEU), NATO (both in 1948) and the Council of Europe in 1949. Objectives of these organisations were not merely defence against the Soviet threat, but also the protection of values such as freedom, democracy and human rights.

A last but not least incentive for West European integration was formed by the 'German question'. After two world wars, a completely independent Germany was considered to be a potential danger to peace. A solution to this problem would be to link the newly established Federal Republic of Germany as solidly as possible to the other European countries.

This question became urgent in the light of what was seen as the increasing Soviet threat to Europe. A strong Europe, both in the military and the economic sense, was thought to be absolutely necessary. A German contribution to the strengthening of Western Europe was of great importance, though care had to be taken to avoid allowing Germany once more the opportunity to dominate its neighbours militarily and politically. For these reasons the French Minister of Foreign Affairs Jean Monnet came up with his plan in 1950 to place the European coal and steel industries under one single supranational authority and to establish a common market in this field. This plan would enable a rapid expansion of these industries, which are of vital importance for the defence industry and overall economic development, without allowing the new West German state full control over them. Besides France and Germany, other European countries were also invited to participate in this arrangement.

As a result, the European Coal and Steel Community (ECSC) was established (*Treaty of Paris*) in the spring of 1951 by France, the Federal Republic of Germany, Italy, Belgium, the Netherlands and Luxembourg. The foundation for the construction of a much more extended European Community was laid. For several reasons important countries like the UK stayed out for the time being. Attempts to arrive at a common army by the same six countries (the European Defence Community (EDC)) in the beginning of the 1950s failed, however. It would have required a supranational political power, which was too advanced a notion at that time. Co-operation was first sought, then, in the economic field on a more modest basis. So the Six founded the European Economic Community (EEC) and the European Atomic Energy Commission (Euratom) in 1957 by the *Treaty of Rome*. Euratom was designed for the peaceful development of nuclear energy. The treaties came into effect on January 1, 1958.

1.2.2 *Towards an economic and political union*

A major difference between the ECSC and the EEC at that time was that the EEC was hardly equipped with supranational powers; the main decision-making body within the EEC was the Council of Ministers (of Foreign Affairs), leaving considerable powers to the national authorities. Important decisions could only be taken by unanimity.

Despite this, the Treaty of Rome envisaged progress towards a kind of economic union. Article 2 of the Treaty of Rome states that:

> The Community shall have as its task, by *establishing a common market* and *progressively approximating the economic policies of the Member States*, to promote throughout the Community a harmonious development of economic activities, a continuous and balanced expansion, an increase in stability, an accelerated rise of the standard of living and closer relations between the States belonging to it.

The three Communities (ECSC, Euratom and EEC) duly amalgamated in 1967 to form the European Community (EC).

According to Article 8 of the Treaty of Rome a Common Market was to be reached within 12 years (from 1958). The members came nowhere near reaching this target. A *Common Market* can be defined as an association of nations with free trade among its members, a common external tariff and a free mobility of production factors. If in addition the economic policies are harmonised then the association is called an Economic Union.

By 1970 only the first two of these objectives had been met; the removal of all internal tariffs and quota restrictions and the erecting of a common external tariff. Free mobility of production factors and a substantial harmonisation of economic policies were not realised before 1970 and even not as yet (1990). A number of factors can be held responsible for the slowness of the integration process.

First, there is the question of national interests. A real economic union means that the bulk of national power should be transferred to supranational authorities. This would imply a substantial loss of national sovereignty for member states. From the very beginning of the EEC in 1958, however, individual member states have been reluctant to accept this idea. According to the Treaty of Rome, decision-making by unanimity should have been replaced in 1966 by qualified majority voting for a wide range of issues. Because of the French opposition, however, member states kept a right of veto in situations where vital national interests are involved (the Luxembourg compromise of 1966). In the 1970s and 1980s it was mainly the UK which tried to slow down the integration process for nationalistic reasons.

A second factor preventing rapid progress towards economic union was the frequent enlargements of the EC. The UK, Ireland and Denmark joined the EC in 1973, Greece in 1981 and Spain and Portugal in 1986. These enlargements shifted the political attention to other questions and made the negotiations on common policies even more complicated.

Third, the economic crises of the 1970s and the beginning of the 1980s created an unfavourable climate for free trade. National governments were inclined to return to protectionist policies and to support national industries in order to counter the effects of the international crises upon the national economy.

In the early 1980s, however, the drive towards European integration received new impetus. During the economic crises of these years it became clear that the problems in Europe were intensified because producers in the Community were losing ground to their main competitors in Japan and the USA. The fragmented home market of the Community was seen as a major reason for this development, and a call for the speeding up the integration process was made. A single European market, it was argued, would stimulate economies of scale in production, marketing, research and development and also strengthen competition, enhancing efficiency and competitiveness of European industry.

A necessary condition for accelerating the completion of the internal market was a change of the Community decision-making process, which till then required unanimity on most issues. This condition was met by the adoption of the *Single European Act* in 1985, whereby in matters concerning the internal market the condition of unanimity was replaced by a qualified majority. The Act, which after ratification of all 12 members came into force in 1987, also contained the provision that the internal market should be completed before the end of 1992. In addition to setting a timetable for the completion of an 'internal market without frontiers' the Single Act also amended the original Treaty of Rome by adopting policies in the field of economic and social cohesion, environment, monetary and political co-operation etc. The Single Act can be seen as a major, but not as the last step towards the final goal of an economically united Europe.

This goal is supposed to be achieved by the establishing of an Economic and Monetary Union (EMU), which requires a far-reaching co-ordination of monetary and economic policies of the Member States. Monetary policy, for instance, should be largely transferred from national authorities to an independent European Central Bank (*Eurofed*) and national currencies replaced by one common currency, for which Eurofed will set the interest rates. In the field of fiscal policy national governments will keep more autonomy, but their control will be considerably limited by common policies and restrictions.

In the EC summit meeting of October 1990 broad outlines of the treaty on EMU were set. EMU should be reached in three stages; the last one should be completed by the second half of the decade. As control has to be surrendered for a great deal to supranational powers, EMU can in fact not be realised without *political integration*, at least to some extent.

That is why not one, but two inter-governmental EC conferences were held in December 1990 to work out the plans on further integration: one on EMU and the other on political union. At these conferences, it was decided that a new constitution for the EC should come into force in January 1993, at the same time as the completion of the internal market. The constitution will provide for an introduction in stages of EMU and political union, based on two new treaties. Guidelines for the contents of these treaties were established. In the political field for instance, the European Parliament should be given more law-making power. For EMU the three-stages plan, developed by the EC commission, headed by the Frenchman Delors, will serve as a draft treaty. Definite decisions by governments will be taken on new summits in 1991, leaving the year 1992 for national parliaments to ratify them.

It is not certain that all plans will really be carried out. Many problems have to be solved and it is not clear yet if all participants (governments, parliaments) will fully agree with the proposals, but the trend towards some kind of *federal Europe* seems to be irreversible.

1.3 Main objectives and policies of the European Community

1.3.1 *A free and single market*

The overall objective of the European Community is, according to Article 2 of the Treaty of Rome, the promotion of a harmonious development of economic growth and the accelerated increase of welfare and the standard of living in its Member States. Such an objective could be reached in different ways. But it is crystal clear that the Community opted for *the free market* as the main instrument to achieve its goals and not planning or other state interventionist strategies. A large, free and competitive market is expected to create improved efficiency of production, more economies of scale, an optimal allocation of factors of production, and to stimulate research and development. This would, in turn, lead to lower unit costs and increased competitiveness of European industry. Government involvement, on the contrary, is generally considered as detrimental to competition and the optimal allocation of the factors of production. For this reason Article 2 focuses on the establishment of a Common Market as the main tool for the achievement of a higher level of welfare. The necessity of approximation of economic

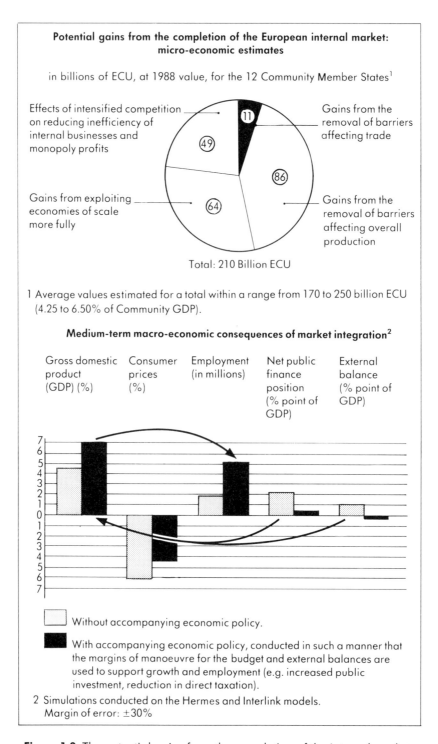

**Potential gains from the completion of the European internal market:
micro-economic estimates**

in billions of ECU, at 1988 value, for the 12 Community Member States[1]

Effects of intensified competition on reducing inefficiency of internal businesses and monopoly profits

Gains from the removal of barriers affecting trade

Gains from exploiting economies of scale more fully

Gains from the removal of barriers affecting overall production

Total: 210 Billion ECU

1 Average values estimated for a total within a range from 170 to 250 billion ECU (4.25 to 6.50% of Community GDP).

Medium-term macro-economic consequences of market integration[2]

Gross domestic product (GDP) (%) Consumer prices (%) Employment (in millions) Net public finance position (% point of GDP) External balance (% point of GDP)

☐ Without accompanying economic policy.

■ With accompanying economic policy, conducted in such a manner that the margins of manoeuvre for the budget and external balances are used to support growth and employment (e.g. increased public investment, reduction in direct taxation).

2 Simulations conducted on the Hermes and Interlink models.
Margin of error: ±30%

Figure 1.2 The potential gains from the completion of the internal market
Source: Commission of the European Communities

policies (also in Article 2) is based on the idea that harmonisation of national policies is required to ensure fair competition and to avoid uncertainty in international trade relations. For instance, different tax systems create unequal production costs and profit opportunities and hence discriminate between producers of different Member States. The same applies to subsidies, environmental policies, social security policies, health and safety standards and quality controls.

The stress put on the free market as a method to gain a higher level of productivity, income and employment and to reduce costs and prices is also embodied in the European Single Act. In the so-called Cecchini Report, prepared by order of the European Commission, the benefits of the internal market will be derived in a large part from *enhanced competition* within a deregulated internal market. A second factor is the *increased scale* of production. Competition and scale are mutually reinforced by each other. See Figure 1.2, where the potential gains from the completion of the internal market (according the Cecchini Commission) are summarised.

In the report, the medium-term economic advantages from 1988 (within 5–6 years) were estimated to be within a range of 170 to 250 billion ECUs, the real Community GDP would go up by an extra 5 to 7% and there would be an additional employment creation of 2 to 5 million jobs.

Competition will be encouraged by:

- the removal of entrance barriers erected by national frontiers;
- the opening of (national) public procurement markets;
- the elimination or reduction of (national) monopolies;
- market deregulation and liberalisation; for instance in the area of financial markets.

This enhanced competition is expected to lead to a fall in production costs, gains in efficiency and price reductions.

Besides the static effects there are also dynamic effects to be expected from the completion of the internal market.

A more competitive environment is an essential element determining the pace of technological innovation, according to the Cecchini Commission. Pursuit of economies of scale and competition together will encourage the emergence of large, truly European companies, better equipped to compete with US and Far Eastern companies and to conquer strong market positions. Hence the internal market will eventually affect economic structures which, in turn, will produce an accelerated growth.

It has not been said that there is no room for the role of government in a united Europe. The Treaty of Rome already explicitly identifies a number of common policies to be adopted, e.g. in the field of competition, agriculture, transport, monetary relations, external trade, taxation and social security. Implicitly it also deals with regional policies. In addition, the European Single Act mentions common policies in the area of environment and scientific and technological development. Most of these policies are intended to:

- ensure free competition on fair terms;
- guarantee stability and
- provide (quasi) public goods.

1.3.2 *Common policies*

Competition rules

The Community has adopted, for instance, rather strict *competition rules*. These forbid restrictive agreements and practices, which affect trade between Member States and the abuse of a dominant position by firms and (national) government aid to businesses. EC competition law has precedence over national legislation, but it does not replace it. It is mainly intended to secure free competition. National regulations are generally much more tolerant, with clear exceptions in the cases of Germany and the UK.

Taxation, social and environmental policies

As has been said before (common) *taxation, social* and *environmental policies* are adopted principally to guarantee fair competition, because taxes, social security contributions and pollution standards, for instance, affect costs of production. Harmonisation and standardisation of tax rates, pollution norms, health requirements and so forth are primary objectives of these policies. The provision of social services, health services and education are to be left to national governments; they are considered to be an accepted matter of national sovereignty.

Environment protection, however, has received greater priority recently, especially since the adoption of the Single Act. The increasing pollution problem does not stop at frontiers and is therefore automatically a matter of common concern. A clean environment can also be considered as a public good, which probably can be secured most appropriately through the intervention of a supranational authority.

So far, however, there has not been great progress in the harmonisation of taxes. Decision-making with respect to taxation requires unanimity of the Council of Ministers, even after the adoption of the European Single Act. This is so because taxation affects preeminently the sovereignty of national states.

Transport policy

For international trade *transport costs* are of vital importance; they are in fact part of production costs. In many countries, however, elements of the transport sector are heavily subsidised. This is so because transport generates considerable external benefits, e.g. in the field of environment protection, energy conservation, infrastructure and industrial development. Transport can, in fact, be considered as a quasi public good: although the criteria of non-rivalry in consumption and non-excludability of benefits are not applicable in this area, it is nevertheless at least partly provided by government. Without a common policy in this respect, production costs could be distorted by differences in national policies.

Monetary policy

The Community's *monetary policy* was introduced primarily to eliminate uncertainty in international economic relations. Wildly fluctuating currencies have a negative impact on international trade, because they make international transactions more risky. The call for a European stabilisation policy especially arose after the collapse of the Bretton Woods' fixed exchange rate system in 1971. After some earlier attempts to reach a common arrangement, the European Monetary System (EMS) came into force in 1979. All Community countries of that time became members, except for the UK which entered only in October 1990. Of the later entrants (Greece, Portugal and Spain), only Spain has joined the system (in 1989).

Within the EMS arrangement, currencies are only allowed to fluctuate within narrow ranges of ± 2.25% around a central rate (Spain and the UK temporarily ± 6%). These bilateral central rates are calculated on the basis of the ECU (European Currency Unit), a weighted average of all existing currencies (the Luxembourg and the Belgian franc are considered as one currency). Fixed exchange rates have very wide repercussions on other economic policies.

With the exchange rates more or less fixed, it becomes very difficult for Member States to conduct independent economic policies. Exchange rate management (or tariffs) cannot be used any more to adjust balance-of-payments imbalances. So inflation and productivity rates and taxes must be brought into line with each other. Monetary integration cannot be realistically envisaged without economic and even political integration.

This is one of the reasons why the Community is trying to establish an Economic and Monetary Union (EMU) in which the EMS should be incorporated. It is intended to reach EMU in three stages. The first stage includes the completion of the internal market and the free movement of capital. In the second stage, beginning in 1993, it is intended to create a European Central Bank (Eurofed) and closer economic convergence. In stage three a common European currency should replace the national currencies. A great deal of national fiscal and other economic policies would have to be transferred to Community authorities by then.

The conclusion so far is that most of the common policies support the working of the free market rather than hindering it. They create, in fact, the necessary conditions for the operation of the market or are intended to reduce market imperfections.

Agricultural policy

There are some major exceptions, however, like the agricultural policy and the regional and industrial policies.

The Common Agricultural Policy (CAP) is very important in the Community. It is responsible for almost three-quarters of the expenditure of the Community Budget (which, apart from that, is fairly small). Agriculture is heavily subsidised and highly protected within the Community; it is certainly not left to the forces of the market. The main reason for this policy is that the Community wants to stay self-sufficient in food production, which is of vital interest for any society. As a consequence of this principle, producers are guaranteed a fair standard of living, mainly be setting minimum prices and the levying of tariffs for food imports. Other goals of the CAP are the stabilisation of markets, regular supplies and reasonable prices for consumers. The latter would, however, be much lower in many cases if there were no CAP at all. The CAP is heavily criticised, because of its interventionist approach, which causes high costs and has discriminating effects on non-EC suppliers; but there is also a strong political lobby in its favour.

Regional policy

Like agricultural policy, *regional policy* is also not in line with the general market orientation of the Community. It is mainly adopted to support weak regions within the Community. As can be seen in Figure 1.3, there are large regional differences in terms of wealth within the Community.

Portugal, Greece, Spain and Ireland have *per capita* incomes far below the EC average for all regions. The poorest region is situated in North Portugal, with a *per capita* income of about 45% of EC average (in 1986).

Among some of the more wealthy countries considerable regional disparities are to be found. The peripheral regions of the UK (including Scotland, the North of England, Northern Ireland and Wales) and the South of Italy are notable for their lower levels of income, emigration and limited job opportunities compared to the national average. *Per capita* income in Italy's *Mezzogiorno* is only two-thirds of the EC average. In most cases lower income regions are less developed rural areas (Portugal, Greece, Spain). Other regions have problems due to decline in the staple industries, such as coal and steel, textiles, shipyards (North of

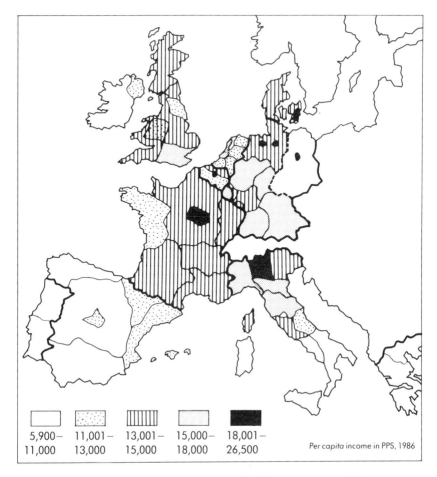

Figure 1.3 GDP in purchasing power standards per region, 1986
Source: Eurostat, European Commission

England, Wales, parts of Belgium and North of Spain), or because of an unfavourable geographical position (e.g. too far away from the centres of economic activity).

Wealth is generally concentrated in large urban areas, like the Paris region (Ile de France) with a *per capita* income of 165% of EC-average, the region around Milan (Lombardia, 137%), Hamburg (183%) and Bremen (147%), London (the South-East of England, 125%), Brussels (155%) and Copenhagen (138%). So the disparities between the different regions are very substantial. The problem is that in practice they have a natural tendency to intensify. The prosperous centres are more attractive for new industries because of the availability of a developed infrastructure, skilled labour, suppliers, output markets and generally also because of their accessibility. This produces a very unbalanced development.

Free movement of labour and capital within the EC can worsen this situation, because these factors of production are seeking the highest yields. The conclusion is that economic integration can even reinforce regional imbalances; but these imbalances in turn can be a (political) threat to further integration. Convergence in economic performance is of great importance for integration.

For this reason the EC applies regional policies to counterbalance the unequal development and to support the weaker regions.

These policies are additional to national policies and consist of public aid to local industries, investment in infrastructure, loans for restructuring industries etc. An important role in the regional policy is played by the European Regional Development Fund (ERDF), which was set up in 1975 to channel the aid. Funds are also distributed by the European Investment Bank, the European Social Fund and other institutions.

The effects of EC regional policies are limited, however. The EC funds set aside for these purposes are fairly small; only a fraction of the CAP budget, for example, and much smaller than the national funds.

Industrial policy

Industrial policy (apart from competition policy) can be defined as government actions to influence industry and thus be considered as a state interventionist policy. It is a highly debated issue within the Community. On the one hand it used to be heavily supported by countries with a rich national tradition in this respect like France and Italy, while countries like Germany (the FRG), the Netherlands and the UK were generally more in favour of liberal economic policies.

Industrial policy was not explicitly included within the Treaty of Rome. In the first decades of the Community's existence it was mainly used to restructure declining industries like coal, steel, shipyards, textiles and clothing. In terms of money Community involvement with industry was of limited significance in this period though.

In the 1980s attention shifted to the more advanced industries such as information technology, telecommunications and nuclear energy. Several programmes were adopted to promote Research and Development for high-technology industries. The ESPRIT (European Programme for Research and Development in Information Technology) was launched in 1983 to support joint private R&D in the information industry. It has been followed by further programmes such as ESPRIT II, RACE and BRITE, supporting private joint R&D in the field of advanced technology.

Since 1984, co-operation between companies in the area of R&D has been granted a 'block exemption' from competition rules. In the Single European Act the Treaty of Rome was changed in order to give this technology support a legal basis. In so-called 'Framework Programmes', with a duration of four years, goals are defined and budgets assigned. The Framework Programme of 1987–1991 is provided with a budget of 6.5 billion ECU.

The main ground for this heavy emphasis on technology support is that the Community fears it will lose the technology race to Japan and the USA.

Advocates of this policy argue that there are substantial external benefits and economies of scale related to R&D. These market imperfections can be offset by government support to industry in this respect.

Opponents stress that state intervention constitutes a potential danger for free international trade, because subsidies distort prices and provoke similar reactions by the governments of trading partners.

1.3.3 *Conclusion*

The European integration process is based on a market-oriented approach. Besides some clear exceptions, most of its policies are designed to realise a large, free, internal market characterised by a strong and fair competition.

This approach is not very remarkable when we put it in a historical context. The very start of the integration process was made right after the war, with the adoption of the Marshall Plan, which strongly reflected American free-market ideas. During the era of the Cold War attempts were made to build up a strong counter force to the Communist threat in Europe and to defend freedom and democracy. In the beginning the general idea was that this should be a military and political power, as was reflected by the proposals for the European Defence Community and the ECSC during the early 1950s. But in a later stage, emphasis shifted to economic power. The large and free market should play an important role in the development of such a power as can be observed in the Treaty of Rome for instance. The adoption of the European Single Act finally can be considered as a European attempt to keep up with the USA and Japan; countries with very large competitive home markets. The Act was brought about in a period in which free market ideologies were generally very dominant.

The bringing into line of national and EC policies constitutes a major challenge over the coming years. Although most EC countries have shifted their policies towards less state intervention and more supply-side oriented practices, considerable differences still remain in their approaches, e.g. between France on the one hand and Germany on the other (see part C of this book). Another problem undermining the market-based integration is the disparities between regions. Spain and Portugal were granted a transition period to the end of 1992 to adapt their economies to the more developed EC standards. But if the inequalities do not disappear, or are even reinforced, then the pressure for state intervention and protectionist measures will grow. The last decade, clearly, has not been marked by a tendency towards economic convergence, although some progress has been made in the second half.

1.4 The EC: size and relative importance

As a single entity, the European Community is one of the three dominant economic blocs in the world. With a GDP of 4729 billion ECU the EC surpassed, in 1990, the USA, which had a GDP of 4311 billion ECU in that year. Japan followed (still) at some distance with 2264 billion ECU. These figures, however, are strongly dependent on exchange rates (the

Table 1.1 Main economic indicators 1990 EC, USA, Japan

	EC	USA	Japan
Population (millions)	345	251	124
Gross domestic product (GDP)			
current market prices (billion ECU)	4728	4311	2264
per head, PPS, EC = 100%	100	151	120
Unemployment rate	8.5	5.4	2.2
average 1981–1990	9.6	7.1	2.5
Inflation			
(average GDP deflator 1981–1990)	6.8	4.2	1.4
Gross fixed capital formation	20.8	16.0	33.9
(% of GDP at current market prices)			
Private consumption	61.5	66.7	56.3
(% of GDP at market prices)			
Nominal unit labour costs	87.4	101.4	117.0
(relative to 19 industrial countries			
double export weights, 1980 = 100)			
Exports of goods and services	9.1*	9.9	13.9
(% of GDP at current market prices)			
Imports of goods and services			
(% of GDP at current market prices)	10.1*	11.2	12.5
Current balance	−0.3	−1.7	1.6

* External exports/imports

Source: European Economy December 1990
Figures based on European Commission estimates, November 1990

dollar and the yen depreciated considerably against the ECU in 1990). In terms of population, also, the EC leads with 345 million inhabitants compared to 251 million in the USA and 124 million in Japan (in 1990). United States citizens are on average by far the richest in the world. Measured in purchasing power index figures their average income was 151 in 1990, Japan being second with 120 and the EC third with 100. Nevertheless, the EC, and especially Japan, are catching up (the latter very rapidly); in 1960 the USA was still leading with 189 against 100 for the EC and only 56 for Japan.

The relative strength of the Japanese economy can also be seen in the very favourable unemployment and inflation figures and the large current account surplus. The negative trend of the double-weighted unit labour costs are not caused by internal factors but largely by the strong appreciation of the yen at the end of the 1980s.

Notable also is the large proportion spent on investment in Japan and the relatively low level of spending on consumption. Gross fixed capital formation amounted to 33.9% in 1990; the estimated figure for the whole decade is about 30%. This indicates that Japan puts heavy stress on technical innovation and the growth of its production capacity. The Japanese stance is in strong contrast to that of the USA, where gross investment is relatively low and consumption high. The EC occupies a position in between, but it is closer to that of the USA.

A break-down at industry level shows that the Community, compared with Japan and the USA, has the largest market shares (in terms of value-added) in industrial activities with a moderate or even weak growth in demand. Examples of these industries are: food products, tobacco, beverages, textiles, leather, clothing and metal products. In strong demand sectors, like office and data processing machines, electrical and electronic goods and chemical products, the Community is clearly surpassed by the United States and, despite its bigger size (in terms of GDP and population), its market share is hardly bigger than that of Japan. The conclusion is that the proportion of Community industry in the strong demand sector in relation to the whole of Community industry is obviously smaller than that of the two other blocs. Products of industries in strong demand sectors generally have a high technological content and require huge R&D investment. They are normally only produced on a very large scale to cover development costs. A large home market is a prerequisite for these products.

The awareness of a growing gap between the Community and its two rivals in the field of fast growing high-tech industries had become a major driving force behind the speeding up of the integration process within the Community at the end of the 1980s. The Community's industries can only keep up if they operate within a large unfragmented internal market, as is proposed by the 1992 initiative. Relative backwardness in the

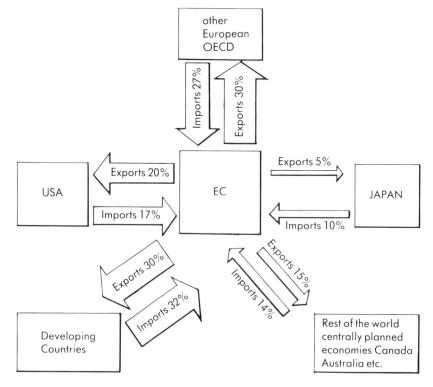

Figure 1.4 Extra-Community trade in percentages in 1988. Total exports: 366 billion ECU; Total imports: 383 billion ECU.

technological field also explains the recent emphasis on joint R&D research in the Community's industrial policy.

The current account of the EC is in balance; in contrast with that of Japan which over many years has shown a large surplus and that of the USA, which has a large deficit (see Figure 1.4).

Exports and imports of goods and services constituted about 10% of GDP in the three blocs (besides the 13.9% exports of GDP of Japan) in 1990.

Developing countries and other European OECD (non-EC) countries are by far the most important trading partners for the Community, each accounting for about 30% of extra-Community exports and for 32 and 27% respectively of its imports (in 1988, see Figure 1.4). Exports to the USA and Japan accounted only for 25% of total EC exports and imports from these countries for 27%. The trade deficit with Japan reached 23 billion ECU in 1988.

The Japanese trade pattern is completely different. About 58% of total exports of the country of the Rising Sun went to the EC and the USA and 32% of its imports originated from these areas.

The trade between the three dominant blocs is clearly out of balance; a problem which has provoked many disputes. The USA reproach the EC for using unfair trade practices like subvention and protection, especially in the field of agriculture. Americans fear that despite its free market rhetoric, the EC will construct a 'Fortress Europe', with little access for foreign exports. The EC, for its part, complains about limited access to the Japanese market due to non-tariff barriers and feels itself flooded with Japanese high-tech products (electronics, cameras, cars, computers and so on). But the EC's main orientation towards less developed countries and countries in its neighbourhood obviously shows a lack of competitiveness in the advanced strong demand sectors. A structural weakness which among others may be overcome by a more integrated large single market within an integrated European economy.

1.5 The five major European countries

Germany

Of the five major EC-countries *Germany* is by far the largest. Even before the German unification, with a population of 62.0 million, the FRG was slightly ahead of France, Italy and the UK and its GDP is more than a quarter higher than that of these three countries (1989, see Table 1.2). But if we add the population and the (roughly estimated) GDP of the former German Democratic Republic (East Germany) to the West German figures, we get a total German population of 78.7 and a combined GDP of 1242 billion ECU (15% higher). Obviously Germany will be the leading economic force within the EC.

The populations of France, Italy and the UK are roughly comparable (57 million) and their GDPs do not differ very much; France is still the richest, while, compared with the other countries of the 'big five', Spain is much smaller in terms of population and GDP.

The Western part of Germany (the former Federal Republic of Germany) is also leading with respect to GDP per head; it had the lowest unemployment and inflation rates and its competitiveness and export performance are impressive. Nevertheless, its real GDP growth rate in the 1980s was among the lowest of the five (together with that of France); but it is a very stable and balanced economy. The prospects for the German economy are hopeful but uncertain: on the one hand the German unification offers many new opportunities in terms of market enlargement, investment and economies of scale. The European unification and the economic transformation in Eastern Europe are also positive

Table 1.2 Main economic indicators, 1989
Federal Republic of Germany, Spain, France, Italy, United Kingdom

	FRG	SPAIN	FRANCE	ITALY	UK
Population (millions)	62.0	39.2	56.0	57.6	57.2
Gross domestic product (GDP) current market prices (billion ECU)	1080	342	857	793	746
average real growth rate in % 1981–90	2.1	2.9	2.1	2.5	2.4
GDP per head, PPS, EC = 100%	113.3	75.7	108.5	105.1	104.6
Unemployment rate average 1981–1990	6.3	18.6	9.4	9.7	9.8
Inflation	2.7	9.3	6.3	10.1	6.1
(average 1981–1990)					
Gross fixed capital formation (% of GDP at market prices)	20.7	24.4	20.5	20.1	18.8
Private consumption (% of GDP at market prices)	60.3	62.5	59.9	60.9	62.6
Nominal unit labour costs (relative to 19 industrial countries double export weights, 1980 = 100)	87.4	93.7	81.8	120.8	92.5
Exports of goods and services (% of GDP at market prices)	31.3	19.5	23.3	20.3	24.9
Imports of goods and services (% of GDP at market prices)	25.7	22.0	23.3	20.2	28.7
Current balance	2.8	−1.0	−0.5	−0.8	−0.8

Source: European Economy Eurostat/OECD

factors for the competitive German economy. On the other hand the integration of the East German economy will involve high costs for restructuring, cleaning up the environment, infrastructure, education, and measures in the social field (unemployment, retraining and retirement).

Spain

The Spanish GDP per head is still the lowest among the five countries considered, but it is catching up very rapidly. The Spanish economy showed a lot of imbalances in the 1980s, e.g. high unemployment, interest and inflation rates. Due to the policies of the Franco era it was a raher closed, protected, regulated and monopolised economy. Recent Spanish governments, however, have quite successfully implemented policies to prepare Spain for full integration in the Community in 1993. The Spanish economy is much more competitive now and possesses a large growth potential. For instance, a much greater part of female production could be integrated in the labour force. Investment is very high, much of it financed by foreign capital.

Italy

Italy is another fast grower of the 1980s. The economy of the Milan region (Lombardia) in particular boomed in the second half of the 1980s. A very remarkable feature of the Italian economy is the large presence of small and medium-sized companies, which moreover turned out to be one of the major driving forces behind the Italian success. The growth lacks in terms of balance, however. The gap between the northern and the southern parts is even widening. Full exposure to international competition within a united Europe may even fuel this development. Other significant problems are the inefficient public sector, the large budget deficit and the high inflation rate.

United Kingdom

The United Kingdom succeeded in the last decade in bringing to an end a long period of poor performance. In the 1960s the average UK growth rate was only a meagre 2.8% against 4.8% for present 12 EC members; in the 1970s the 2.0% was still behind the 2.9% of EUR-12. But in the 1980s the 2.4% was slightly above the then average EC-12 rate of 2.3%. So the UK is on its way back. Especially the financial service sector is very strong; the UK has become the financial centre of Europe. Like Italy, however, there remain strong imbalances in the UK economy, such as regional disparities, high interest and inflation rates and a large current account deficit. The latter can be considered as the result of a structural weakness in competitiveness; an aspect which may partly explain the UK's reluctance to join the EMS and to support other steps leading in the direction of economic unification of Europe.

France

France finally has recovered from a severe recession at the beginning of the 1980s. While the other countries adopted policies of strict austerity and supply-side policies in response to the crisis, France experimented with Keynesian-inspired reflation policies and state intervention strategies. Whatever may be said about the current relevance of Keynesian demand management, it certainly does not work if it is carried out by only one country with a rather open economy, and not big enough to dominate its international economic relations. So the result was a large trade deficit, inflation and rising unemployment. Since 1983, France has made a major shift in its economic policies towards more liberal and free-market approaches; together with the improving world economy this caused a speedy recovery of the French economy. French industry is in general well developed and passably flourishing. But it has also some important weaknesses such as its lack of specialisation and the unfavourable geographical orientation of some sectors.

In the next part of this book the above developments will be discussed in more detail. It will become apparent that large differences in policies, industry structure and economic performances still exist.

Part B

Country Surveys

2 | Federal Republic of Germany

Professor Rudi Kurz

2.1 Institutional and historical context

2.1.1 Introduction and historical overview

Germany's economic success has been attributed to a large extent to the particular economic system that was established after World War II – the *Soziale Marktwirtschaft* (social market economy). It is essential for anyone who wishes to understand the German economic miracle to become acquainted with the major features of this system. Everyone who plans to do business in Germany should understand how it works, because not only does it grant basic economic freedoms but also it defines the conditions that apply to the use of private resources in business and the obligations that have to be met. The *Soziale Marktwirtschaft* is intended to be efficient and humane (W Eucken). It is an attempt to achieve a balance between market efficiency and social interests (A Müller-Armack). To adapt this system to changing conditions in the process of economic development is a permanent challenge.

The post-war economic development of West Germany may be subdivided into the following three periods:

- 1948–65 A reconstruction period characterised by high growth rates, price stability, the regaining of full employment and the establishment of a strong position in international trade. Distributional and environmental issues caused little concern.
- 1966–79 A state interventionist period characterised by the Keynesian principle of a guarantee of full employment and an extension of the welfare state. Deficiencies inherent in the basic ideas and two oil price shocks brought this period to an end.
- 1980–90 A period of liberalisation characterised by the withdrawal of the state on all fronts: the policy of full employment was replaced by a policy of long-term growth, government intervention in the

market by deregulation and privatisation and the levelling off of
increased expenditure on social security and subsidies.

In the 1990s a new period is beginning which is characterised by new
challenges and which will demand unconventional approaches without
ideological restraints. Liberalisation will no longer be adequate as a label
for this period – rather it is going to be *perestroika (Umbau)* without the
sacrifice of liberal principles. Among the challenges are environmental
protection, disarmament and conversion of some sectors of the defence
industry and giving aid to the Third World. However, in the near future
these international challenges will be subordinated to coping with the
problems of German unification.

Unification makes it difficult to describe the state and the prospects
of the German economy at this moment. While reliable data are available
for the old (west) German states (*Bundesländer*), it will take a considerable time for comparable economic data to become available for the five
new (east) German states which are in the process of rapid transformation. However, we perceive a marked division between the development
of the prospering West and the depressed East. Given these circumstances it is not yet possible to describe Germany as an integrated entity.
Therefore the following text refers primarily to the old Federal Republic
of Germany (FRG) – which still represents about 80–90% of the German
gross national product (GNP) – with remarks on special problems of the
new states throughout the text and in a more general perspective at the
end of the chapter.

2.1.2 *Major characteristics of the German economic system*

Constitutional principles

The German constitution – the *Grundgesetz (GG)* of 1949 – does not
codify the *Soziale Marktwirtschaft*. It is open to changes in the economic system. However, there are narrow boundaries to such changes
because any economic system has to be compatible with inalienable
human rights (Art. 1–20 *GG*) and the decentralised political structure
(strong position of states and local communities). Private property is
guaranteed. Its use has to serve the general welfare of the community.
Expropriation and adaptation to social use are possible (Art. 15 *GG*) if
they benefit the community and if a financial compensation is paid. In
Art. 20 *GG* the FRG is defined as a democratic and social federal state
(*demokratischer und sozialer Bundesstaat*). This is to emphasise the
significance of social justice for the long-term existence of a market
economy and to protect the federal structure of the state. The latter is

defined by attributing specific functions and sources of revenue to every level of state activity. With regard to the division of labour within the government sector the principle of subsidiarity (*Subsidiaritätsprinzip*) applies whereby decision-making is delegated to the lowest possible authority: state (*Bundesländer*) and federal involvement occur only when local authorities (*Gemeinden*) are unable to cope. Decentralisation creates problems of co-ordination, but experience shows that the advantages of flexibility and autonomy are dominant factors.

Law relating to competition

Competition is based on the freedom to make agreements and to form enterprises. However, both may be restricted in order to protect consumers or competition itself as an institution. The most important law protecting competition is the *Gesetz gegen Wettbewerbsbeschränkungen* (*GWB*). Its major components are as follows:

- cartels and concerted actions by combines are in principle forbidden, with some exemptions defined by the law (paras 2–8 *GWB*);
- the conduct of monopolies (*marktbeherrschende Unternehmen*) is controlled in order to prevent them from abusing their market power;
- large firms are subject to provisions governing mergers. If the cartel authority (*Bundeskartellamt*) disallows a merger, the Minister of Commerce may grant permission if the economic advantages outweigh the disadvantages of restricted competition (e.g. the case of Daimler-Benz/MBB in 1989).

In addition to the general laws governing competition, a large number of specific rules (market regulations) for entry into or competition in various markets exist. To mention only a few examples:

- Some industries such as transportation, mail and telecommunications, public utilities (electricity, gas, water), banking, insurance, agriculture are partly exempted from the *GWB* and subject to the control of specific regulatory authorities. Market entry and pricing in these industries are not free from regulations. However, these regulations are expected to change significantly over the next few years, especially under pressure from the EC.
- Shop closing hours: shops are allowed to open from Monday to Friday from 7 a.m. to 6.30 p.m. and on Saturday from 7 a.m. to 2 p.m. (the first Saturday of each month until 4 p.m.). After lengthy debate this has been liberalised and shops may now remain open until 8.30 p.m. every Thursday. A more comprehensive liberalisation is unlikely to take place because unions and small and medium-sized enterprises (SMEs) are opposed to it.

- Craft codes (*Handwerksordnung*): craftsmen have to have special training and a formal qualification (*Meisterprüfung*).

The numerous codes of practice (partly in guild tradition) are an example of the German inclination to order going awry. Many of these regulations will have to be adapted in order to allow for more (international) competition and to improve the German economic system (regulatory reform).

Financial system

The *Gesetz über die Deutsche Bundesbank* of 1957 rules that the *Deutsche Bundesbank* is autonomous, i.e. independent from the Federal Government. The *Bundesbank* is obliged to support the economic policy of the *Bundesregierung* only to the extent that it is compatible with the *Bundesbank's* sole goal: the stabilisation of price level. By defining minimum reserve standards, changing conditions of refinancing (discount rate) and open market intervention, the *Bundesbank* controls the liquidity of banks and the supply of money in circulation. The *Bundesbank* may provide credit for public budgets only within well-defined, narrow limits (to bridge liquidity gaps). Because of the great importance of the banking system, this industry is subject to specific control by a regulatory authority (*Bundesaufsichtsamt für das Kreditwesen*). The FRG is a member of the European Monetary System and hence the *Bundesbank* is obliged to intervene in order to stabilise exchange rates (within margins of fluctuation of ±2.25%). For all other currencies flexible exchange rates apply.

Legal foundations of labour markets

(1) The freedom to design individual labour contracts is restricted by the existence of collective agreements between unions and employers (*Tarifverträge*) from which individual labour contracts may deviate only if such deviation is to the advantage of the employee (*Günstigkeitsprinzip*). Laws on labour conflicts do not exist and so the courts have to resolve any conflicts.

(2) Lay-off protection: every employee who has worked for more than six months in a firm may not be laid off without good reason. To prevent the circumvention of this rule labour contracts which are for a limited period of time may not last longer than 18 months. Temporary workers may not be employed in the same firm for more than six months. In cases of mass lay-offs (more than 10% of a firm's employees), a social plan (*Sozialplan*) has to be negotiated between management and employees. The equivalent of several months' pay has to be awarded to those who are laid off.

(3) The working time of employees is restricted by various legal rules: Sundays and public holidays are in principle free and only work which is in the public interest may be performed (e.g. in hospitals) and in rare special cases also for economic reasons (e.g. maintaining continuous production). For juveniles specific restrictions apply (e.g. piece-work is not allowed). Women are granted a paid holiday of six weeks before and eight weeks after the birth of a child. Normal working hours may not exceed eight per day. The number of days paid holiday per year must be a minimum of 18. Many of these provisions are of little practical relevance because collective agreements in most cases go far beyond these minimum standards (e.g. as regards working hours per week and paid holidays).

(4) Employees are granted extensive rights of co-operation and co-determination. For all enterprises with more than five employees the *Betriebsverfassungsgesetz* of 1972 applies. This law grants employees and their elected representatives (*Betriebsräte*) comprehensive rights of information and consultation (working hours/breaks, workplace design, etc). For large corporations, of which there are about 500 (*AG, GmbH* with more than 2000 employees) the *Mitbestimmungsgesetz* of 1976 goes far beyond that. It stipulates that half of the members of the board (*Aufsichtsrat*) shall be elected by the employees. In stalemate situations the vote of the chairman (who is a representative of the capital-owning side) counts twice. This means that we do not have full parity in employee's co-determination.

Social security system

The FRG built up one of the world's most advanced (and most expensive) social security systems, which contributed significantly to the avoidance of social conflicts. Its main elements are as follows:

- Pension fund: for all employees with an income of less than 5700 DM per month membership of the scheme is mandatory. Contributions amount to 18.7% of gross income and are paid half by employers and half by employees. Individual pensions depend on the amount of contributions made and the general increase in incomes of the active workforce (*Generationenvertrag*). Pensions are index-linked, i.e. they increase according to the level of average net income.
- Health insurance: all employees with a monthly income of less than 4275 DM must have health insurance. Contributions are paid half by employers and half by employees and amount to about 13% of gross income on average.
- Unemployment insurance: all employees have to contribute to the scheme regardless of the amount of their income. Contributions amount to 4.3% (from a maximum of 5700 DM per month) and are

paid half by the employers and half by the employees. Based on his or her contributions a worker who becomes unemployed receives up to 68% of his or her last net income (but not more than 2400 DM) for a maximum period of one year and contributions for pension fund and health insurance are paid. After one year of unemployment payments are reduced to a maximum of 58%.

- Social aid: this aims at enabling everyone to live with dignity even if they are without income. It is paid only if no other source of income is available (e.g. from property or family members). Social aid is paid by the local authorities.
- Insurance against accidents in the work place: employers are obliged to pay for rehabilitation and damages in cases of accidents in the work place. To cover this risk, employers pay contributions to an insurance scheme (*Berufsgenossenschaften*). The rates of contributions depend on the risks in the firms and on the employees' incomes.

2.1.3 *Participants in policy formation*

Parties and their political power

Political development in the FRG has been dominated by three political parties: the *Christlich Demokratische Union (CDU)*, and its affiliate in Bavaria (*Christlich Soziale Union (CSU)*), the *Sozialdemokratische Partei Deutschlands (SPD)* and the *Freie Demokratische Partei (FDP)*. *CDU/CSU* and *SPD* are '*Volksparteien*', trying to address all groups in the electorate and currently both have a potential share of the votes of about 40%. The *FDP*'s following is the upper middle class; as a consequence this party now and again has difficulty in obtaining the minimum of 5% of the votes necessary for representation in federal and state parliaments. However, this small party played an important role because none of the major parties had an absolute majority and hence they depended on coalitions with the *FDP*. In recent years only one party has successfully challenged this structure; the Green Party, which is focusing on environmental and armament problems and has a potential electorate about the size of the *FDP*'s. Extreme right-wing parties (*NPD, Republikaner*) had only very short-term successes. Now the *PDS*, the successor to the communist *SED* which governed the German Democratic Republic (GDR) for forty years, is struggling to become an additional left-wing player in the party system—with little success so far.

The economic policy of the post-war period is characterised by stability and continuity. Most of the time Conservatives and Liberals set the course. When Social Democrats participated in the Federal Government from 1966 to 1982 there were no radical changes, partly because they had to compromise with their coalition partners (*CDU* or *FDP*). This political continuity has been one of the positive conditions in the framework of the FRG economy. In the social-liberal era the welfare state was elaborated and Keynesian strategies of full employment were applied – with the consequences of an increasing public deficit. After 1982 when the *FDP* formed a new coalition with the *CDU/CSU* ('*Wende*') emphasis has been given to eliminating deficits and on improving conditions for long-term economic growth (supply-oriented economic policy). The government also relies on that concept as a guide for the 1990s.

Major lobby groups and business associations
(1) A large variety of organised groups participate in formulating economic policy employing formal (e.g. hearings) and informal (e.g. financial support and lobbying) methods. Most important are the unions with about nine million members organised in various industries and 7.8 million of them united in the *Deutsche Gewerkschaftsbund* (*DGB*). Traditionally, unions have a close relationship with the *SPD*. However, this affinity is declining. Employers organise themselves in industry-specific associations where membership is voluntary. The most important umbrella organisations are the *Bundesverband der Deutschen Industrie* (*BDI, Köln*) and the *Bundesvereinigung der Deutschen Arbeitgeberverbände* (*BDA, Köln*).

(2) All enterprises are mandatory members of regional chambers of commerce (*Industrie- und Handelskammer, Handwerkskammer*). These serve as bodies of self-administration, organise examinations on completion of apprenticeships and for qualification as foreman, give consultations to and educate young entrepreneurs, settle internal industrial disputes and undertake public relations work. The umbrella organisations are the *Deutsche Industrie -und Handelstag* (*DIHT*, Bonn) and the *Deutsche Handwerkskammertag.*

2.2 Main economic characteristics

2.2.1 *Population, labour force, employment*

Even before unification the FRG had the largest population among all EC countries (see Statistical Annexe, Table D6). The new states add a population of about 16 million, so that the total population of Germany is almost 80 million. Population density is high but has declined somewhat owing to unification (from 247 inhabitants per square kilometre to about 225). In West Germany the population was decreasing after 1975 and has only recently reached the level of 62 million again. This number includes about 4.6 million (7.5%) foreigners, of whom 1.6 million are in employment. During the last three years more than one million emigrants from Eastern Europe have had to be integrated. The age structure of the population is changing significantly. The proportion of older people in relation to the active part of the population (people 65 and older/people 15–64) in the FRG – as in other European countries – will increase dramatically, from the current 25% level to more than 45% in 2040, and this will cause serious economic and social problems during the coming decades. The participation rate of the labour force declined from the mid 1950s to the late 1970s by five percentage points. It then started to increase and is now 47.5% (see Statistical Annexe, Table D7). According to the results of the population census in 1987 the West German labour force is 29.8 million. About three million of them are self-employed or family workers. Participation rates of the labour force in the GDR have been high (about 54%) but this may change significantly. We therefore do not know how many persons the new states will add to the labour force.

Two million of the West German labour force are unemployed. The unemployment rate reached its peak in 1985 and has steadily declined since then (see Statistical Annexe, Table D9). However, it is still higher than it was ten years ago. Although the rate of unemployment, as well as the actual numbers, have not improved much, one has to take account of the fact that during the last seven years one and a half million new jobs have been created (see Figure 2.1). But this has not been sufficient given the rate at which the labour supply has been increasing.

The resolution of the unemployment problem has been rendered more difficult as a consequence of an adverse selection process. The pattern of unemployment is creating more and more problems because an increasingly greater proportion of the unemployed are older people who have health problems or who are without qualifications. As a result one-third of the unemployed are out of work for a year or more (*Langzeitarbeitslose*). There are large regional differences in unemployment rates (between 2% in the south west and about 10% in the north) and these are not disappearing because mobility of labour is limited. Furthermore, there are large differences with respect to qualifications and these differences continue to exist because the amount of training and retraining undertaken is insufficient to meet the need. As a consequence firms face a severe labour shortage in certain regions and also a shortage of people with certain qualifications.

Unemployment causes high costs. The costs per unemployed person are calculated to be 26 500 DM and almost 60 billion DM in total (expenditure plus revenue losses). A greater emphasis on existing

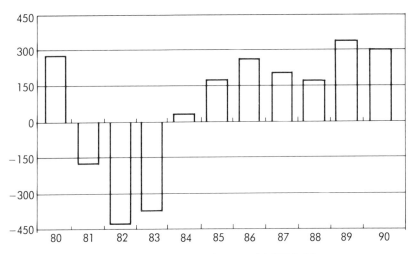

Figure 2.1 Change of employment (in thousands) 1980–90
Source: Bundesminister für Wirtschaft, 1990, p. 14

programmes of active labour market policy, including retraining, job-creation schemes, wage cost subsidies, could have contributed towards reducing these costs as well as the social costs which the unemployed and society have to bear. During the transformation period in the East German states the number of unemployed could rise to a total of 3–4 million, i.e. to more than 10% of a prospective labour force of 38 million.

A sectoral break-down (see Statistical Annexe, Table D8) reveals that the percentage of the labour force employed in industry is still very high at about 41.2%, i.e. the highest proportion among all EC nations. There has been a long-term decline from 44% in 1980 and 49% in 1970. Also declining is the proportion employed in agriculture (now less than 5%). Government employment has expanded significantly but has recently begun to stagnate at about 15%. An increasing number of people (40% of the labour force) work in the service sector (including trade and transportation). There are hopes that this sector could absorb even more people and thus make a greater contribution to curing unemployment. Within the industry sector, small and medium-sized enterprises (SMEs) with less than 1000 employees provide 60% of all jobs, large firms (2% of all firms) 40%.

2.2.2 *Growth and business cycles*

(1) The FRG's gross domestic product (GDP) at current prices is 1180 billion ECU (1990, excluding the former GDR) (see Statistical Annexe,

Table D10). This is about 52% of the GDP of Japan and 27% of the GDP of the USA. How much the new states will add to the GDP is not exactly predictable at the moment; over the next few years it may be no more than 10–15%. Within the EC the West German GDP *per capita* is surpassed only by Luxembourg; it is twice as high as in Greece or Portugal. However, the GDP *per capita* of the USA is still considerably higher (see Statistical Annexe, Table D12). GDP *per capita* in Germany will decline as a consequence of unification.

Real GDP growth rates showed a declining trend over the 20 years following the end of the reconstruction period. The 1980s brought a continuous expansion at an average rate of 2.1%. Declining growth rates do not imply economic decline: in 1989, for example, real GDP increased by 30 billion ECU, i.e. by 3.8%. In the early 1960s this would have been an 8% increase. The continuous expansion which started after the recession of 1981/2 is still going on and in its eighth year no signs of a recession are in sight. Compared with the EC in total, the German growth performance is average; Germany has not been an engine of growth in the recent past but neither has it been retarding economic growth in Europe. The continuous expansion with only minor changes in the growth rates of real gross national product (*'Wellblechkonjunktur'*) does not conform with traditional theories of business cycles. The difference in pattern is related to the change in the paradigm guiding economic policy. Since the early 1980s the emphasis has been on stimulating long-term growth (supply-oriented policy) rather than on trying to reduce un-employment by means of Keynesian deficit spending. As a consequence there was no spectacular boom and no significant reduction of unem-ployment. However, the economy became more robust and has been able to absorb exogenous shocks such as the stock market crash of 1987. Whether the economy will also resist the negative impacts caused by the structural adjustment crisis in the new states is currently debatable.

(2) A demand-side analysis of the last few years reveals that all compo-nents of aggregate demand contributed to the expansion.

Stable expansion of private consumption, which amounts to about 60% of aggregate demand (see Statistical Annexe, Table D13), provided a solid foundation for the long-term expansion by growing at an average annual rate of more than 3%. Within the last five years consumer demand increased by 50 million ECU to approximately 500 billion ECU (in real terms). This stimulus was most favourable for the automobile, furniture, tourism and food industries. The personal saving rate (personal savings divided by disposable personal income) recovered from its minimum of 12.2% in 1983 to almost 14%. The increase in both consumer expendi-ture and the personal saving rate is based on the steady increase of mass incomes. Higher real wages, overtime working and tax reduction contributed to that. The growth of government consumption has been reduced significantly in the second half of the 1980s, and hence it declined relatively to GNP (13% for government without social insurances).

From 1986 on, the formation of capital, especially investment in equipment, provided for the dynamics of growth (see Statistical Annexe, Table D16). Throughout the five-year period 1986–90 investment in equipment grew at an annual rate of 6.5%. The major reasons for the investment boom, were a high rate of capacity utilisation (up from 88% in 1982 to 98% in 1989) and a significant increase in profits after 1983. After 1988 investment in construction picked up and this is likely to continue because of a pressing housing shortage in the FRG and low housing quality in the new states of the former GDR. In 1988 the manufacturing industry invested 4 billion ECU in environmental protection (about 8% of this sector's investment). Gross investment amounted to 240 billion ECU in 1989. As a share of GNP (21.5%) it is now almost as high as it had been in the 1960s.

The surplus in the balance of exports and imports of goods and services increased to almost 70 billion ECU, which is more than 6% of GNP. Exports grew by more than 20% over the last three years (i.e. by 85 billion ECU). This increase is due mainly to the strong growth of world trade and the competitive prices of German products caused by relatively low inflation rates.

(3) Income distribution: over the last decade incomes from profits have doubled and now amount to 300 billion ECU. The growth of income from labour was slower with the consequence of a declining labour share in the figure for national income (66.4% in 1989 compared with 72.4% in 1982). Despite the economic expansion the number of people in need of social aid increased continuously during the 1980s. In 1989 3.3 million people received social aid (50% more than in 1980) resulting in costs of 28.7 billion DM. This is one indicator of the fact that in the midst of wealth poverty is increasing. If all the people receiving less than half the average income are defined as poor, the poverty rate in the (old) FRG is 10% and is even higher for Germany as a whole. For comparison, the official poverty rate in the USA is 13%. Financing the social security system incurs a government expenditure of 330 billion ECU per annum (5000 ECU *per capita*); related to GNP (*Sozialleistungsquote*) this is 30% (up from 25% in 1965 with a maximum of 34% in 1975).

(4) Inflation: for a while it seemed as if inflation had been completely defeated in the FRG. From 1985 to 1988 the consumer price index increased by only 1.2%. However, since the end of 1988 the risk of inflation revived as a consequence of higher import prices (oil, raw materials), the depreciation of the DM (against the US $ and the yen, see

Statistical Annexe, Table D24), increases in indirect taxes, fees for government services and sectoral bottlenecks (e.g. in house construction). The inflation rate is now 3% and may increase further. Unions have negotiated wage increases of about 6%. This leads to higher costs and higher demand, which, together with the pressure of demand from the former GDR may generate a wave of price 'hikes'. However, the *Bundesbank* will not tolerate a new price–wage spiral and will react by imposing monetary restraints and higher interest rates. Price stability continues to be given a high priority on the economic agenda, and this specifically German emphasis of such a priority, which has economic as well as historical foundations (the Weimar experience), will be an important issue in the emerging European Economic and Monetary Union.

(5) Prospects for further economic growth in Germany are bright. Real GNP growth in 1990 is expected to be about 4%. Conditions for investment are favourable, private consumption stable and foreign trade is prospering. Uncertainties concerning the near future stem mainly from the German integration process. Currently, this is a source of hope as well as concern, with more emphasis on hope. Reconstructing East Germany (infrastructure, machinery, buildings, environment) is a huge task with many opportunities for business activity. Given a suitable economic environment this should attract private capital from all over the world and thus limit the burden on public budgets. But, even under these conditions, opportunities for further reductions in taxes, government activity and deficit as well as for lower interest rates have diminished. Positive effects are expected to result from the EC 1992 common market project, although some economic activity might emigrate to Europe's sun belt.

2.2.3 *Cost of production and productivity growth*

(1) The FRG has the highest labour costs in the world. At 35.74 DM per hour the rate recently surpassed that of Switzerland. This figure is made up of two components: wages are 19.29 DM/hour and additional labour costs, such as (half of the) social security contributions, paid holidays, bonuses, etc., which are 16.45 DM/hour, i.e. roughly 85% of wages. The latter component is much higher than in any other nation. It is the result of a most elaborate set of social security and fringe benefits. Total labour costs in the UK and in France are about two-thirds of those in Germany, in Portugal they are only 18%. Japan has lost its status as a cheap labour economy; its labour costs have already climbed to 83% of those in Germany.

(2) The increasing labour costs are in part compensated for by productivity growth, which has been about 2.5% per annum over the last five years. Combined with the moderate wage policy of the unions this growth has led to a decline in real unit labour costs (see Statistical Annexe, Table D15). In this respect German competitiveness has actually improved over recent years – within the EC as well as compared with the USA and Japan. The question is whether German productivity, reliability and quality can maintain a competitive advantage large enough to pay for the high additional labour costs in global markets. At least more flexibility in terms of the number of hours worked may be necessary. The effective number of working hours in the FRG is the lowest in the world: 1620, i.e. 31.2 per week (including 1.6 billion hours overtime). However, the FRG is also among the nations with the fewest number of working hours lost through strikes.

(3) The acquisition of financial resources, especially venture capital, in the FRG has been burdened with high capital costs caused by various taxes on capital transactions. These taxes are eliminated at the end of 1990 and 1991 (*Finanzmarktförderungsgesetz* 1990). This represents part of the effort to make the FRG a more attractive international financial marketplace and to reduce the discrimination between equity and debt financing.

(4) Although the cost of electrical power represents only a small fraction of industry's expenditure, a great deal of attention is given to it in political discussion. Commercial users of electrical power in the FRG pay the highest prices in Europe. In France prices are only about two-thirds of those in Germany, and in Denmark they are even lower. In some countries industry prices are cross-subsidised and hence private households pay more than in Germany. Prospects for lower energy prices in Germany are not good: environmental considerations (especially the greenhouse effect) demand energy saving and this requires higher energy prices. More competitive energy markets could contribute to lower energy prices.

2.2.4 Economic structure

(1) *Sectoral structure.* The analysis of economic activity by major sectors reveals that manufacturing, most importantly automobiles, chemicals, machine tools and electrical engineering, still has a dominant position. Its share in gross value added is 33% (down from 40% in the 1960s). Construction, mining, energy and water supply have a combined share of less than 10% now (13% in the 1960s). Agriculture's share is

only 1.5% (5.5% in the 1960s). The share of trade and transportation has been declining slightly (to 15%). The government's share increased until the early 1980s, has declined since then and is now approaching 10%. The only sector which has expanded its share markedly is the service sector, including banks, insurance and other services. Within the span of 30 years its share has doubled and is now almost 30%.

(2) *Industry structure*, concentration and firm size. The investigations of the *Monopolkommission* (1988) reveal no clear trend towards concentration in Germany industry. While concentration ratios have increased in some branches, they have either remained unchanged or have declined in others. The most concentrated industries are (market share of the ten largest firms): tobacco (98%), air and space (95%), oil (94%), mining (92%), computers (88%), automobiles (74%), iron and steel (74%), shipbuilding (71%), rubber (62%), and pulp and paper (56%). The number of mergers and acquisitions has increased significantly since 1983 (when the *Bundeskartelamt* registered 586). This is in part interpreted as a reaction to the challenge of EC 1992. Small and medium-sized firms still play an important role in the FRG economy and are crucial to its strength and flexibility. Their position is not endangered, although the interdependence of large enterprises and SMEs is increasing, for example as a consequence of just-in-time production.

(3) *Regional structure.* Based on indicators such as unemployment rate and GDP growth, there seems to be a north–south gradient in the FRG with prospering regions concentrated in the south (the states of Baden-Württemberg and Bavaria). More recently the debate of this question has ceased, primarily because it became clear that the south is still in the process of catching up, in terms of *per capita* income, and some inherent limitations to development for the booming regions in the south became apparent, such as sky-rocketing real-estate prices and rents, traffic congestion, problems with waste disposal, etc. While the regional disparities within the old FRG have been small compared with European standards, this changed significantly with the incorporation of the new states. Average income in the new states is only a third of that in West Germany. Environmental damage, unemployment, quality of jobs, etc, all combine to widen an already huge gap in the quality of life between the two regions. In order to avoid a large migration to the West, major regional development and restructuring efforts are urgently needed.

2.3 Government involvement in the economy

2.3.1 *Government expenditure, taxes and deficits*

(1) Government expenditure, including social insurance, as a share of GDP reached its peak in 1982 (49.4%), has steadily declined since then and is now approaching the level of 45% (see Statistical Annexe, Table D18). The decline in the government's share is a consequence of the change in political concepts and of improved economic performance (higher employment). The decline could continue because no serious reductions in government subsidies, for example for declining industries, have taken place so far. German economic integration does not necessarily have to stop that decline if the political will to reduce government subsidies and military expenditure is strong enough, and if efforts to privatise public undertakings are intensified, for example in rebuilding the infrastructure in the new states.

(2) A total government expenditure of about 500 billion ECU is shared between the Federal Government, which accounts for 28%, the states, 27% and local communities, 18%; the rest is the net expenditure, after eliminating government transfer payments, on social insurances. Federal expenditure of about 140 billion ECU is primarily for social security (one-third), defence (one-fifth) and interest payment on federal debt

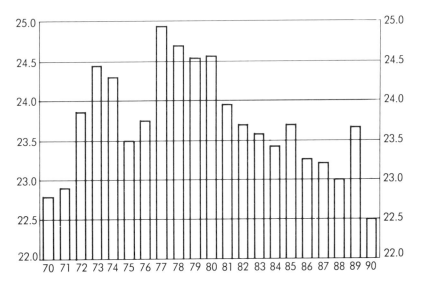

Figure 2.2 Tax revenues as share of GNP, 1970–90
Source: Bundesminister für Wirtschaft, 1990, p. 31

(one-tenth). Government subsidies, according to the official statistical data (*Subventionsbericht*), amount to 23 billion ECU. Some estimates state that the figure is more likely to be 50 billion ECU. The most subsidised sectors are agriculture, energy and transportation.

(3) The sum of taxes and compulsory contributions to social security insurance increased significantly during the 1970s until the mid-1980s. The trend was then reversed and the gap between the averages for the FRG and the EC is becoming smaller. From the average employee's perspective, the burden of government taxes and contributions drains about a quarter of his or her gross income. The most important government receipts are income taxes (about 50% of all tax revenues) and value added taxes (about 25%). Taxes as a share of GDP have been declining since the late 1970s and are now about 22% (see Figure 2.2).

(4) The taxation rate of profits in Germany is 70% of pre-tax profit and hence is higher than in all competing nations. This high rate results from high (personal or corporate) income tax rates (up to 53%) combined

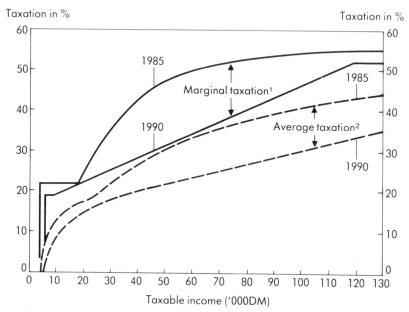

1. Per cent taxation of marginal income increases
2. Average per cent taxation of total income

Figure 2.3 Reform of the personal income tax schedule
Source: OECD, 1989, p. 87, based on German Ministry of Finance data

with taxes which are not profit-related, such as local trade tax on business capital (Gewerbekapitalsteuer) and wealth tax (Vermögensteuer). This figure of 70% is, however, misleading because the calculation starts only with taxable profits and does not take account of tax allowances which enable firms in Germany to reduce significantly the amount of 'profit' on which they are finally taxed. Moreover, the level of subsidies and the infrastructure provided by the government should be included in the analysis in order to arrive at a balanced judgement. A major tax reform which was implemented in three phases from 1986 to 1990 resulted in a net tax relief of almost 25 billion ECU. The most important part of this reform was a flattening in the curve of income tax progression (see Figure 2.3). This progression has arisen, because as a consequence of inflation, medium-level incomes have been growing and entering the higher tax brackets over the years. This 'hidden progression' had reduced incentives to work (especially for qualified persons) and encouraged the 'black' economy. The tax reform reduced the top marginal rate from 56% to 53% for annual taxable income of 120,000 DM (24,000 DM for married couples) and over. The corporate income tax rate on retained profits has been lowered from 56% to 50% (the rate for distributed profits remains 36%). Among the tax expenditures reduced or abolished to compensate in part for the cost of tax reforms are provision for R&D, investment in energy saving and residential building.

The taxation of businesses has so far been left unchanged. It is doubtful whether the major reform (including a reduction of the top marginal and the corporate income tax rate, the elimination of the wealth tax and the reform of the local trade tax) announced in this field for the next legislature period (1991–4) will actually take place, considering the high cost of overcoming the economic and environmental disaster in the new states. The kinds of tax incentive that should be provided to stimulate investment in the new states are the subject of controversial debate.

(5) Public debt accumulated from deficits in central, state and local budgets amounted to 500 billion ECU in 1990 (43% of GNP). The Federal Government is responsible for more than half of that debt; the rest has been incurred at state and local levels. A significant part of the public debt (100 billion ECU) is foreign debt and hence directs interest payments of about 7 billion ECU abroad annually. Total interest payments on government debt are 30 billion ECU per annum. Public net borrowing (including social security insurance) as a proportion of GDP has declined from a maximum of 5.6% in 1975 to zero in 1989 (see Statistical Annexe, Table D19). The deficit in central, state and local budgets has been reduced to 10 billion ECU in 1989 (less than 1% of GDP). Deficits will, however, rise in the next few years in order to

finance the costs of German economic integration. For 1990 and 1991 respectively, public deficits are expected to be higher than 50 billion ECU.

2.3.2 *Industry and technology policy*

(1) Total R&D expenditure in West Germany is about 32 billion ECU (1989), i.e. 2.9% of GNP (2.6% in 1981); 63.5% is privately financed (up from 55.4% in 1981). The public share is divided between the Federal Government (21%) and the eleven states (14%). The Federal Government share is not concentrated in one department but is at the disposal of various departments: in dominant position is the Federal Ministry of Research and Technology (*BMFT*) with more than half of the Federal Government R&D spending, followed by the Ministry of Defence (about a fifth) the Ministry of Education and the Ministry of Commerce with less than 10% each. In real terms the *BMFT* budget has shown no significant increase during the last eight years.

(2) A large part, about 20%, of the Federal Government's R&D spending goes into basic research, for example to the *Max-Planck Gesellschaft, Fraunhofer-Gesellschaft, Deutsche Forschungsgemeinschaft*. Another 20% is devoted to military research. The rest is widely spread over a variety of purposes summarised under the headings 'preventive research' and 'key technologies':

- air and space technologies 12%;
- energy research and technology (primarily nuclear power) 10%;
- information technology (including production engineering) 6%;
- environmental, climate, safety research 5%;
- research on materials, physical and chemical technologies 4%;
- biotechnology 2%;
- subsidies for R&D activities and improved basic conditions (investment in R&D, R&D personnel, technology-oriented new firms, technical information) 4%.

Only weak elements of industrial policy, i.e. targeting of specific technologies or industries can be identified based on these figures, for example, air and space and nuclear technologies.

(3) The role of small and medium-sized enterprises. To support and stimulate innovation on the part of SMEs the Federal Department of Commerce (*BMWi*) provided 1.6 billion ECU between 1979 and 1987 in order to subsidise employment of R&D personnel (*Personalkostenzuschuss-Programm*). Owing to a shift in concept, that programme has not been renewed. Instead the Federal Government relies primarily

on more favourable general conditions for innovation in SMEs. Among these, besides low interest rates, stability of prices, etc. are:

- the income tax reform which, in three phases 1986/1988/1990, brought significant tax reductions for nine out of ten SMEs (which are unincorporated);
- universities and colleges are given more freedom and incentives to co-operate with SMEs;
- SMEs benefit from the reduction in regulations (market entry) and bureaucracy costs;
- in public procurement there will be a greater insistence on employing SME sub-contractors, for example in the Airbus programme or in space projects;
- assistance with consultancy and access to technological information for SMEs has been improved and is subsidised.

Moreover, some funds are available to compensate for specific problems experienced by SMEs. The *BMFT* continues to provide about 100 million ECU annually for additional R&D personnel in SMEs. SMEs also benefit substantially from the indirect-specific *BMFT* programmes such as the one on CAD (computer-aided design), robotics and CIM (computer-integrated manufacturing). In 1984 a pilot project for new technology-oriented firms was started and will continue to make up the deficiency in seed capital.

The Federal Government attaches great importance to SMEs receiving a greater share of public funds (28%) in comparison with their share of total private enterprise R&D expenditure (15–20%).

(4) Elements of industrial policy in competition policy and regulatory reform: Competition policy has been adapted in various ways to prevent it from becoming an obstacle to innovation, for example, joint R&D ventures will only in rare special cases cause anti-trust problems. For example, the Daimler-Benz/MBB deal was strongly opposed by the *Bundeskartellamt*, but approved by the Minister of Commerce who has the final decision. Recently, large West German corporations have been taking over former state-guaranteed monopolies in East Germany, thus protecting their position against new competitiors in the new states.

Progress in deregulation or regulatory reform is slow in Germany. Much of the deregulation which has been and will be enacted is due to the EC 1992 internal market programme. Rate-setting in surface transportation has been abandoned (in 1989) and has been replaced by reference rates. But control of market entry (concessions) still exists. As a precondition for deregulation in the trucking industry the German government requests the harmonisation of taxes, safety and social standards in order to provide a level playing field for competition with the Netherlands, Italy and other EC countries. In telecommunications a major step has been made in opening up markets for private innovators. The *Deutsche Bundespost* has been divided into three public enterprises (telecommunications, mail services, banking services) and free market entry has been liberalised in telecommunication equipment, value-added services (e.g. data transmission) and the networks of satellite and mobile radio transmission. The monopoly is maintained in network transmission and telephone services. Some social welfare regulations have been reduced in scope in the labour market, for example employment protection. The number and extent of environmental regulations have increased, for example on emission control, waste water, chemicals, noise, biotechnology, but little has been done to minimise costs by applying economic measures that are less restrictive to innovation than the command-and-control approach.

2.4 Financial system

2.4.1 *Structure of financial institutions*

(1) A characteristic of the German banking and financial systems is the dominant role of universal banks which, unlike the specialised banks in other countries, engage in all kinds of bank business: short-term and long-term deposits, short-term and long-term credits, issue of and trade in bonds and stocks. In addition most banks engage in insurance, building-society and real estate activities. This system has advantages for the customer; many firms rely on only one bank (*Hausbank*). However, it also causes problems because of the concentration of information and economic power. There has recently been a revival of the debate on restricting the banks' share of stocks of industrial firms and their activity in the boards of competing firms.

The German banking system, with a total business volume of about 2 trillion ECU (sum of balance sheet), consists of different bank groups focusing on different kinds of business and customers. The three large banks (*Deutsche Bank, Dresdner Bank, Commerzbank*) have a share of 9%, dependencies of foreign banks a share of less than 2%; regional savings banks and savings and loan associations and their institutions (*Girozentralen, DG-Bank*) have a dominant position with about half the business volume and a large network of branch offices. In general, the density of branch offices in Germany is very high; 1500 inhabitants per office as compared, for example, with almost 4200 in Italy.

(2) Money and capital markets in the FRG. About 2100 stock corporations exist but only 500 of them are in the stock market. Moreover, about 500 foreign stocks are traded in German stock markets. There are eight exchange centres, the main one being Frankfurt. The role of stock

markets in business financing has traditionally been relatively minor, but the volume of new issues has steadily increased over the last few years. The exchange turnover in the FRG is the second highest in Europe, next to the UK. The major issuers of bonds are (large) banks and the government, primarily the Federal Government. This is the most common method by which banks refinance the credits they grant to the business and public sector. Interest rates are low compared to international standards, primarily because the rate of inflation is low. Moreover, government programmes provide interest rate subsidies for certain projects, such as creating new business ventures and house building.

(3) The structure of firms' financing. On average firms finance their activities to about 20% from their own capital resources, 60% by credits and 20% through reserves, especially for firms' pension funds. Credits are primarily short-term with a large share of the credits being granted by suppliers. Capital market credits play only a minor role. In the early 1980s there was an intense debate about the declining capital resources of firms relative to the sum of the balance sheet. It was stated that, as a consequence, firms will be unable to invest in new ventures which typically involve high risks and for which banks are reluctant to provide financing. Hence, low capital endowment of enterprises was identified as a major obstacle to innovation and growth. Since the mid-1980s, with profits being higher, the capital resources of firms improved and the debate lost its momentum. The average share of capital resources, relative to the sum of the balance sheet, is about 20%; in large stock companies the share is above average and there is a lot of variation between industries. Above average are chemicals, automobile, electrical engineering; below average are textiles, steel and the retail trade.

(4) Trends and perspectives. The universal bank idea has been extended to create *Allfinanz*, the merging of banking and insurance activities. New financial super powers are emerging but there is also fresh competition between giants like *Deutsche Bank* and *Allianz* which have up till now operated in separate markets. Control of these super powers will also come from foreign competitiors who may extend their activities in the FRG when banking and insurance markets are liberalised as a consequence of the EC 1992 project.

2.4.2 *Money supply, interest rates, exchange rates*

(1) After the crash of 1987 the *Bundesbank*, like most other central banks, provided additional liquidity to the banking system and low interest rates in order to avoid a spill-over of the crisis. Then, in the middle of 1988, the *Bundesbank* changed its course and returned to a

more restrictive policy by significantly increasing central bank interest rates (e.g. discount rate from 3% to 6%). As a consequence the level of interest rates rose generally: consumer credits are charged almost 13%, housing loans are up to almost 10%. Higher interest rates in the FRG were also a necessary reaction to high interest rates in the USA, which attracted considerable amounts of German capital, and hence contributed to a revaluation of the US $. This, however, would not have been sufficient to reduce the disproportions in both the German and the USA trade balances. Compared with those of other European nations, interest rates in the FRG are low (see Statistical Annexe, Table D20). Countries with external deficits and a high inflation rate have to offer higher interest rates to attract international capital. It is accepted that, as a consequence of the huge amounts of capital needed in East Germany, interest rates in Germany will be high for a considerable period of time. However, the demand to lower central bank rates may increase with the growing number of unemployed in Germany.

(2) The *Bundesbank*'s attempts to reduce excessive liquidity in the banking system from 1988 on have been only moderately successful. From 1986 on, the *Bundesbank* did not meet its monetary target for three years in a row. M3 growth overshot the target. Commentators fear that, as a consequence, an inflationary potential has been built up. The monetary target for 1989 was an M3 growth of 5%; for 1990 it was 4–6%. The *Bundesbank* has made clear that it is not going to tolerate a creeping inflation as a side-effect of the German unification process.

(3) The exchange rate of the DM within the European Currency system has remained almost unchanged over the last few years. This is primarily due to the success achieved by the European partner countries in coping with inflation. From late 1987 until mid-1990 there has also been relatively little change in the US $–DM exchange rate, although there have been significant fluctuations. In total, the value of the DM compared with 18 other important currencies steadily increased until the end of 1987, then was weak for about two years and then picked up again in late 1989 (see Statistical Annexe, Table D24 and monthly reports of the *Bundesbank*, Table IX 9).

(4) Germany's international reserves amount to 32.6 billion ECU (net). Gold reserves (rated at the low original purchasing costs) amount to 6.6 billion ECU, dollar reserves to about 25 billion ECU. The DM's role as an international reserve currency increased considerably during the 1980s. Among the international reserve currencies the DM is second to the US $ with a share of about 20%.

2.5 International relations

2.5.1 *Foreign trade by industry and by country*

The FRG's foreign trade volume (exports and imports) is about 9% of the world trade (France and the UK 5.5% each). From 1958 to 1988 the share of German exports to EC countries increased from 37.9% to 54.1% (see Statistical Annexe, Table D21). The share of exports to all other regions decreased, with the exception of the USA and Japan: 53.3% of German imports came from EC countries in 1988. The proportion from all other regions, with the exception of Japan, declined, for example, the imports from developing countries from 17.2% to 9.4%. Germany's major trading partner is France (exports of 34 billion ECU and imports of 25 billion ECU). France is followed by the UK and Italy on the export side and by the Netherlands and Italy on the import side. The countries most dependent on German imports are Austria (44% of all imports are of FRG origin), Switzerland (34%) and the Netherlands (26%), while less than 20% of France's imports and less than 5% of those of the USA and Japan come from Germany. The FRG shows a trade deficit with only a few countries, such as Japan (6 billion ECU), Brazil, Norway, Libya, Taiwan, Ireland (all less than 1 billion ECU). Eastern Europe until recently, had only a share of less than 5% in the FRG's foreign trade. The trade volume may increase significantly in the future; so far the euphoria caused by the unexpected transformation to market economies in Eastern Europe has not been borne out by business records.

The structure of foreign trade by sector
Exports are concentrated in four sectors: automobile industry (17.5%), machinery (15.3%, chemicals (14.1%) and electrical and electronic engineering (11.2%). Imports are less concentrated: chemicals amount to 10.5% of imports, electrical and electronic engineering to 9.5%, textiles to 9.4%, automobiles to 8.1%, oil, gas and petroleum products to 7.2%, agricultural products to 6.9% and food to 6.2%.

An increasing share of exports is in technology-intensive goods. Recently producers of machinery, automobile exporters and even steel producers have been very successful. Industries such as textiles and leather goods are losing market share to international competitors. Its own protectionism, especially in coal mining, steel, agriculture, food and textiles, cost the FRG billions of DM and thousands of jobs. Protection does not pay off, even in terms of jobs. However, well-organised, special-interest groups block any moves towards a more rapid structural change.

2.5.2 *Balance of payments*

German economic policy continues to miss the goal of external equilibrium (see Statistical Annexe, Table D23). From 1982 on, the current balance has been in permanent surplus reaching a peak in 1989 at 50 billion ECU (i.e. 4.6% of GNP). These surpluses result exclusively from the surpluses in the trade balance (65 billion ECU in 1989). No significant surpluses occur in the service balance primarily because Germans spend about 14 billion ECU per year as tourists abroad. The balance of unrequited transfers (transfers by foreign workers and payments for international organisations and grants) shows significant deficits.

Related to the surplus in the current balance are large exports of capital. In short-term capital flows, assets increased by 50 billion ECU faster than liabilities (1989), compared to only 8 billion ECU in 1987. Long-term capital flows show, with the exception of 1988, no such dramatic increase. Net capital export in 1989 was 11 billion ECU. The increase of German direct investment abroad (from 8 billion ECU in 1987 to 12 billion ECU in 1989) has raised concerns about the attractivity of the FRG for investors. However, this increase should not be interpreted as a flight of capital but rather as complementary to increased exports; it is marketing- and sales-oriented rather than production-oriented. These concerns seem to be supported by relatively low new foreign direct investment in the FRG. Actually, the increase of foreign direct investment was 1.7 billion ECU in 1987 and is 5 billion ECU in 1989. Moreover, the changes in Eastern Europe improved the attractivity of Germany as a location for business activity and investment. In total, German direct investment abroad now amounts to more than 72 billion ECU, the largest part of it (about 40%) in the USA. Foreign direct investment in the FRG is about 53 billion ECU (see *Statistisches Bundesamt*, Table 24.5).

2.6 Special issue: German economic integration

The single most important challenge which Germany is currently facing is the integration with the East German states. German integration is part of the historic transformation in Eastern Europe, especially in the Soviet Union, and hence part of the integration of a larger Europe. Since the peaceful revolution in the GDR starting in autumn 1989, this process accelerated to a breathtaking speed. After opening the border and the wall in Berlin, the next important step was the currency union which came into being in July 1990. The first problem was choosing a proper conversion rate for Mark into DM which would safeguard the people's assets and income without ruining the competitiveness of the East German economy (wages, interest on debt). The compromise solution was as follows:

- Wages 1:1. Average wages were 1200 M per month (FRG 3500 DM per month) and productivity was 30–40% of that in the FRG.
- Pensions 1:1. As the average pension in the GDR would have been 380 DM additional provisions were necessary here.
- Bank deposits and debt 1 DM : 2 M, except for an amount of 4000 M *per capita* which was exchanged 1:1.

As from the 3rd of October 1990 the GDR no longer existed. The East German states joined the FRG in accordance with Art 23 of the *Grundgesetz*. If the economic integration process is successful, Germany's position as an economic super-power will be significantly reinforced, maybe by 20%. However, in order to make German integration an economic success story, a large number of difficult problems will have to be resolved in future years.

(1) First of all, private property rights have to be restored and guaranteed in order to stimulate investment and to attract West German and foreign capital. Nobody knows whether entrepreneurial 'animal spirits' (J M Keynes) have survived 40 years in an autocratic system and hence if they will stimulate significant internal development. Attracting outside private initiative is crucial because public budgets alone cannot provide the resources that are necessary to rebuild the GDR. Most of the GDR firms (*Kombinate, Landwirtschaftliche Produktionsgenossenschaften*) were public or social property and have to be privatised. All this property has been converted into a huge public institution (*Treuhandanstalt*) which is now organising privatisation.

(2) Price reform has to be continued and accelerated. All subsidies, for example for food, housing, transportation, etc. have to be abolished or reduced in order to reach realistic, i.e. cost-oriented, prices and to end shortages (sellers' markets). Prices will go up and may cause open inflation. With net incomes increasing only slowly, the standard of living may decline and poor people will experience real problems. Therefore, substantial direct subsidisation of incomes will continue to be necessary in the near future.

(3) It will be necessary to deal with unemployment. Most products and production technologies in the GDR were not competitive in the international market in which firms had to survive from one day to the next. Most firms had no chance of coping with this challenge, particularly given a management that had no idea of what a market economy is all about and consumer preferences turning rapidly towards Western products. Shut-downs and unemployment are the consequences. To overcome this situation it is necessary:

- to increase labour productivity. This requires more capital investment because the level of capital equipment per worker in the average workplace in the GDR was about a third of that in an equivalent workplace in the FRG. Significant tax incentives would be helpful in attracting private investors. The new states must become an attractive location not only as a market but also as production centres in order to avoid regional imbalances in the long run.
- to retrain and qualify the labour force on a large scale, beginning at the shop floor and extending right up to top management. This is not possible without government involvement and government support for private initiatives, and it will cost billions of DM.

(4) The burden on public budgets. The East German states will cause huge deficits in public budgets because they are participating in most government programmes on equal terms but are unable to contribute to revenues. Unemployment and low incomes give rise to high social security expenditures. Low revenues result from the sluggish economy and from the absence of effective tax authorities. The German Unity Fund, which will be raising 115 billion DM from the (old) FRG states and the capital market until 1994 will not be sufficient to cope with the infrastructure problems. Estimates state that 250–500 billion ECU are required to rebuild the rail, road and telecommunication systems. The only quick solution can come from attracting support from private investors. If strong economic growth continues in the FRG (increasing tax revenues by 6–7% or 20 billion ECU per annum) this may bring some relief, but it is not the solution.

(5) The GDR regime left behind an environmental disaster of huge and not yet fully explored dimensions. Among the consequences of this disaster are the following:

- the need for immediate closures of some industrial plants (because of highly toxic or dangerous waste products, e.g. in the chemical industry and nuclear power plants);
- the need for investment in 'end-of-the-pipeline' technologies, such as scrubbers for brown coal power plants and purification plants for processing drinking water;
- the need for a change in the ecological structure: the closing down of almost all the chemical industry based on coal, increasing energy efficiency, the introduction of interdependent livestock and crop farming;
- the urgent need to clean up hazardous waste dumps, which over the years have provided a cheap method of dumping hazardous waste from East and West Germany.

(6) While the FRG may successfully take care of the former GDR, it would be overtaxed if it also had to take care of the rest of Eastern Europe. Here is where the EC and the USA come in. Both should provide financial support now because this will prevent a revival of the old political antagonisms and so save a lot of money in future defence expenditure. The Bank for Economic Recovery and Development in Eastern Europe represents a first step in forming a strategy like the Marshall Plan. Gorbachev's economic adviser, N Petrakov, is right when he states: 'Unfortunately Westerners have so far acted largely as if they were watching in a stadium to see which team would win. You must understand that you are in the game, on the same field' (*Fortune*, 7 May 1990, p. 87).

2.7 Trends and developments

(1) The international competitiveness of Germany is excellent, as the surplus in the trade balance suggests. However, Germany is, and will remain, a country where production is expensive. The most important strength of the German economic system may be summarised in the following three points:

- a qualified labour force at all levels of employment (from the shop floor to the research laboratory) with a unique work ethic and know-how;
- a highly developed infrastructure making mobility, communication and distribution easy;
- social, political and monetary stability reducing the uncertainty in calculating the return on investments.

The main problems of the German economic system seem to be:

- rigid institutions defended by well-organised interest groups (in part the other side of the stability coin);
- high costs (of labour, government taxes, social security, energy, environmental protection), higher than justified by the advantages of the system;
- diseconomies resulting from agglomeration (real estate and housing costs, traffic congestion).

All of the problems are closely related to the strength of the system. This sounds paradoxical, but it is due to the German way of overdoing things, the tendency to become too sophisticated, the desire to be perfect.

Production will be profitable in Germany only for those firms who rely on those particular resources which Germany can offer: a highly qualified and motivated labour force, an excellent infrastructure, a

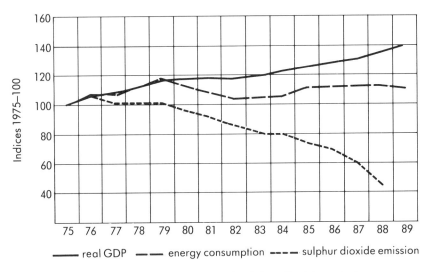

Figure 2.4 GDP, energy consumption and sulphur dioxide emission
Source: Bundesminister für Wirtschaft, 1990, p. 45

differentiated industry structure (with innovative and reliable suppliers), a market-place with high purchasing power, social consensus (as evidenced, for example, by the very few working days lost through strikes) and an attractive natural environment. Purchasing power will increase further in years to come, because throughout forty years of peace and thriftiness an enormous amount of wealth has been accumulated. Consumers will become more discerning and competition more intensive as efforts to deregulate and to open up markets continue.

(2) With respect to addressing future problems and making provisions to deal with them, there is a reluctance in Germany to address future problems with vigour. These will be problems such as the essential restructuring of the economy in order to save energy, the redefinition of the role of labour (becoming more flexible, retraining, greater participation) and of social security (more private initiative) as well as the implementation of a culture of social dialogue on the consequences of new technologies. The Federal Government, occupied with unification issues, addresses only some of these problems but displays no positive leadership. The new challenges of the deterioration of the natural environment and world climate do not receive due attention. There are some success stories, such as the reduction in sulphur-dioxide emissions (see Figure 2.4). But these challenges demand dramatic increases in productivity of energy and resources which would require a redirection and a broader concept of government economic policy. In this respect economic policy in other EC countries, such as Denmark or the Netherlands, is more 'modern' than in Germany.

(3) The process of German unification will add more problems than stimulating effects to the German economy, at least in the short term. Increasing deficits will raise pressure for budget cuts, and important investments in the future, such as R&D expenditure and environment protection, will be among the victims. Only in the longer term may the stimulating effects, emerging from new 'brains' and entrepreneurs, predominate, creating opportunities for a pool of unexploited inventions in, for example, optics, electrical engineering and mechanical engineering. Moreover, the role as bridgehead in East–West trade may contribute to Germany's prosperity. As a former front-line state Germany is among the nations that will be major beneficiaries of the dividends of peace.

In summary, Germany as a nation, or rather as a region within the global economy, must be aware that it, like most of her firms, is located at the high-quality, high-price end of the market spectrum. Furthermore, it is no longer in the position of an imitator adapting to trends originating in the USA. Germany is expected to participate in a world leadership role. This opens up new opportunities but also implies unknown risks. Pioneers often face high costs and it may be more convenient instead to be a close second. Germany has not yet lived up to the demands of this new role. No doubt so far almost nowhere in the world has a better combination of economic success and social justice been found. However, environmental problems have added a new dimension to the 'big trade-off' (A. M. Okun) between efficiency and equality. Global leadership should deal with this new 'magic triangle'. The existing 'Model Germany' could not be generalised: its high performance it still based on too high an energy consumption and too high a level of environmental pollution. If the whole world were to adapt to that standard, collapse would be the consequence. Politicians from all parts of the political spectrum are now debating the transformation of the German economic system into a social-ecological market economy. The vision is that of a peace economy: minimum military power, resolution of social conflict and harmony with nature. This, truly, is the new challenge which will, hopefully, be addressed once the haze of German unification has evaporated.

2.8 Bibliography and sources of information

Literature

Bundesminister für Wirtschaft (various years): *Jahreswirtschaftsbericht der Bundesregierung*, Bonn

Commission of the European Community (1989): *Panorama of EC Industry 1990*, Brussels/Luxembourg

Deutsche Bundesbank (various years): *Geschäftsbericht* (Annual Report), Frankfurt

Donges, J. B./Schmidt, K.-D. et al. (1988): *Mehr Strukturwandel für Wachstum und Beschäftigung. Die deutsche Wirtschaft im Anpassungsstau*, Tübingen

Kroker, R. (1990): *Lohnstückkosten im Verarbeitenden Gewerbe im internationalen Vergleich, iw-trends* 17. Jahrgang, Heft 1, D1–D12

Klodt, H./Schmidt, K.-D. et al. (1989): *Weltwirtschaftlicher Strukturwandel und Standortwettbewerb. Die deutsche Wirtschaft auf dem Prüfstand,* Tübingen

Lampert, H. (1988): *Die Wirtschafts- und Sozialordnung der Bundesrepublik Deutschland.* 9. Aufl., München

OECD (1989): Economic Survey Germany 1988/1989, Paris

Sachverständigenrat zur Begutachtung der gesamtwirtschaftlichen Entwicklung/Council of Economic Experts (various years): Jahresgutachten (Annual Report), Wiesbaden

Soltwedel, R. et al. (1986): *Deregulierungspotentiale in der Bundesrepublik,* Tübingen

Statistisches Bundesamt (various years): *Statistisches Jahrbuch für die Bundesrepublik Deutschland,* Stuttgart/Mainz

Stolper, W. F./Roskamp, K. W. (1979): Planning a Free Economy: Germany 1945–1960, *Zeitschrift für die gesamte Staatswissenschaft* 135, 374–404

Vaubel, R./Barbier, H. D. (eds. 1986): *Handbuch Marktwirtschaft,* Pfullingen

Wirtschaftsgesetze. *Textsammlung für Juristen und Wirtschaftsfachleute,* München

Sources of information

Arbeitsgemeinschaft deutscher wirtschaftswissenschaftlicher Forschungsinstitute, Poschingerstr. 5, 8000 München 86

Bundesanstalt für Arbeit, Regensburger Str. 104, 8500 Nürnberg 30

Bundesministerium der Finanzen, Graurheindorfer Str. 108, 5300 Bonn 1

Bundesministerium für Wirtschaft, Villemombler Str. 76, 5300 Bonn 1

Bundesverband der Deutschen Industrie (BDI), Gustav-Heinemann-Ufer 84–88, 5000 Köln 1

Deutsche Bundesbank, Postfach 1000602, 6000 Frankfurt 1

Deutscher Gewerkschaftsbund (DGB), Hans-Böckler-Str. 39, 4000 Düsseldorf 30

Deutscher Industrie- und Handelstag (DIHT), Adenauer Allee 148, 5300 Bonn 1

Presse- und Informationsamt der Bundesregierung, Welckerstr. 11, 5300 Bonn 1

Statistisches Bundesamt, Postfach 5528, 6200 Wiesbaden 1

Umweltbundesamt, Bismarckplatz 1, 1000 Berlin 33

3 Spain

Professor Milagros García Crespo
Professor Arantza Mendizábal
Dr Marisol Esteban

3.1 Institutional framework and historical context

In analysing the institutional framework and historical context of the Spanish economy two years are of great significance. In 1978 the Constitution was approved and the democratic system, suspended since the 1936–39 Civil War, was re-established. Two aspects of the Constitution are specially relevant for our analysis here: first, the adoption of the market economy model in the context of an *état de droit*, and second, the transition from a very centralised economic and political system towards a high degree of decentralisation. The Spanish territory was divided up into 17 Autonomous Communities responsible for many aspects of local economic activity.

The year 1986 is significant since it marks the recognition of Spain as a member of the European Community. This relatively late entrance is being compensated for by the determination of Spain to catch up in the European integration process. EC integration requires the Spanish economy to eliminate, over a transition period of six years, the complicated system of protectionism which historically has influenced and conditioned the evolution of the Spanish industry. Entrance into the EC coincided with a period of economic growth which made it possible to reduce the high levels of unemployment which had prevailed in the Spanish economy since mid-1979.

The new economic model embodied in the Constitution substantially modified the economic management system prevailing during the 40 years of Franco's dictatorship. The Franco period falls into two main periods, from 1939–59 and 1959–75.

The 1939–59 period was characterised by (a) the project to build an autarchical economic system, (b) extensive public intervention in the economy, (c) the international blackout, and (d) the insignificance of international trade activities. During this period, basic goods were

55

rationed, productivity levels and income *per capita* decreased significantly, and there were no institutional channels for working-class claims to be negotiated. The civil war and its aftermath meant that the production levels of 1936 were not regained until 1951, when US financial assistance flowed in following the installation of US military bases in Spain. In 1955 Spain was accepted as a member of UNO.

The beginning of the second period is marked by the '1959 Stabilisation Plan'. This Plan signalled a new economic approach involving greater use of the market mechanism and thus initiated a slow and somewhat belated process towards liberalisation of both internal activities and outside relations. In the event, it proved easier to replace strict state control of the economy with a more liberal approach than to give up the authoritarianism and centralism so entrenched in post-war Spain. The liberalisation process implied the entrance of the Spanish economy into the OECD as well as the devaluation of the peseta and the acceptance of foreign investment into the Spanish economic system.

This liberalisation process, however, proved difficult to maintain and a well-developed protectionist system was established together with privileged financial circuits for several industrial sectors and high customs duties for an extensive range of imports. Pressure for protection was exerted by the main enterprise groups, and as late as 1968 the average customs duty for industrial goods reached 31%.

Parallel to the rise of protectionism and the preservation of the national market for home production, a period of economic growth commenced in 1960, with sharp increases in GDP real rates (averaging 8.6% during 1960–65). During the 1960–65 period fixed capital investment increased at a real rate of 14% per year. This growth was based upon the migration of workers to other countries in Europe and tourist activities, which provided for the necessary foreign currency to pay for the structural trade deficit and generated surpluses in the balance of payments.

During this period a contradiction manifested itself between the economic evolution, characterised by growth and capitalist concentration, and the politics of the Franco regime. A 'peculiar' socioeconomic change occurred since the sharp economic growth (in terms of GDP increases) was not followed by the development of a welfare state and a democratic political system.

In 1964, indicative planning was initiated inspired by the French model. The three 'four-year plans' (1964–75) basically consisted of macroeconomic forecasts, which were compulsory for the public sector and indicative for the private sector. These plans introduced a certain rationality into public sector activities. However, as the 1960s progressed and the protectionist system was erected, GDP increases weakened, with an average annual growth rate of 5.9% between 1968 and 1973 (see

Statistical Annexe, Table D 11), and a lower rate (7.4%) of fixed capital investment (see Statistical Annexe, Table D 16). At the same time, inflation, which had been controlled in the 1960s, was allowed to increase reaching 11% in 1973 (see Statistical Annexe, Table D 17). The expansive phase was artificially prolonged throughout 1974, although the international economic crisis had manifested itself and most industrial countries had already adopted restrictive measures in their economies to counteract the effects of the sharp increases of oil prices.

With the death of Franco in 1975 the period of economic growth came to an end and the process of political transition towards democracy began, even though the country was in the middle of serious economic problems.

The 1973 oil crisis did not modify the economic strategy pursued by the Spanish government. Not only did it fail to adapt to the recession, but continued to implement an expansive policy relying on currency reserves and borrowing capacity in anticipation of eventual international recovery. Thus, the Spanish economic cycle ran counter to international tendencies; GDP increased by 5% in 1974 (see Statistical Annexe, Table D 11), but a pronounced trade deficit was registered and the rate of inflation rose to 17% (see Statistical Annexe, Table D 17). Neither output (by using restrictive policies) nor the level of prices (by modifying the exchange rate) were adjusted. On the contrary, an excess of production capacity was generated leading to reductions in productivity levels together with increases of average costs and prices. As a consequence, external debt rose and foreign reserves were significantly reduced.

These trends in the major economic indicators continued and even worsened through the following years, so that by the end of 1977 an inflation rate of 35% was expected. The government was eventually obliged to undertake a set of corrective short-term economic measures, together with others of a structural and institutional nature.

Inflation was brought under control by the management of public sector expenditure, liquid assets in the hands of the private sector and controls over wage increases. Simultaneously, unemployment levels began to rise (see Statistical Annexe, Table D 9). In 1978, GDP increased by 1.4% (see Statistical Annexe, Table D 11) while there were 300,000 more unemployed.

The adoption of the market economy model in the context of an *état de droit* in 1978 meant at last the recognition of political parties as the expression of political pluralism together with the acceptance that both trade unions and employers' associations contribute legitimately to the defence and promotion of their economic and social interests. This late evolution allows us to understand the already poor role of trade unions in economic life, or the difficulties encountered when negotiating with the employers' associations who have lost the privileges enjoyed in

Franco's dictatorship. This is the expression of the fact that Spain is a country recently introduced to democratic practice.

Moreover, the 1978 Constitution led to a new territorial organisation of the State, since it recognises the right of historical nations and regions to autonomy. This has allowed a high degree of political decentralisation.

The public sector has a relevant presence in the economy, accounting for more than 40% of GDP by the late 1980s (see Statistical Annexe, Table D 18). Yet not all the activities generated by public expenditure are carried out by central administration. On the contrary, it is necessary to differentiate at least two levels of the administration: a first level, called 'central administration' and constituted by the administration of the central State, other autonomous public organisations and the social security; the approval of their budgets and the control of their functioning is a task of central Parliament; and a second level, called territorial administrations, and constituted by 17 Autonomous Communities and the local administration (local and provincial authorities). The autonomous Parliaments in the case of the Autonomous Communities, and government bodies of local administrations are responsible for establishing their budgets and activities.

The decentralisation of public expenditure, measured in terms of the amount administered by Autonomous Communities, has significantly increased since 1984 (see Table 3.1), as a consequence of the transfer of responsibilities from central administrations and the increasing role of local authorities in the Spanish political system. Yet, the distribution of public expenditure still remains far away from the desired distribution 50, 25, 35. Nevertheless, it is clear that the decentralisation process has been pursued at a pace not met by any other Western political structure.

Table 3.1 Public expenditure by administrative level (%)

Year	Central State	Autonomous Communities	Local Authorities
1984	75	13	12
1989	65	21	14

The responsibilities transferred to the Autonomous Communities range from health, culture and education to housing, urban planning, roads and other infrastructures, several elements of industrial policy and training programmes, and even tax control in some Communities (e.g. Navarre and the Basque Country).

Although Spain had been trying over a long period of time to integrate itself in the EC, it was not until 1978, with the transition towards democracy, that its candidacy was taken seriously into consideration by Brussels. The first and very important consequence of entry to the EC was the need to dismantle the protectionist system behind which Spanish industry had traditionally sheltered. From that moment onwards, the need to improve the competitiveness of Spanish production and the urgent need to carry out the restructuring of many industrial sectors became a priority for economic leaders.

This need to undertake a restructuring of the production system came at a time of recession lasting from1979 to 1985. During this period GDP grew at an average annual rate of only 1.5%, with a positive contribution from the foreign sector, a stable level of internal consumption and a negative rate of investment (see Statistical Annexe, Tables D 11 and D 16). The most important result of this demand and production crisis was the loss of over 1 million jobs, over 3 million people unemployed, equal to an unemployment rate of more than 20% by 1985 (see Statistical Annexe, Table D 9). Furthermore, the inflation rate remained close to 10% (see Statistical Annexe, Table D 17), and the weak economic activity together with an increased demand for social services affected both the income and the expenditure of the public sector, public deficit thus reaching 6% of GDP by the mid-1980s.

While experiencing these severe economic difficulties Spain became a member of the EC in 1986. Right from the start, the Spanish economy embarked on a period of expansion that has gradually overcome the most important economic disequilibria. Significant increases in private and public consumption and, more importantly, a rise in fixed capital investment have resulted in an increase of internal demand of over 6% per year in the late 1980s. While unemployment has fallen in recent years to 17.6% on average in 1989 (see Statistical Annexe, Table D 9) and the public deficit has been reduced to 2.6% of GDP (see Statistical Annexe, Table D 19), the expansion has been accompanied by rising inflation (see Statistical Annexe, Table D 17) and serious deficits in the balance of trade (see Statistical Annexe, Table D 2). Nevertheless, there is confidence on the part of investors in the Spanish economy, giving rise to appreciation of the currency.

3.2 Main economic characteristics

3.2.1 *Human resources*

Population
The Spanish population in 1986 (the date of the last available census) amounted to 38.6 millions (see Statistical Annexe, Table D 6). The country experienced the process of 'demographic transition' (the shift from a situation with high death and fertility rates to another one where low death and high fertility rates prevail) later than Northern European

countries. This has produced a radical change in the age pyramid which has gradually become narrower at the base and wider at the peak.

However, while birth rates in the 1960s and early 1970s were relatively high in the context of a process of intense economic growth, during the late 1970s and 1980s birth rates have drastically dropped. Nowadays, Spanish demographic trends mirror general trends in Northern and Central Europe. The reasons for this change are not clear. Undoubtedly, the economic crisis and the subsequent insecurity are at the roots of this shift, but other social and attitudinal changes are also considered by experts as the inability of economic recovery to modify birth rate trends demonstrates. Nevertheless, the major economic consequences of this change will only be noticeable in twenty years' time.

Active population

During the 1960s the active population registered a significant increase, approximately one million people over the decade, representing by the end of the period 38% of the total population. This increase of the active population, however, was not accompanied by the generation of a sufficient number of jobs, a factor which in turn provoked a slight increase of unemployment.

The industrialisation process of the 1960s provoked a shift of the labour force from the agricultural sector towards industry and service activities. However, these sectors were unable to absorb the flow of workers from agriculture. The alternative and effective safety valve for the Spanish economy was the constant emigration to Northern and Central European countries until 1974 when the international economic crisis brought this process to an end (see Table 3.2).

Throughout the recession, the entire industrial sector was seriously affected. This circumstance linked to the closure of foreign labour markets for Spanish workers led to a severe increase of unemployment levels, which led, in turn, to the stabilisation of the active population. The economic recovery from 1985 together with demographic reasons (the baby-boom of the 1960s) have induced a steady increase of active population rates, even if Spanish levels remain lower than the EC average,

Table 3.2 Spanish migration to Europe, 1959–74 (number of migrants)

Years	Emigration	Immigration	Balance
1960–64	658,848	254,068	+404,780
1965–69	324,784	216,584	+108,200
1970–74	462,276	396,400	+65,876
1975–79	69,089	336,500	−267,411
1980–85	99,246	91,006	+8,240

Source: Instituto Español de Emigración

especially for women. Yet, a major change of the recent past has been precisely the integration of women into the labour market even though female activity rates remain in 1990 below 30%.

Employment

Throughout the 1975–85 crisis period, employment decreased by more than 2 million jobs, falling to 10.5 million jobs in 1985. From that year, with the economic recovery, 1.7 million net jobs have been generated (see the evolution of annual percentage change in Statistical Annexe, Table D 2). Self-employment has remained stable, while wage jobs have absorbed most of the employment growth. Both the public and private sector have contributed to this employment recovery, even if the private sector has shown a high dynamism.

Ongoing structural change means that employment in agriculture continues to fall (14% of total employment in 1988; see Statistical Annexe, Table D 8), even though the weight of agriculture is still significant compared to EC average levels. Industrial employment, on the contrary, dropped drastically during the late 1970s and early 1980s, but since 1987 has experienced a relative revival. The construction sector, in particular, has shown up very strongly indeed with a 47% increase in employment since 1985, though in absolute terms the service sector, with an increase of 342,000 jobs (more than 25% increase) has made the greatest contribution.

Unemployment

The proportionately large number of young people in the labour market, the fact that the post-war demographic explosion took place in Spain in the 1955–65 period, ten years later than in the rest of European countries, has meant the integration of a large number of young people in the labour market during the crisis, together with the late integration of women in the labour market have intensified the effects of employment loss during the 1975–85 decade. Unemployment levels reached a peak of 3 million people (22%) in 1985 (see Statistical Annexe, Table D 9).

Unemployment figures show an irregular distribution by age and sex. The rate for women (25%) is significantly higher than that for men (13%). By age group, youth unemployment is by far the most acute, even though in relative terms it is the group which has shown the fastest recovery. This adverse situation may be due to (1) the fact that in periods of crisis, starters are in a very unfavourable position and (2) a neglect of the public sector, since the relatively lower rate of unemployment among the older age groups is due to an extensive use of early retirement practices, while employment programmes specially oriented towards the youth of the country are not very developed in Spain.

3.2.2 Major production indicators

Gross domestic product (GDP)
The economic crisis seriously affected the entire economic system as the evolution of GDP growth rate demonstrates (see Statistical Annexe, Table D 11). Between 1975 and 1980, Spanish GDP grew at rates significantly lower than the rest of developed countries. However, in the 1981–84 period, a general recession period, this magnitude increased at comparable rates. From 1986, the Spanish economy has been growing again at the highest rates among the EC countries. The intense growth in terms of GDP per head increases that characterised the Spanish economic boom of the 1960s can be seen again since 1986.

Throughout the 1955–74 period, when the Spanish economy underwent the fastest economic growth of its history, employment and production structure changed drastically. The importance of the primary sector diminished in favour of industry, and more especially in favour of construction and service activities.

Later on, with the economic crisis, the proportionate loss of agriculture and industry was significant, as the service sector expanded to account by 1985 for over 50% of total employment and more than 55% of GDP. If the reduction of the primary sector in relative terms may be seen as a component of the process of modernisation of the economy, the fall of industrial activities can be explained both by the crisis of the sector and a restructuring of production. The contribution to GDP of the secondary sector fell by more than five percentage points. There were also important changes in the structure of industrial production. Table 3.3 analyses this transformation, breaking up industrial activities into 25 industrial sectors and classifying them into three main groups: strong, medium and weak demand at the international level. According to this classification, Spanish industrial structure in 1970, and even nowadays, presents the characteristics of that of a developed country of intermediate level, with a reduced weight of strong-demand industries, an important presence of medium-demand activities and still a significant influence of weak-demand industries.

However, the evolution of the recent past shows an increase of strong demand sectors—over 3 percentage points between 1970 and 1986—with the rising presence of two new sectors—office equipment and computers and electronic material—and the lower weight of electric machinery and chemistry. The group of medium-demand sectors has increased its share in total production by 4.4 percentage points in the same period. This increase is due mainly to the automobile sector, machinery and equipment, foodstuffs and oil refineries. The group of weak-demand sectors has lost its share, falling by 7.7 percentage points since 1975. This fall is general with the exception of steel activities, and relates especially to shipbuilding, leather, and clothing and shoes.

This evolution allowed Spain to achieve an industrial value-added growth rate which, compared with that of the EC countries, was similar from 1975 to 1985 (higher from 1976 to 1980, and lower from 1981 to 1985). The rapid increase of internal demand from 1985 onwards, with the recovery of private consumption and especially investment, gave rise to an outstanding industrial growth, well above the average of European countries.

The service sector exhibits three main characteristics in Spain: (a) it has been the most dynamic in terms of employment generation and production growth, (b) it is the main sector in terms of its share of GDP and total employment, and (c) little is known about its main structural characteristics since any study on service activities in Spain encounters countless limits imposed by the available statistics.

Table 3.3 Structure of industrial production, 1970–86 (%)

Sector	1970	1986
Strong demand sectors	11.2	14.5
1 Aircraft	0.2	0.4
2 Office equipment and computers	–	0.6
3 Electrical equipment and components	3.1	3.4
4 Electronic material	–	2.0
5 Precision instruments	0.3	0.4
6 Pharmaceutical products	1.0	1.5
7 Chemistry	6.6	6.2
Medium demand sectors	49.0	53.4
8 Rubber and plastics	2.8	3.1
9 Automobiles	4.8	4.1
10 Mechanical equipment	3.8	4.1
11 Railway transport equipment	0.5	0.2
12 Other transport equipment	0.4	0.3
13 Foodstuffs, drinks and tobacco	21.4	22.9
14 Oil refineries	10.4	10.2
15 Paper	5.0	4.5
Weak demand sectors	39.8	32.1
16 Steel	5.7	8.5
17 Non-ferrous metals	2.7	1.6
18 Shipbuilding	1.8	0.7
19 Metallic products	4.5	6.0
20 Non-metallic mineral products	4.2	3.7
21 Wood and cork	4.3	3.1
22 Textile	5.9	3.4
23 Leather	1.2	0.7
24 Clothing and shoes	7.9	3.4
25 Other manufacturing industries	1.5	0.9
Total industrial sectors	100.0	100.0

Table 3.4 Contribution of service activities to the generation of gross value added, 1985 (%)

Commerce, maintenance and repair	23.85
Restaurants, hotels and bars	7.73
Transport	7.49
Communications	3.01
Credit and insurance	10.41
Renting of buildings	12.70
Education and research	5.18
Health	5.33
Services to firms, other services and domestic services	12.28
General services of public administration	12.03
Total services	100.00

A detailed analysis of the contribution of different service activities to the generation of gross value-added can be found in Table 3.4. According to this division, the most important sectors nowadays are: commerce, maintenance and repairs; renting of buildings; services to firms, other services and domestic services, and general services of public administration.

The activity branches with the highest growth rates during the 1980s are: air transport, communications and public administration services, each increasing by over 4% per annum at constant prices. At the same time, there are some branches which have been fairly stable, such as commerce, maintenance and repairs, railway transport and passenger transport by road. A small number of activities have contracted during the period, such as seaway transport, and the private activities of education and health, which contrasts against the significant increase in the public activities in these same branches. To conclude this section on the service sector, it has to be taken into account that the economy's dependence on the service sector is not caused by public services financed through the public budget, the relative weight of which is three percentage points lower in terms of GDP than the EC average. The major importance of the service sector is the result of tourist activities and the weakness of industrial activities themselves.

Consumption and saving

In the last 15 years, and taking into consideration the relative stability of these macroeconomic aggregates, private consumption, from initially high levels, increased by two percentage points its share in the GDP between 1981–84. From 1985, along with the economic recovery, private consumption has gradually declined towards EC average levels, thus liberating resources for saving. Public consumption has shown a steady upwards movement, and thus has had a moderately countercyclical effect, though it has not reached the average level of the rest of the European countries.

The level of saving has developed following consumption require-ments. Thus the saving level exhibits a depression which coincides with the hardest years of the crisis, since lower levels of production and employment loss made it necessary to dedicate a higher percentage of resources to consumption. After five years of economic recovery, it seems necessary to encourage internal saving and restrict consumption, both to control inflation and reduce the deficit in the balance of trade.

Gross fixed capital formation

The evolution of gross fixed capital formation appears to be very different from that of most EC countries. This aggregate, in Spain, has exhibited a negative behaviour in the period 1975–84 with a sharp recovery since 1985. Since the mid-1970s public investment has worked in a countercyclical way, maintaining its share in the GDP in the critical years. It is clearly private investment that has been influenced to the greatest extent by economic stagnation and recovery.

The study of Table D 16 in the Statistical Annexe shows some interesting results. The average annual increase during the 1961–70 period reached 11%, almost doubling the average rate of the twelve EC countries. Conversely, in the depression of 1975–85, it experienced a very negative evolution, to come again to the top of EC growth in the past five years (13% against 6%, EC average). The possibility of Spanish economic growth approaching average European levels depends precisely upon this capacity to generate investment.

Income distribution

The distribution of national income among different components is important because of its effects upon social welfare and also because it affects the dynamics of growth itself. In Spain, the variation of income distribution has been rapid and far-reaching.

The *per capita* income of the Spanish population increased from US $337 in 1960 to US $2275 in 1974. During the recession, real income grew very slowly at an annual average rate of 1.2%, and real *per capita* income at 1.16%. This situation has notably changed since 1985. In 1986, *per capita* income in Spain amounted to 57% of the EC average (76% of Community's average, if income data are corrected to take account of differences in real purchasing power).

The unquestionable income expansion and the radical change of the productive structure were accompanied by particular problems. In the first place, economic growth did not generate enough employment, thus inducing the migration of over two million people in search of work abroad (see section above). Another feature was the lack of a modern public sector able to satisfy the collective needs of the country and to correct the uneven distribution of rent and wealth.

Distribution by factor income

An interesting analysis of the various aspects of income distribution can be made by studying the respective income shares of labour, capital and entrepreneurial activities. However, national accounting does not provide the information necessary to analyse this issue. In the case of Spain, however, the reports of the Bank of Bilbao provide significant information to which we turn now. Some aspects need some discussion:

1   The relative importance of wages and salaries grew until 1980 to gradually decrease after that year. Two facts have contributed to this apparently surprising situation: (a) the higher weight of social security contributions which have been applied to finance the increasing social benefits, especially after 1975; and (b) the reduction in the number of employed people, which can be numbered in more than 1.5 million people between 1975 and 1985.
2   The capitalisation process of the Spanish economy together with the obsolescence of the productive system leads to an increasing level of amortisations as a percentage of GDP (12% in 1985).
3   In the evolution of mix rents (rents from self-employment activities), the fall of agricultural rents contrasts with the maintenance of rents of other professionals and private entrepreneurs.
4   Capital rents have shown a behaviour coherent with the economic development. In contrast to the stability of incomes from rented accommodation, both firms' savings and interests and dividends fell during the crisis to increase again after 1985.

3.2.3 *Wages and productivity*

Real labour costs experienced a significant increase from 1970, especially from 1974 until 1980, when different measures obliged them to fall at varying rates. This evolution of real labour costs has been primarily the result of the evolution of wages and salaries. Net real wages over the 1970s grew constantly because of the strength of trade unions throughout the political transition. During the 1980s, however, the rate of increase has been systematically reduced. Another factor which has contributed to this increase of labour costs is the evolution of social security contributions which gradually account for a bigger share of total labour costs.

As far as productivity is concerned, during the 1960s, a sharp increase of labour productivity took place, mostly in the industrial sector. Since 1975, the increases of productivity are mainly due to employment reduction in an attempt to offset wage increases.

Until 1973, the evolution of labour costs and productivity went parallel while in the 1973–79 period a pronounced gap developed as a consequence of the sharp increases of real labour costs and the stagnation of productivity. Since 1980, the gap between the evolution of labour costs and productivity is being reduced favouring the recovery of working margins. On the one hand, labour costs experience a decrease due to a lower rate of wage increase; on the other, the increases of productivity of industrial activities also make their contribution. However, productivity increase has not been the result of an increase of production levels, which have remained stagnated, but the outcome of a reduction of industrial employment and the closing down of a large number of unproductive firms. It was only as recently as 1985 that a real economic recovery took place with increases of production without significant reductions of employment levels.

Nevertheless, the competitiveness of the Spanish economy in the European market, in terms of nominal unit labour costs (see Statistical Annexe, Table D 15), remains problematic if one takes into consideration the range of labour intensive sectors which still are predominant in the economy.

3.3 Government involvement in the economy

3.3.1 *Fiscal policy*

The public sector inherited from Franco's dictatorship was small, centralised and extremely interventionist. The welfare state as known in most European countries never existed, and thus health, education, social benefits or the provision of infrastructures were and still are undeveloped.

In the first two years of the political transition, until 1977, economic policy in general was not a concern for the political leaders, even less budgetary policy. Between 1977 and 1982 an expansive fiscal policy was carried out, manifested in a sharp increase of public expenditure (see Statistical Annexe, Table D 18). It must be remembered that the crisis provoked the adjustment of many private and public firms, with the transfer of costs from the private to the public sector through subsidies and other financial transfers to firms. Simultaneously, there were important increases of taxes and social security charges in order to finance unemployment subsidies to an increasing number of unemployed workers. As a result of this passive adaptation to the crisis the necessary fiscal and financial reform process was postponed, financing public expenditure via increasing deficits, mostly covered directly by the Bank of Spain (see Statistical Annexe, Table D 2).

Thus, when the Socialist Party came to Office in 1982 the budgetary situation was characterised by a large public deficit (5.6% of GDP), caused by the absence of a fiscal reform, the demographic and financial crisis of the social security system, the costs of economic restructuring and the outburst of social claims which had been suppressed during the dictatorship's period.

It was necessary to re-establish the basis for future economic growth, the only way to create new employment. In order to attain this, the entire economic system had to be stabilised and modernised. Briefly, the major tasks were: (a) to restructure public firms, (b) to balance the social security budget, and (c) to decentralise public income and public expenditure, as ordered by the 1978 Constitution.

The '1984–1987 Medium-term Economic Programme' contemplated a general reduction of real wages, a very restrictive monetary policy, and a budgetary policy designed to reduce public deficit at a moment in which industrial restructuring was to have important effects on the budget. The income raised through the tax system was to be primarily directed at the objective of deficit reduction. Fiscal policy was to take second place behind wage control policy and the demands of monetary policy.

The evolution of public sector expenditure can be seen in Statistical Annexe, Table D 18. Throughout the 1977–82 period, public expenditure increased ten percentage points, going from 27% to 37% of GDP. Between 1982 and 1990 two periods can be clearly identified: the first one, lasting until 1985, in which public expenditure continued to rise, reaching its peak at 42%; and a second one, lasting until 1990, in which public expenditure has been finally stabilised at 41%.

This evolution contrasts clearly with that of other EC countries. Despite this sharp increase in public expenditure, Spanish levels are still low compared with EC average levels. Moreover, while most of the other countries built up the welfare state during the period of economic expansion after the war, Spain has had to attempt this task in the middle of economic recession.

Public income has experienced a clear boost, going from below 25% of GDP in 1975 to 38% in 1990. The factor which explains this behaviour is the evolution of tax income that went from 25% of GDP in 1982 to 32% in 1990 after a much needed tax reform. Yet, it still remains four percentage points below EC average. If one compares the increase in tax pressure and the evolution of public expenditure, the consequence can only be a reduction of public deficit.

The evolution of public deficit can be found in Statistical Annexe, Table D 19, which shows three different periods: (1) between 1977 and

1982, public deficit went from 0.6% to 5.6% of GDP, (2) between 1982 and 1985, the efforts to control it being unsuccessful, it reached a maximum of 7% of GDP; and (3) from 1985, public deficit drops constantly to 2.4% in 1990, below EC average.

The analysis of the evolution of the three most important budgetary variables shows that the objective of stabilisation has been attained to a great extent. If the integration in the Community requires the co-ordination and convergence of economic policies, Spanish budgetary policy should be directed at selectively increasing the dimension of the public sector and improving the financial position of the tax system by combatting tax evasion in order to reduce the structural deficit.

The important deficits registered in the last decade have consider-ably increased the weight of public debt and interests to be paid by the government. Yet, they have been brought under control in the recent past as shown in Statistical Annexe, Table D 2. The level of public debt in Spain (if measured in *per capita* terms) is not high compared with the rest of EC countries, and only a small part is financed in the international financial markets.

Every international economic organisation has evaluated positively the evolution of Spanish public budget in the 1980s. On the income side, fiscal pressure has been increased avoiding, however, significant in-creases of *per capita* fiscal pressure. Besides, the integration in the European Community in 1986 obliged Spain to introduce the VAT system which subsequently entailed a radical reform of the entire indirect tax system. The growth of public expenditure has been re-strained while the number of people who benefit from social services has been augmented by increasing the efficiency of the system. Moreover, this general appraisal appears to be even more favourable if one considers that during the period restructuring and re-industrialisation measures absorbed more than one billion pesetas.

Spanish economic recovery started in 1985 when public deficit reached 7% of GDP. This level of deficit was justified by the need to finance a public expenditure dominated by transfers to families and firms, with investment just reaching 5% of total expenditure. The key factor that explains the reduction of the deficit to 2.6% of GDP in 1989 is the economic recovery which allowed the reduction of expenditure related to the crisis (subsidies and benefits) and the increase of income via taxes.

The above evolutions partially explain the Spanish gap in terms of public facilities and services as in Italy, where there is a clear disequilib-rium with most European countries. In order to attain a satisfactory level of public facilities, is it necessary to increase public expenditure? To answer this question, one must take into account that what in Western Europe is known as 'a rejection of the State' is a phenomenon which has appeared when public expenditure represented more than 50% of GDP since 1980. In Spain, public expenditure reached a maximum of 42% in 1985 due to the reasons mentioned above. This different behaviour has allowed Europe to enjoy a much higher level of infrastructures, public facilities and services than that which exists in Spain, a factor that may hinder Spanish development in the future.

3.3.2 *Industrial policy*

It is commonplace nowadays that the economic crisis undergone by all developed countries since 1974 has been a structural crisis, especially affecting industrial systems and strategies. Sectors such as shipbuilding, steel works or household equipment, characterised by a standardised and hardly sophisticated technology and a not very highly qualified, labour intensive process, faced a substantial excess capacity in all industrialised countries.

The crisis focused, in general terms, on those sectors in which the Spanish economy had specialised during the 1960s where most of the efforts had been concentrated. As a consequence, among other things, of increasing costs resulting from oil price increases together with the emergence of the so called 'Newly Industrialised Countries (NIC)' in the international context, Spain lost the relative advantage achieved in those sectors.

In this context, while most of the countries affected by the crisis reacted rapidly, adapting their productive structures to new market demands by reducing productive capacity and channelling resources towards new activities, Spain reacted slowly. This contributed to further losses of competitiveness at the international level. This situation notwithstanding, industrial policy, between 1975 and 1982, was aimed at stimulating export activities and supporting foreign investment as a way of mitigating the excess capacity and the shortage of internal investment, without paying any attention to technological issues. Moreover, the absence of an adequate macroeconomic policy together with the passivity of most directly affected economic agents—trade unions and entrepreneurs—made even more difficult the undertaking of a determined strategy of an industrial restructuring process. The measures adopted during this period were merely defensive, in an attempt to adapt to the crisis and, therefore, to freeze the sectors most directly affected. This reveals the belief in the soundness of the industrial structure prior to the crisis as an adequate foundation for a future recovery of the Spanish economy.

Clearly opposed to the strategy just described which, nevertheless, comprised some measures to solve the most acute problems of certain big firms, industrial policy from 1982 was primarily aimed at facilitating industrial restructuring processes. This policy was carried out in the context of the 'Restructuring and Re-industrialisation Law' of July 1984, addressed to the so-called 'mature' or 'traditional' sectors. These sectors were: steelworks, shipbuilding, textile, electronic components, shoes, electrical equipment for the automobile industry, fertilisers, iron-alloys, foundry products, copper products, etc. The main objectives of this law and strategy were:

1   to adapt industrial supply to the new market conditions, with the subsequent adjustment of excess capacity in order to secure an adequate dimension;
2   to rationalise production processes, which implied both technology modernisation and a shift in production specialisation;
3   to correct the financial structure of the different firms affected; and
4   to put a halt to the de-industrialisation process undergone by the Spanish economy since the beginning of the crisis, that is, to programme a re-industrialisation process.

Behind these objectives lies the attempt to raise the competitive level of these firms in order to meet European standards and re-establish Spain's position in the new international division of labour that emerges from the crisis.

The most relevant instruments which support this restructuring process are:

1   *labour measures:* mainly early retirement facilities and improved unemployment benefits and conditions for people made redundant by the restructuring of firms;
2   *financial measures:* which include apart from grants and subsidised credits to firms, equity participation by the public sector;
3   *regional measures:* appropriate regional incentives were introduced to mitigate the spatial impacts of the restructuring process since the firms affected presented a high degree of geographical concentration. Thus the 'Urgent Re-industrialisation Areas' were created to enhance re-employment opportunities of redundant workers;
4   *measures to support technological development:* which provide finance and other services to generalise R&D activities among industrial firms; and
5   *measures to support small and medium-sized enterprises:* basically by providing long-term finance and stimulating the emergence of associative strategies (e.g. common marketing or R&D strategies).

By 1988, restructuring plans had almost been completed, with generally satisfactory results: 791 firms had been included within these plans (683 in the textile sector alone, but one must take into consideration the varying dimension of firms in different sectors), with a total investment of 650 thousand million pesetas and an employment reduction of approximately 84,000 jobs (over an initial workforce of 280,000). Most of the restructured sectors show a clear tendency towards recovery (productivity increases, financial soundness, profits, . . ., even if for some sectors, e.g., steel or shipbuilding, the results fall far short of the objectives.

Nowadays, once the restructuring process of traditional sectors has officially come to an end, Spanish industrial policy develops around three major lines of action. First, the integration in the EC as a full member in 1992 forces Spanish industry, if it wants to compete as an equal with the rest of European firms, to make a supplementary effort to adapt the productive structure to the new competitive requirements. In a 'Europe without barriers' the temptation to rely on protectionism (the reserve of the national market for products which do not find a market abroad) no longer exists. Second, the process of technological innovation becomes a central element in facing not only the above challenge, by increasing productivity levels, but also in guaranteeing a continuous economic recovery in the long run. Finally, in recent years a substantial effort has been made to attract direct foreign investment with the double objective of helping in the process of technological innovation and complementing internal saving, which has been insufficient since the 1960s to finance the process of economic growth in Spain. Obviously, this last strategy entails the risk of further increasing the dependence of Spanish industry on assistance from abroad, which is already a matter of concern as many critics argue.

3.3.3 *Social policy*

As has been argued above, there are close interrelations between fiscal policy and the expansion of social expenditure. The aim of this section is to discuss the structural reform currently under way of the social assistance system in Spain. This process has been partially induced by fiscal difficulties but also by the obvious need to build up a welfare system.

Before entering into the reform issue, it seems appropriate to explain briefly the main traits of the social assistance system before the crisis. This analysis will show sharp differences with most countries within the Community, which in turn will allow us to understand the relevance and difficulties of the current reform.

The making up of the social security system
The 1964 'Social Security Law' and its later developments in 1967 are the starting point of the social security structure which is under reform nowadays. The aim of this Law was to build up a fee-based, social assistance network which would guarantee the general benefits relating

to retirement, health, unemployment and disablement, following the German model. The protected groups, according to the chosen system, were the wage-earning population, and, through special schemes, several other working groups on account of the particular characteristics of the sector (e.g., mining workers) or working conditions.

From the financial viewpoint, the system had to meet its needs through social dues paid by workers and employers (mainly the first group) and state contributions. Nevertheless, the system was financed up to 95% through social dues.

Until 1972 when a legal reform took place, the level of protection was fairly weak for the system's financial resources were insufficient. More importantly, and despite this financial shortage, the system was obliged to generate an important volume of savings to finance other activities apart from those to do with social assistance.

The 1972 reform aimed at a radical change. An improvement in the level of protection was attempted by a better management of the available income and an increase of state contributions. This would generate sufficient resources to finance the desired expansion of social expenditure. However, these objectives were not achieved because of the impact of the economic crisis. As early as 1977, the economic policy strategy against the crisis imposed serious restrictions on the expansion of social expenditure. The reform of the social security system was to be implemented on the basis of an immature social assistance structure in which, for example, the guaranteed average retirement pension was below the average official minimum wage.

The 1977–85 transition period

Until the 'Social Security Reform Law' of 1985, the different governments tried to find solutions to the financial problems of the system by working on three different fronts. On the income side, a general reduction of employers' contributions, consistent with a more general strategy of wage restriction, was undertaken together with an increase of state transfers to sustain the system. On the expenditure side, the strategy focused on two lines of action. On the one hand, attempts were made to improve the management of the system, thus cutting down current expenditure levels. On the other, social expenditure was simply frozen. Between 1977 and 1986, with the exception of the expenditure linked to unemployment, total expenditure of the social security system increased by less than 1% of GDP. In 1976, the social expenditure/GDP relationship amounted to 12.3%, while in 1985 this figure dropped to 11.8%. This evolution is especially relevant since it took place at a time when a significant restructuring process was taking place with the subsequent increase of social needs and demands.

The issue of unemployment benefits deserves special attention because of the sharp increase of unemployment levels as we have already seen. It is precisely this issue that was the object of the first legal changes which had the aim of diminishing the level of expenditure by making access to unemployment benefits more difficult. As a result of these successive legal changes, it is estimated that by 1985 only 30% of the unemployed were entitled to get unemployment benefits. This situation can only be understood if one remembers the role played by family relations as a protective network in Spanish society.

The current reform

The 1985 reform law contemplated a whole range of legal changes with the objective of controlling the expansion of social expenditure on retirement pensions. It was an explicit recognition that the financial crisis of the social security system could not be solved by larger state contributions. Public deficit began to create serious economic problems. There was a need to control the magnitude of this deficit throughout all the areas of expenditure and therefore social expenditure.

The next step of the reform came with the 1987 Budget Law. From this moment, state transfers to the social security system were to be used to finance health expenditure. Pensions were to be financed exclusively from social contributions. A complementary step had already been taken in 1985 with the regulation of pension funds, thus allowing the private sector to enter into an area reserved until that moment for the state.

The final step in this reform is still being debated by the Parliament at the time of writing this chapter. It refers to what in Spain are called 'not paid through contributions' pensions or welfare pensions, that is the pensions received by those people who are not entitled for various reasons to get a pension from the traditional system.

3.3.4 *Labour policy*

During the 1980s, the labour market's major characteristics from the point of view of employment generation may be classified into two clearly defined periods: the first one, 1980–85, with a massive destruction of jobs, and the second one, 1985–90, with a distinct recovery of employment, as we have already discussed. Thus, employment evolution and general economic evolution run parallel during the entire period. Employment recovery and economic recovery seem to be the two sides of the same coin, despite the labour policies implemented to improve employment conditions. Notwithstanding this reality, an analysis of the labour market would be incomplete without mentioning the significant changes in labour force management that have taken place during these years, especially, those changes aimed at increasing the flexibility of the labour market. Moreover, there are other structural changes which drive the Spanish labour market towards taking on similar characteristics to those of most European countries, even though the common problems appear to be more severe, given the specific traits of Spain's economic development model.

The emergence of a democratic system in the late 1970s brought major changes to labour management strategies such as the recognition of the right of trade unions and employers' organisations to sign collective labour agreements within the different sectors of the economy. However, the real basis of labour policy in Spain is defined by the 1980 'Employment Law' and the 1980 'Workers Statute', which developed the general rights written down in the Constitution. Both laws modified significantly the previous legal framework, by introducing into labour relations management a considerable degree of flexibility by allowing the possibility to sign part-time contracts and contracts for a limited time period in all sectors of the economy and for any worker.

The result of these changes has been the design of a whole range of flexible contracts, which have given the Spanish labour market the highest degree of flexibility in the entire Community. By the end of 1989, 26% of all wage jobs were carried out under a part-time contract. Furthermore, almost all the jobs linked to the recovery are associated with the different forms of temporary contracts. An increase of this degree of flexibility is not foreseen, due to the serious macroeconomic consequences, in terms of demand, that an economic recession would bring if such an important group of workers were sent into unemployment.

Finally, it is necessary to mention here those labour policies aimed at adapting labour force qualifications to new job requirements. This strategy has been designed by the 'General Council of Occupational Training' constituted by representatives of workers, employers and the administration. It is being carried out through the 'National Training Programme' financed by the administration and compulsory contributions from employers. The issue of training is becoming central in discussions over economic and social perspectives, as a recognition of the shortage of qualified workers faced by many sectors which may hinder future economic growth and employment generation

3.4 The financial system

3.4.1 *Institutions, markets and the most relevant financial assets*

The Spanish financial market has been changing since the beginning of the crisis. During the last ten years its major characteristics have become very similar to those of other national markets within the European Community.

The presence of public institutions in the market is led by the Central Bank, *Banco de España*, and the *Instituto de Crédito Oficial (ICO)* which aggregates several (state-owned) banking institutions, each one specialised in financial transactions for specific economic activities such as industry, shipbuilding, agriculture, etc. The activity of these banks has little importance if compared to that of the private sector, but they distribute that part of the public resources earmarked for investment. There are also the *Cajas de Ahorros*, owned by local authorities, which have evolved from their ancient savings-bank financial activity to their present fully banking business and the volume of their deposit liabilities represents nowadays more than 40% of the entire system. The *Cooperativas de Crédito*, operating locally, are private institutions initially created for aiding regional development and presently running as banks.

By the early 1960s, the private banks were legally divided into two groups, commercial and industrial. The purpose of the authorities was then to encourage bank specialisation, either on financial transactions related to industrial investment (industrial or business banks), or on banking for day-to-day transactions of particulars and firms (commercial or deposit banks). As a matter of fact, owing to the particular characteristics of Spanish economic development, private banks became 'mixed', half-industrial and half-commercial, rather than specialised in one way or another. In this sense, private bank lending to small and medium-sized companies, mainly for investment plans, constitutes an important feature of the Spanish economy for it also took place in the form of banks acquiring majority interests in many of those firms.

The 'big six' of Spanish banks, namely Bilbao-Vizcaya, Central, Banesto, Hispano-Americano, Popular and Santander, ignoring their associated institutions concentrate more than 60% of peseta bank credits. Foreign banks were allowed to create branches under strongly restrictive regulation in 1978, but since then conditions of entrance and restrictions to their activities have been relaxed. In this sense, usual comparisons between domestic and foreign institutions based on absolute figures are not relevant and other references like business profitability or growth ratios per employee tend to reflect a certain superiority of foreign competitors.

As the industrial crisis deepened throughout the late 1970s, a bank crisis occurred in Spain. From 1978 to 1985, 58 private banks failed or became bankrupt representing 27% of total bank liabilities. According to experts, major causes of this crisis have to be found in the real system crisis and in management errors ranging from unorthodox practices (the RUMASA case is a good example) to general undervaluation of financial assets due to high inflation rates and failures of enterprises.

Also remarkable is the lack of legal devices allowing the *Banco de*

España to supervise banking activities. The very first measures were taken by 1978, when the problem arose. Since then, there have been several initiatives enlarging Central Bank control and power over dubious institutions. Simultaneously, there has been a need for other banks to co-ordinate and co-operate, also with the authorities, in order to prevent the crisis from worsening (the much feared 'domino effect'). Therefore, the *Corporación Bancaria* was created. This is a banking institution jointly owned by the private banks and the *Banco de España*, which took control over some failing banks so that it could sell them after re-establishing their profitability.

As a collateral offset of this and other inter-bank relations, a process of mergers began with total support from the public authorities. However, it has resulted so far in only two really important amalgamations, namely that of the *Banco de Bilbao* and the *Banco de Vizcaya*, thereafter called *Banco Bilbao-Vizcaya*, and the *Caixa de Barcelona* and the *Caixa de Pensiones*, still in process, which would become the first credit institution in Spain. In the Spring of 1991, two new major mergers took place: *Banco Central* with *Banco Hispano*; and the creation of the *Corporación Bancaria de España* (CBE) grouping all public banks.

Other financial intermediaries, like insurance, leasing, factoring companies or pension funds, have grown under the control of private banks. They have supplied the necessary funds in the absence of a developed financial market outside the banking system.

The *Sociedades Mediadoras en el Mercado de Dinero*, monetary market intermediary firms, are non-banking monetary institutions which operate between banks and other agents selling and buying various short-term assets.

The monetary market, based on the Central Bank operations with reserves, includes inter-banking and other monetary intermediaries' transactions with short-term financial assets. The efficiency of this market is very important in the control of money supply as policy measures are spread to the economy through the credit strategy changes (reactions) of involved monetary market institutions. In this sense, the authorities have already completed the scheduled plan for developing this market and its gaining in efficiency and have shifted their attention to the stabilisation of the capital market.

The stock exchange market (*Bolsa de Valores*) had been underdeveloped in Spain because of traditional interrelations between financial and industrial capital. Similarly, capital markets were restricted to long-term credit institution loans. The relative low levels of revenues and savings and the role of financial intermediation performed by banking institutions, had been causes of the meagre importance of the stock exchange market in the Spanish economy until the 1980s. Since 1985, capital inflows from abroad and the change in Treasury deficit funding have been contributing to the strengthening of the stock exchange market. Nevertheless, this has not been so easily done because of the problems created by the obsolescence of market organisation. It was a matter of transaction timetables (less than 15 minutes for each group of assets), market accessibility (brokers had to be civil servants), market integration (strictly speaking, there were, still are, four different stock exchange markets in Spain at Madrid, Barcelona, Valencia and Bilbao, where the same security may have four different prices, one in each market), and the lack of advanced technological support for processing and transmission of information and the decisions of agents.

Instead of preparing, as in London, a 'sudden big-bang' for the technological *aggiornamiento* of the stock exchange market operations, the Spanish government began by creating a treasury bill market where there were no 'physical' transfers of titles but accounting records on books of the institutions involved (*Mercado de títulos de deuda pública anotados en cuenta*). That was a crucial step if we consider the importance of public sector financial flows in the economy. As private agents and banking institutions were getting used to the new device, mostly in monetary market payments, the reform of the stock exchange market included its application to the transactions of any other financial asset. The *'mercado continuo'* (continuous market) was born, in which trade begins at 9.00 a.m. and ends at 5.00 p.m. for all assets (between 5.00 and 8.00 p.m. under some special restrictions).

According to the step-by-step approach adopted by the government, firms and other borrowers on the stock exchange market are allowed to trade their issues either on the continuous market or on any of the four markets until the end of 1992. The task of surveying the solvency and fair play of the agents is carried on by the *Comisión Nacional de Valores*, presently led by former Minister of Industry, Carlos Croissier, which will replace the old organisation after the reform.

The main financial assets traded on those markets are short-term treasury bills (*Pagarés* and *Letras del Tesoro*), commercial paper issued by major firms and various bonds and mortgage securities offered by credit institutions.

3.4.2 *Monetary policy in the 1980s*

Since the Spanish Socialist Party took office in 1982, monetary policy has tended to reduce the pace of money supply growth by means of instruments related, either to Central Bank activity in the money market (i.e. leading to increases or decreases of reserve balances of credit institutions), or to different legal devices of credit control called *coeficientes*, obligatory rates to be maintained between different parts of their balance sheet by domestic banking institutions. This system has been usually described as a fractional reserves system, where monetary policy is applied on a two-level basis. The changes in monetary (intermediary) target are induced by the Central Bank changing the monetary base, the quantity of central money or reserves, forcing the credit institutions to change their credit policy in order to respect, among other things, the obligatory reserves rate of *coeficiente de caja*. Nevertheless, these latter instruments are being removed while another policy step is taken towards state monetary neutrality and private banking freedom.

The 'traditional' state monetary intervention in Spain was the imposition of domestic interest rates, non-competitive in foreign markets. In addition, restrictions on international financial transactions were usual in order to prevent foreign competitors from penetrating into the Spanish financial markets.

In that sense, the monetary policy applied by the Socialist government has changed both internal and external conditions for financial activity. With regard to national monetary market excesses of liquidity, up to 1985 owing to non-orthodox Treasury financing and, thereafter, as a result of intervention on foreign exchange markets, where the peseta was appreciating under the pressure of capital inflows, it was more difficult to establish monetary control by means of an operative target (namely, the growth of Central Bank reserves).

Thus, monetary authorities have implemented a number of measures in the context of general economic policy aimed at the modernisation of the Spanish economy, which implicate at least the following interrelated objectives:

1 *To reinforce competition in the financial market,* in order to increase general efficiency in national financial markets and also to counterbalance the pressure on interest rates originated by public sector borrowing requirements. The merger process may be included as another factor for increasing efficiency and competition.

2 *To improve monetary policy efficiency:* active policy on money supply rather than on interest rates, and a strong belief in free-market efficiency also in financial payments generated by public sector deficit are the major elements of this strategy. The interventions of monetary policy authorities take the form of bids by credit institutions for reserve credits or treasury bills to the Central Bank, which usually decides the total tradable amount and distributes it to each institution depending on the interest rate offered or demanded. The lowest rate to the Central Bank in each intervention is known as the 'marginal rate', that is, the lower rate when increasing reserves and the higher rate when lending them to the credit institutions. It is a well-established policy 'signal' for credit institutions and domestic and international investors.

3   *To reinforce market liberalisation* without endangering national
     credit institutions' stability and solvency, in the context of the
     European single market.

Financial innovations, like new financial products or institutions mentioned above, have been developed by the Treasury and other financial
institutions, helping in the creation of new financial markets, in order to
obtain resources directly from particular sources for financing expenses
in excess of revenues. Financial 'des-intermediation' can be seen as a
main feature of the changes undergone in domestic monetary policy, for
it expresses government's commitment to improving the general efficiency and competition of the financial system at large.

   Another thread of Spanish monetary policy can be analysed in
relation to the different steps taken towards the free movement of capital
flows within the European Community, that is, the liberalisation of the
European financial market. In that respect, however, the removal of
barriers to capital inflows has not been equally applied to capital
outflows in order to prevent disequilibria in foreign currency markets.
Yet, by the end of 1992 all restrictions will be completely removed.
Special restrictions on foreign credit institutions' activities are to be
removed according to the issues of the negotiations within the general
process of the European Union.

   During the 1980s, and due to financial innovation, the definition of
the money supply under control (intermediate objective) has been
enlarged, from ancient near-money aggregate (M3 or *Disponibilidades
Líquidas*, bank money) to M4 (M3 plus other short-term assets issued by
the Treasury or major firms on the monetary market). The main reason
was the lack of accuracy of price movement forecasting based on M3
evolution in the early 1980s. The development of new financial products,
short-term, and the emergence of non-banking financial institutions,
trading them on the markets, shifted the patterns of portfolio distribution, so that near-money assets were no longer included uniquely
among bank liabilities and their evolution did not reflect the total
monetary buying power in the economy.

   According to the well-known monetarist theory, the evolution of
price inflation relied upon the evolution of M4, also called ALP, from the
Spanish words for liquid assets in the hands of the private sector. During
the last decade, many factors have intervened to maintain a high rate of
money supply growth: public sector deficit, high rate of economic
growth (increasing aggregate demand) and foreign capital inflows. At the
same time, especially at the beginning of the Socialist government, policy
measures have tended to reduce the rate of money supply growth by
increasing the banks' obligatory *coeficientes* and the rates of interest of
Central Bank credit operations.

   The strength of monetary growth and the relative inefficiency of short-term fiscal policies, given the public sector deficit, have induced the authorities to use restrictive monetary policy as the most important anti-inflationary instrument. Government and Central Bank officials yearly estimate the growth of M4, based upon real growth and inflation forecasting. Taken into account the current fluctuation of monetary variables, monetary authorities do not intervene to correct the rate of M4 growth if it maintains itself within the 'path' defined along a 1.5% range around the target rate. However, it was not until early 1990 that monetary targets were being respected without heavy interventions on the part of monetary authorities. These interventions have been seen, generally, as the major cause for the high interest rates prevailing on the Spanish market.

As already said, by the end of the 1980s, improvements in general economic indicators (unemployment, inflation, reduced public sector borrowing requirements, investment) have encouraged the government to ease legal restrictions of banks' credit operations by reducing all *coeficientes*. The legal cash rate, fixed at 5% with a maximum of 7%, is a good example. In spite of this last measure, interest rates are still very high and the causes of this are not clearly determined by experts. In addition to the alleged public sector role, namely the impact of public sector borrowing upon the evolution of interest rates, another factor may be the importance of international financial interdependence.

In this sense, full membership of the Spanish European Monetary System imposes, since mid-June 1989, some restrictions related both to maximum interest rate differentials between member countries and to the maximum fluctuation of the peseta exchange rate against other European currencies. Exchange rate evolution in foreign currency markets seems to obey international capital flows rather than current account balances. Therefore, interest rates jointly with tax regulations on capital revenues constitute a necessary tool for guaranteeing stability in the exchange market.

Consequently, the Spanish Government hesitates before reducing national interest rates fearing domestic credit expansion, which may fuel price inflation, current account imports and foreign capital outflows which, in the presence of current account deficit, may endanger exchange-rate stability and the financial soundness of the whole Spanish economy.

3.5 International relations

3.5.1 *Trade policy*

Unlike other countries in Western Europe, Spain did not undertake a rapid process of liberalisation of foreign trade after the end of the Second

World War. It was not until 1959 that, together with the internal liberalisation process, the Stabilisation Plan initiated a slow process of foreign liberalisation, after twenty years of 'economic autarchy'. This fact and the absence of political democratic liberties until the end of the 1970s excluded Spain from the process of European integration as already said. Thus, and despite the fact that in 1970 a Preferential Agreement was signed with the Community, Spain did not become a member until 1986, as stated above. Therefore, it is necessary to analyse first the main characteristics of the Spanish trade policy until the end of the 1970s, and then to discuss the major changes induced by the integration in the EC.

The most important feature of the tariff protection system of the Spanish economy is its complexity, due to continuous modifications of the 1960 tariff system. In spite of this, the liberalisation process resulted in a significant decrease of tariff barriers, which went from an average of 16% in 1960 to 7% in 1974, to increase slightly in the second half of the 1970s, and decrease again during the 1980s to reach 5.5% just before the integration of Spain in the EC.

Besides the tariff system, several 'trade regimes' co-existed (trade of State, bilateral, global and exempted) which made distinctions between various imports depending on the type of goods or their origin in establishing import quotas and restrictions. In 1960, only 40% of total imports came under the category of 'exempted trade', but in 1974 this percentage had increased to 85%, while the 'trade of State' (the most restrictive category) had become marginal by 1965.

This protectionist network was complemented by the *Impuesto de Compensación de Gravámenes Interiores (ICGI)* (Tax to Compensate for Internal Taxation), theoretically introduced to tax import products as home products, but which in practice meant a protection level of two or three per cent.

On the other side, Spanish authorities designed several instruments to support export activities, which in many cases concealed dumping practices. Thus, together with special tariffs for goods in transit, credits to exports, export insurance and other instruments, a very special form of tax reduction for exports was at work. This reduction was an adjustment at the border in line with the ICGI. While this tax overestimated Spanish indirect tax levels, it also overestimated tax reductions. So, in fact, it was a concealed subsidy to exports. Hence, some fiscal adjustment at the border, theoretically neutral, became in practice a very important instrument of Spanish trade policy over the years.

The integration of Spain in the EC has introduced many changes in the regulations of Spanish trade policy. Among them, the various trade regimes of foreign trade have been substituted by the general regime in force in the EC with all the countries of the GATT, and fiscal reductions to exports and the ICGI have given way to just applying the VAT system at the border. This, in fact resulted in a reduction in the level of protection of Spanish production and a significant loss of competitiveness of several industrial sectors such as steel or shipbuilding.

Yet, the most important innovation for the Spanish economy is the application of the Common Tariff System with countries outside the EC and the progressive elimination of tariff barriers in relation to other Community members. Thus, at the end of the transitory period, envisaged in the Accession Treaty for the end of 1992 (with the exemption of some agricultural products), Spain will be a full member of the Tariff Union.

Taking into account the structure of Spanish foreign trade, this means that more than 75% of total imports, which come from Community countries or other countries with which the Community has signed preferential agreements, will enter into Spain exempted from any tariffs or duties. Moreover, tariff barriers will be significantly diminished for the remaining 25% of imports, because Spanish tariffs prior to the integration were three points above Community levels on average. In sum, the full integration at the end of the transition period will result in a substantial reduction in the level of protection of the Spanish economy. The first outcome of this fall of tariff barriers is already noticeable, in the form of a significant increase of imports, as will be discussed below.

3.5.2 *The structure of foreign trade*

A. *The territorial structure of foreign trade*

Western Europe has always been the most important market for Spanish exports and, in a smaller proportion, it has been the major supplier of the Spanish economy (see Statistical Annexe, Table D 21). This fact has been accentuated during the 1980s, especially as a consequence of the integration into the EC. Thus, more than 60% of total exports go into other countries within the Community, while a slightly lower percentage of total imports come from them. The rest of the countries of Western Europe only account for 5% of total Spanish exports and 6% of its imports. These percentages are surpassed by the USA which ranks first in both cases among non-European developed countries, despite the rapid increase of imports from Japan. Yet, exports to Japan only account for 1% of total exports.

During the 1980s among developing countries, both in terms of imports and exports, a clear downward tendency can be observed in the OPEC countries, due to the fall of oil prices which has reduced its buying capacity. The loss of importance of the Latin-American countries is also significant. This traditional market has fallen from 8% of total exports in 1980 to 3% at the end of the decade. The crisis of foreign debt is the origin of this phenomenon since it has limited their opportunities to pay in any foreign currency. Imports arriving from Latin-America have also lost relative weight, mainly because they are energy goods. On the other hand, the newly industrialised countries (NIC) of the Asian Coast still account for a small part of Spanish imports and exports (1.4 and 2.6% respectively in 1988), even though the growth rate has been very high in recent years.

The volume of trade with countries which come under the 'trade of State' system is unimportant for the Spanish economy. Imports have remained at around 3% of the total during the 1980s, whereas exports have gradually fallen to approximately 2% at the end of the decade.

The already mentioned concentration of Spanish foreign trade in the EC market is so pronounced that the largest four countries accounted in 1988 for 46.2% of total Spanish exports and 46% of its imports. Yet, France ranks first as far as sales are concerned, while West Germany becomes first in relation to purchases. Portugal, Spain's neighbour, deserves special attention since, despite its relatively small economic potential, it receives more than 5% of total Spanish exports. Thus, Spain is Portugal's second trade partner just behind the powerful West German economy. In fact, Portugal is the only country in the European Community for which imports from Spain become relevant at all (13% of its total imports in 1988, followed at a great distance by France with a 4%).

B. The sectorial structure of foreign trade

From the imports viewpoint, Spain has always presented three major sources of foreign trade dependence: energy products, intermediate products and capital goods. In the first group, the lack of oil resources leaves a clear imprint on Spanish imports. In 1981, energy imports represented 42% of total imports, a culmination of the climbing tendency initiated in 1974, where they doubled the value of the previous year (25% against 13% in 1973). Afterwards, a noticeable drop took place, and if in 1985 they still amounted to 36% of the total, in 1988 they were only 11%. Obviously, this evolution has been clearly influenced by an oil price evolution.

Intermediate products, in contrast to energy products, represented in 1981 40% of total Spanish imports, steadily increasing their share throughout the decade to reach 47% in 1988. The fact that a sizeable part of imported intermediate products are of an agricultural nature needs to be highlighted. In the industrial sector, almost every sector shows a high level of dependence on foreign intermediate products.

Capital goods have significantly increased their presence in the structure of Spanish imports in the last years. In 1981, they represented just over 9% of total purchases from foreign markets; in 1985 11% and in 1988 were 21% of the total. This is a good indicator of the high level of technological dependence of the Spanish industry.

Finally, consumer goods accounted in 1988 for 20% of total imports. It is interesting to highlight the rapid increase in the pace of purchases from abroad for direct consumption since the integration in the European Community, especially in the automobile sector.

On the exports side, intermediate goods, other than energy products, play the major role in the Spanish trade, since they represented in 1981 almost 49% of total exports, and they still were 46.7% in 1988. If energy products are included, they surpass the 50% barrier. The other main export sector is constituted by consumer goods (37% in 1988). Within this group, foods gradually lose their share (41% in 1981, 35% in 1988), while durable consumer goods increased their importance (30% in 1981, 38% in 1988). The automobile sector is responsible for over 75% of exports of durable consumer goods and these represent 11% of total Spanish exports. As far as capital goods are concerned, they represented just below 12% of total exports during the 1980s.

The joint analysis of foreign trade by geographic area and type of product shows that the trade pattern in industrialised countries is very different from that in developing countries. Spain exports in relative terms more consumer goods to the OECD countries and capital goods and intermediate products to developing countries. Among exports to the Community countries, durable consumer goods (especially cars) dominate, for they represent 20% of the total; non-durable consumer goods constitute the most important item of the exports to the USA (approximately 30%); and food items are the major component of sales to Japan. Among developing countries, the export of capital goods becomes more relevant for the Latin-American countries than for other markets.

In so far as imports are related, the Spanish economy gets capital goods from OECD countries, where it also buys most of the durable consumer goods. From the developing countries, Spain purchases raw materials, especially energy products, with the exception of the NIC where durable consumer goods are mostly obtained.

3.5.3 The balance of payments

Despite the fact that the opening of the Spanish economy is still below the average in the Community (see Statistical Annexe, Table D 22), the growth rate of exports of goods and services has been surmounted during the 1980s by only two other countries in the EC, Ireland and Portugal. However, Spain endures a lasting trade deficit (see Statistical Annexe, Table D 23), that traditionally has been covered by surpluses of the balances of services and transfers. During the 1980s this trade deficit reached problematic levels between 1980 and 1983, due to the oil bill, and from 1987 as a consequence of the integration in the EC together with the economic recovery.

The positive results of the balance of services derive mainly from the income from tourist activities, that represents over 60% of total income from services. On the contrary, investment income and technical assistance have always displayed a negative balance, because of the dependence of the industry on foreign technology and investment. Nevertheless, in aggregate the positive balance on services compensates for the trade deficit.

The balance of transfers always shows a positive outcome, due to emigrants' remittances. The presence of more than a million Spanish people in Europe contributes to compensating the deficit in the balance of trade, even if in a lower proportion than the receipts from services.

Because of this compensatory effect of services and transfers, the current account balance occasionally displays surpluses, and, in any case, significantly shorter deficits than the balance of trade. In fact, once the impact of oil price increases in the early 1980s had been overcome in 1984, 1985 and 1986, Spain showed a surplus in its current account balance. However, in 1987 and 1988 (see Statistical Annexe, Table D 2), the deficit on current account represented approximately 1% of GDP, rising to 3% in 1989 and reaching 4% in 1990, according to the European Commission's forecasts.

Former examples of this situation can be found only in the mid-1970s, after the first oil crisis. However, in the last few years, the evolution of the oil market could not be better. The increasing trade deficit becomes associated with a declining surplus on services. It is difficult to assert to what extent the worsening situation of the balance of trade (see Table 3.5) is the consequence of the economic recovery, the integration in the European Community, or other factors. In any case, it does not seem possible to continue with this situation in the long term, even if in the short term there are no significant problems because of the persistent increase of reserves since 1986.

A positive assessment of this deficit conveys the idea that this foreign

Table 3.5 Cover rate of Spanish foreign trade (X/M × 100, %)

Year	Total trade	Trade with the EC
1985	81	115
1986	78	93
1987	70	81
1988	67	77
1989	62	73

Source: Calculated from data published by the *Dirección General de Aduanas.*

debt supports the financing of the investment process which in the medium term will improve the production system which, in turn, will enhance the competitive position of Spanish products. A negative view, however, considers that this deficit may generate self-financing difficulties in the long run, strangling economic growth in the future.

Anyhow, the inflow of long-term capital, especially abundant since 1987, is financing this deficit on current account. Thus, the balance on current account and long-term capital has been positive since 1983. If the positive balance on short-term capital is added, an increase of reserves can be observed.

While direct investment (around 40% of total long-term capital inflows) is reasonably stable, portfolio investment (which accounts for a similar volume) is highly volatile. Moreover, it does not seem possible with the European Single Market in prospect, that the Spanish economy can maintain for a long period of time a significant differential of interest rates, with the subsequent loss of attractiveness for long-term capital. Therefore, and without undue pessimism, even if the current trade deficit does not encounter problems in the short run, it must be considered as one of the major concerns for future economic strategy.

The increase of currency reserves had led to the strengthening of the peseta from 1987 even though it is not a hard currency, which undoubtedly does not do any good to Spanish exports. This situation of the peseta has been consolidated by the integration of the Spanish currency in the European Monetary System in mid-1989 for Spain acquired a compromise to maintain the exchange rate. Since this fact has coincided with the large trade deficit, this decision has been controversial. On the one hand, it contributes to finance the deficit since it guarantees to foreign capital a stable currency, which ensures profitability levels. On the other, it does not support the reduction of the trade deficit, which lies at the root of the deficit on current account. And besides, it may compel the differential of the interest rates to be sustained beyond what would be reasonable in order to attract foreign capital to maintain the exchange rate of the peseta. It is, in any case, a risky choice the results of which will only be appraised in the future.

3.6 Special issues

3.6.1 *The future of agriculture*

The future of Spanish agriculture within the EC is still full of uncertainties. Spain has the greatest agricultural potential among Southern European countries, but severe natural deficiencies (climate, altitude) work hand in hand with structural problems, related to the distribution and dimension of agricultural firms (too small in the North, too large in the South and Centre), to make the problem of integration a difficult one. These issues may limit the future competitiveness of several sectors and regions of Spanish agriculture since other EC countries do not suffer from these disadvantages.

Differences in dominant production structures explain differences in specialisation of Spanish agriculture in the EC. EC agriculture is primarily oriented towards cattle raising and cereals while vegetable production is dominant in Spanish agriculture. Moreover, Spanish productivity is significantly lower for most products. Nevertheless, it has to be acknowledged that differences in productivity may be less significant in agriculture than in other sectors since products are highly distinctive. Thus, competitiveness depends less on prices than on quality and services offered by products of different origin. In sum, many Spanish products seem to be highly competitive against Mediterranean products – European and non-European.

The expected reform of the CAP will have diverse effects upon Spanish agriculture depending on the specialisation and level of development of different regions as well as the character of the reform – renationalisation of the CAP maintaining national production levels or increased process of specialisation and competition among countries.

The structural measures to protect less developed regions or those regions most affected by competition from continental production (cereals, meat and milk) may allow them (the North and Centre) to initiate a restructuring process, but the anticipated price fall will give rise to severe difficulties for the future. The most competitive sectors of Spanish agriculture (fruits, vegetables, wine and olive oil), on the contrary, require the removal of protective barriers since their position against other European competitors, in terms of prices and quality, is very favourable.

From the point of view of agro-industrial activities the issues are different. This sector in Spain is characterised by its small dimension, even though a small number of firms concentrate a high and increasing percentage of total sales of the sector. However, the average firm, by volume of sales, differs greatly from the average firm operating in the EC market.

Among big firms, the weight of direct foreign investment has increased in the recent past, penetrating to most activities. The employment and productive structure of these Spanish subsidiaries are similar to those of national companies, but their strategies in terms of foreign trade and technological innovation differ greatly. From a spatial perspective, the location of Spanish agricultural industry seems to favour demand factors, which works against less developed traditional agricultural regions.

In sum, the integration in the EC has provoked a slow and as yet unfinished restructuring process of modernisation and merging of small firms in order to be able to compete with the powerful European companies. The results will vary greatly among sectors and regions.

3.6.2 *Tourist trade*

The tourist trade represents a major source of economic wealth in Spain, resulting both from internal but mainly external demand. By the mid-1980s, the number of foreign visitors to Spain exceeded 40 million per year. Current estimates show that this sector accounts nowadays for over 8% of GDP and 10% of total employment. Moreover, since the 1960s, income from tourism has been a crucial factor in the Spanish economy for it has worked as a counterbalance in the balance of payments, compensating for the traditional deficits in the balance of trade necessary to undertake the process of industrialisation and modernisation of the economy.

Geographically, this sector is highly concentrated in some of the Spanish regions – the Balearic Isles, the Mediterranean Coast and the Canary Isles – where it has been a driving force of economic development. Spanish tourism originates primarily in the EC, France, Portugal, the United Kingdom and Germany being the most important countries (in the mid-1980s tourists from these four countries accounted for over 70% of total foreign tourists).

The development of the Spanish tourist sector has been highly dependent upon the standards of living of EC citizens. Thus, this sector grew steadily from 1960 (when the Liberalisation Plan and some political changes made Spain a more attractive country for tourists) until 1973, due to the effects of the international crisis. The economic recovery of the 1980s resulted in a period of strong growth in terms of the number of visitors, income, employment, etc. However, by 1989–90 the sector experienced a substantial reduction in its activities which seems to be linked not to an absolute decrease in demand but to a shift of the demand away from Spain and directed to other Mediterranean countries.

Nowadays, the tourist trade in Spain is in the midst of a severe crisis and in need of a profound restructuring process. This situation is the result not only of changes in demand but mainly of the way in which the sector has developed since the 1960s.

The sector developed without any special attention from the public sector, as the result of the efforts of the public sector both to increase the supply and to attract the demand. This growth was carried out looking for short-term benefits without any clear long-term strategy and generating all sorts of problem and costs for the future. It was not until 1990 that the government recognised the need to undertake a reform of the sector and initiated the preparation of the 'White Book of Tourism' which will define the major strategies to be undertaken by both the public and private sector to adapt Spanish tourist trade to the challenges it faces.

The major issues which should be confronted even if the solution does not seem to be a simple one are: high concentration of tourist activities in some months of the year, mainly in the summer; 'sun and beach' tourism accounts for over 80% of total demand with a clear underdevelopment of other types of tourism (cultural, professional) despite the existing clear potential, the comparative low price/quality relationship of tourist services in Spain (hotels, restaurants, leisure activities); the environmental 'disasters' in many tourist areas and the underdevelopment of public services and facilities; the lack of invest-ment of many tourist firms; the lack of a clear and co-ordinated policy between central and autonomous governments; the lack of adequate marketing abroad of Spanish tourist attractions, etc.

Despite these major threats to the trade, the prospects for the sector seem to be positive because of the obvious Spanish potential for tourism, the well-developed structures and tradition and the clear shift towards diversification, entrepreneurial management, co-ordination of public and private strategies and policies and the improvement of the quality of services, training schemes and capital investment.

3.7 Conclusion and future perspectives

Three elements commit Spain to a future integrated in Europe: the Treaty of Accession, signed in Madrid in June 1985, the European Single Act, signed in Luxembourg in February 1986, and the integration of the peseta in the European Monetary System in June 1989.

By signing the Treaty of Accession Spain accepted the Community's rules and practices. However, this was to be accomplished through a transition period of seven years, so that total integration will be achieved at the end of 1992. This process of integration of Spain into the European Community was soon effected by the signing of the European Single Act, and reached its full momentum with the integration of the peseta in the Monetary System in the summer of 1989. An exchange rate of 65 peseta/ 1 mark was fixed, with a 6% fluctuation band, similar to that of the Italian lira, due to the inflationist pressures in the Spanish economy. The rapid decisions adopted by the Spanish government were undoubtedly eased by the favourable attitude of Spanish society as shown by the polls on European issues.

As already stated at the outset, the opening up and economic liberalisation of the 1960s made it possible for Spain to enjoy the benefits of the process of economic growth. Yet its pace was subordinated to the existence of favourable internal conditions and the suitability to the political system. By contrast, the aim of the opening up and economic liberalisation in the 1980s is the integration into the European single market. This obliges Spain to accept a very precise timetable and carry it out without hesitation or failure. This integration objective requires Spain to be extremely rigorous both in the process of outward opening and the maintenance of the internal equilibrium, in co-ordination with the rest of the European economies.

The desire of Spain to fully become a European country compels the entire society to undertake a substantial effort if one takes into consideration the existing gap between it and the Community. Because Spain is a European country by right, but not by fact, Spanish GDP *per capita* amounts to less than 76% of the European average. The effects of the crisis were so severe that current economic recovery, initiated in mid-1985, has only allowed Spain to return to the relative position it had with Europe in 1972, on the verge of the oil crisis.

In order to accelerate the approach to European GDP average values, both internal policies and initiatives and European help are needed. From the internal viewpoint, the objective of Spanish economic policy in the near future has to search for the maximum possible increases of GDP *per capita* compatible with the obligation to co-ordinate with and adapt to the economic policies carried out by Central European countries. This, necessarily requires paying special attention to price stabilisation objectives. This task is not an easy one, since the gap in the GDP growth rate can only be situated, in the conditions sketched above, around 1%. Taking a very favourable hypothesis, and if one can project the good results of the 1985–89 period, by the year 2000 the level of convergence will have increased to 85%.

This future task will be favoured by the positive evolutions of the recent past in which there has been a process of marked recovery which has surprised many. It is generally agreed that the integration in the EC has accelerated industrial investment and capitalisation processes so that the country will be better equipped to compete in the future single market. Simultaneously, foreign investment has boomed and it is a major factor in explaining the current recovery.

However, previous discussions have characterised Spain as an intermediate economy whose competitiveness has been based primarily upon a comparative advantage in terms of labour costs. Thus, and despite these positive prospects, the future Single Market brings also major concerns for the Spanish economy. These concerns arise from the lower level of technological development of Spanish firms, which may endanger equilibrium of foreign trade as well as from the process of fiscal harmonisation and the anticipated demand for higher wages and improved social conditions. This may result in a greater fiscal pressure or an increase in public deficit, as a consequence of a major expenditure level. Another factor for concern may be the higher labour mobility for less qualified segments and highly qualified professionals.

Nevertheless, any liberalisation process acting upon the Spanish economy has always produced very positive effects and that induces an *a priori* optimistic attitude towards the impact of European integration, even if it means an increase in competition for Spanish sectors and firms.

3.8 Bibliography and sources of information

Bibliography

The following books provide more information on the issues discussed in this chapter as well as a very complete bibliography on each section.

García Delgado, J.L. (ed.) (1988): *España. Economía*, Madrid: Espasa Calpe.
Ruesga, S.M. (ed.) (1989): *1993: España ante el Mercado Unico*, Madrid: Ediciones Pirámide.
Tamames, R. (1989): *Estructura Económica de España*, Madrid: Alianza Editorial.

Among the periodicals that provide up-to-date information on Spanish economic issues the following may be recommended:

Economía Industrial, published by the 'Ministerio de Industria y Energía', Castellana, 160, 28046 Madrid, Tl. 34-1-4588010.
Información Comercial Española, published by the 'Ministerio de Comercio', Madrid.
Papeles de Economía Española, published by the 'Confederación Española de Cajas de Ahorros', Padre Damián, 48, Madrid, Tl. 34-1-4586158.

Sources of information

Banco de España, Servicio de Publicaciones, Alcalá 50, Madrid, Tl. 34-1-4469055.
Consejo Superior de las Cámaras Oficiales de Comercio, Industria y Navegación de España, Claudio Coello, 19, 28001 Madrid, Tl. 34-1-2752307.
Dirección General de Aduanas, Guzmán el Bueno, 137, Madrid, Tl. 34-1-2543200.

Instituto Nacional de Estadística (INE), Paseo de la Castellana, 183, 28071 Madrid, Tl. 34-1-2799300.

Ministerio de Economía y Hacienda, Paseo de la Castellana, 162, 28046 Madrid, Tl. 34-1-4588664.

4 | *France*

Kirk Thomson

4.1 Institutional framework and historical context

4.1.1 *Introduction*

France has a republican and centralised form of government. The present constitution, the Fifth Republic, dates from as recently as 1958 and, as amended in 1962, provides the directly elected President with consider-able powers. He alone appoints the Prime Minister and the other members of his government and even if traditionally he leaves the day-to-day running of affairs to his Prime Minister, while defining the general pattern of policy, he can, and frequently does, intervene in a direct manner in the decision-making process.

Until very recently, French politics have been marked by a degree of ideological cleavage unusual in a developed industrial state. The election of the socialist candidate, François Mitterand, in 1981 was regarded with concern both inside and outside France on the one hand, and as the opportunity for a fundamental and irreversible change in the French economy and social system on the other. Mitterand's programme, the *Programme Commun*, was one of radical change and was the centre-piece of an uneasy alliance with the then powerful Communist Party.

French economic policy during the 1980s can be subdivided into three periods:

1 The 1981–82 period of reflation launched by the Mauroy govern-ment (Mitterand's first Prime Minister) at a time when other countries were following deflationary policies as a result of the second oil shock.
2 The 1983–85 period of austerity during which France recovered from its balance of payments difficulties and inflation was brought down.

3   The 1986–90 period of quickening recovery, thanks, firstly, to the effects of the fall in oil prices and of the dollar, but also to the beneficial effects of government policy regarding wages and inflation, improvements in business profits, and of a variety of structural reforms. This period also witnessed the period of 'cohabitation' with the right wing Chirac Government from 1986–88. Apart from the policy on privatisation it is difficult to interpret this, or indeed the subsequent left-wing return with Michel Rocard, as representing fundamental shifts in policy.

4.1.2 *The reflation policy of 1981–82*

The main elements of this policy were an expansion in demand brought about by a number of measures:

- increases in the minimum salary, the *salaire minimum interprofessionel de croissance (SMIC)*, which raised its purchasing power considerably in 1981 and 1982;
- increases in various social benefits;
- increases in public investments; housing; aid to the private and public sectors;
- increases in public employment;
- reduction in the working week to 39 hours and an extra week's paid holiday as well as a lowering of the age of retirement.

These measures had a number of characteristics:

- the government made no effort to reduce taxes in order to encourage demand;
- most of the measures were irreversible in nature e.g. increases in public employment, increases in the *SMIC*, early retirement, investments in nationalised enterprises;
- the combination of new taxes on higher incomes and the nature of the other measures involved an important net redistribution effect.

Although the policy of the Mauroy government ensured a moderate rate of growth in 1981 and 1982, it also produced a rapidly growing balance of payments problem and a series of exchange rate crises (October 1981, June 1982 and March 1983). These crises resulted in devaluations and accompanying measures (in particular the wage and price freeze in the Summer of 1982) which culminated in a fundamental policy shift in 1983.

4.1.3 *The 1983 policy change*

The austerity measures introduced in 1983 were designed to reduce aggregate demand in order to bring the balance of payments back into equilibrium. Behind this turnaround lay the constraint of the European Monetary System which is based on the assumption of stable exchange rates. The measures involved three main elements:

1   a compulsory loan of 10% of households' previous tax payments and a special tax of 10% of taxable income to finance the social security system;
2   reductions in public expenditure and incentives to encourage savings;
3   tighter foreign exchange controls.

These measures combined to reduce gross domestic product (GDP) by 0.6% in 1983 and by 0.4% in 1984 and contributed largely to the substantial reduction in the balance of payments deficit in 1983 (this latter improvement was aided by other elements, particularly the excellent results of the food and agricultural exports for that year).

4.1.4 *1984–90 Austerity and recovery:*

The period following 1983 is marked by a degree of homogeneity, despite the March 1986 to May 1988 right-wing interlude. The priority in the 1983–85 period was to reduce inflation and to restore company profits. In terms of budgetary policy the main objectives were to reduce the total level of tax and social security payments and to keep the budget deficit below 3% of GDP. These two objectives were reached, thanks partly to the reduction in oil prices which affected growth and tax revenue from 1986 onwards. The period of 1987–90 has been one of recovery marked by higher rates of investment and growth but continuing difficulties regarding unemployment and the balance of trade.

Following 1983, both inflation and the restoration of business profits were closely associated with the policies pursued by the various governments. The price and wage freeze of June 1982 was an attempt to break the spiral relationship between wage and price increases. In 1983 the government went further in its attempt to achieve 'desindexation' by calling on employers and unions to negotiate annual salary increases in line with a norm fixed in accordance with national objectives instead of quarterly increases which anticipated coming price increases. Negotiations were to be based upon the total payroll of the enterprises rather than of specific salaries, and any increases designed to compensate for a difference between the norm and the inflationary outcome had to take account of the situation of the economy as a whole and of the enterprise.

This policy was effective and was reinforced from 1985 to 1986 by the depreciation of the dollar and the fall in oil prices (which allowed business to re-establish profit margins).

A combination of growth and government austerity has similarly brought about an improvement in public finances. From 1985, budgetary and fiscal policy aimed at reducing the total tax and social contribution take and reducing the deficit. In 1985 and 1986 net tax reductions balanced reductions in expenditure, but from 1987 economic recovery brought about a spontaneous increase in revenue. This coincided with the impact of previous austerity measures which limited the spontaneous growth in expenditure.

These aspects of policy, particularly recent developments are dealt with in more detail below.

4.1.5 *The* 'dirigiste' *tradition*

In considering the French economy, it is important to remember that the relatively recent party political consensus regarding economic policy is developing on the basis of a much older tradition regarding the formulation and implementation of such policy in France. In this respect two elements need to be kept in mind.

1   France has a tradition of centralised economic and public administration, and the administrative dominance of the economy goes back as far as Colbert and Louis XIV. The development of indicative planning at the end of the Second World War was a modern manifestation of an old established reflex rather than an exciting innovation and the painstaking dismantling of the system of controls over the past few years represents a dramatic, although as yet partial, change. Whether recent movements towards more independence in business decision-making have been matched by a fundamental shift in French management attitudes, however, has been questioned by certain observers of French management culture.

2   Very close links exist between the various ministries responsible for the economy and their professional staff on the one hand and the leaders of the business community (especially in banking, insurance and the major public and private enterprises) on the other. Leading professional civil servants complete their career in a 'corps' attached to a ministry and are recruited from specialised and highly selective *'grandes écoles'* run independently from the university system e.g. the *École Polytechnique,* the *École des Mines* and the *École des Ponts et Chaussées.* Large public and private firms try to recruit either experienced civil servants or young graduates coming from these engineering schools and the resulting close interpenetration of

administrative and industrial technocracies has no equivalent in the Western world. That interconnection helps to explain the close co-ordination and mutual trust which exists between administrative and industrial strategies in key sectors.

In considering French economic policy, then, it is important to remember:

(a) that despite ideological differences, particularly in the early 1980s there has been a strong consensus among the decision-making elite, and the political establishment in particular, regarding interventionist policies and national economic objectives;

(b) behind the public political debate a relatively homogeneous corps of highly trained engineers, administrators and managers, sharing a common social and educational background, has been responsible for implementing policy both in the public and the private sectors.

4.2 Main economic characteristics

4.2.1 *Population and labour*

The total population of metropolitan France in 1990 is estimated to be 56,323,000 (Table 4.6). In the period 1982–90 the population was growing at a rate of 0.5% per annum and 80% of this growth came from natural increase as opposed to immigration. Although the rate of growth is low, it stands in marked contrast to that in other comparable EC member states (INSEE, 1 June, 1990).

Previous trends regarding the drift of population towards outer suburban zones surrounding the major cities at the expense of both city centres and isolated rural areas have continued. Paris (2,147,000, 1990) and Marseille (803,000, 1990) remain the largest cities, although both have continued to lose population.

The regions where population growth has been greatest (see Table 4.1) are concentrated along the Mediterranean coast and in the dynamic areas of the Île de France and the Rhône–Alpes region.

This natural rate of growth (relatively high for Europe) is due to a crude birth rate of 13.6°/000 and death rate of 9.4°/000 in 1989.

Although the fertility rate has fallen to 1.8 per woman and is below the replacement rate of 2.1 the figure remains higher than in comparable countries. One explanatory factor may be in the policies aimed at encouraging families by means of tax incentives, social security benefits and plentiful provision for nursery school places. The failure of the French population to grow in line with that of other European nations in the nineteenth and in the early twentieth centuries has left French political opinion favourable to such measures which are designed to encourage population growth.

Table 4.1 Annual population growth %

The French regions	1975–82	1982–90
Languedoc-Roussillon	1.05	1.14
Provence-Alpes-Côte d'Azur	1.08	0.90
Rhône-Alpes	0.69	0.79
Ile de France	0.28	0.70
Aquitaine	0.58	0.63
Haute-Normandie	0.52	0.60
Centre	0.72	0.59
Midi-Pyrénées	0.35	0.54
Pays de la Loire	0.82	0.53
Picardie	0.51	0.49
Alsace	0.45	0.44
Bretagne	0.60	0.39
Basse-Normandie	0.48	0.36
Poitou-Charentes	0.37	0.21
Franche-Comté	0.32	0.15
Bourgogne	0.23	0.10
Nord-Pas-de-Calais	0.07	0.09
Champagne-Ardenne	0.10	0.00
Lorraine	−0.07	−0.09
Auvergne	0.02	−0.14
Limousin	−0.03	−0.23

Source: Le Monde, Saturday, 30 June 1990

Total working population in January 1990 stood at 24.4 million or 43.3% of the total population. Of this population 13.8 million were male and 10.6 million were female. With a male participation rate of 85.5% and a female rate of 45.8% in 1989 the major trends over recent years have been varied (see Table 4.7).

With increasing numbers in full-time education, rates for the 15–24 age group of both sexes have fallen significantly since 1975. Similarly changes in the age of retirement and the possibilities of taking early retirement at 55 reduce male participation rates above 55 and 60 years. Female participation rates, particularly in the 25–54 year age group, have tended to increase. The social and economic reasons for these movements are common to most European nations – increasing desire among women to work outside the home, increasing educational aspirations among the young and a growth in service sector employment. Another important element is the high proportion of women engaged in part-time employment.

Employment structure
The main changes in the employment structures in France have taken place progressively as the economy has adjusted to the new international environment.

Table 4.2 Employment by major industry sector (Millions of people)

Year	Agriculture, fishing etc.	Industry Total	Mfg	Building	Commerce & tradeable ser.	Assurance & finance	Non-tradeable Services	Total
1970	2758.3	5860.3	4965.5	2057.6	5923.4	381.2	3892.6	20,900.4
1975	2185.1	5987.4	5125.6	1958.4	6438.9	504.7	4326.2	21,400.7
1980	1881.8	5631.1	4777.2	1864.7	7123.8	557.5	4788.2	21,847.1
1985	1598.9	4993.5	4129.6	1526.1	7353.1	600.1	5329.1	21,400.8
1988	1443.4	4679.7	3848.5	1554.2	7845.8	606.1	5509.5	21,638.7
1989	1396.4	4669.6	3851.3	1572.9	8099.2	603.9	5549.1	21,891.1

Source: Comptes nationaux

Numbers employed in agriculture, forestry and fishing fell from 2.8 million (13.4%) in 1970 to 1.4 million (6.3%) in 1989. Substantial recent falls have also been apparent in coal-mining (56.3 thousand in 1982 to 27,000 in 1989), iron and steel (150,000 to 98,000) and shipbuilding. Most other changes, however, have been more gradual.

Manufacturing industry as a whole fell from a peak of 5.3 million in 1974 to a low of 3.8 million in 1988. Since that year, numbers have risen slightly although the true figure is somewhat difficult to establish since many manufacturing enterprises made more use than usual in the 1980s of temporary workers hired from agencies (see Statistical Annexe, Table D 8).

Most growth has been noticed in the services sector, both in the market and non-market sector. Most expansion has taken place in commerce, transport, hotels and catering, insurance and financial services, public sector services and, of course, temporary employment agencies (see Statistical Annexe, Table D 8).

Unemployment

The unemployment situation in France remains relatively bleak, although performance has been improving since 1987 when the rate peaked at 10.5% (see Statistical Annexe, Table D 12).

The French statistical office, *INSEE,* traces movements in unemployment in Table 4.3.

Table 4.3 Unemployment by age and by sex, 1986–89 (%)

Age	1986	1987	1988	1989
Men	8.4	8.3	7.7	7.0
15–24	18.6	17.2	15.8	13.6
25–49	6.5	6.6	6.2	5.9
50 +	6.8	7.0	6.7	6.3
Women	13.1	13.6	13.1	12.8
15–24	27.9	27.8	25.9	23.8
25–49	10.5	11.2	11.2	11.6
50 +	7.7	8.6	8.5	8.3
Together	10.4	10.5	10.0	9.5
15–24	22.8	22.0	20.4	18.2
25–49	8.2	8.6	8.4	8.3
50 +	7.1	7.7	7.5	7.1

Source: Comptes de la nation, 1989

These figures show a continuing relatively high rate of unemployment which continues to decline slowly as new job creation slightly exceeds the growth in the working population. The rate for women

(12.8% in 1989) remains substantially above that for men (7.0%). Unemployment remains particularly high for the 15–24 age group (13.6% for males and 23% for females).

Recent improvements in the category have been partly caused by a decline in the participation rate as young people study longer. Another major area of concern relates to the long-term unemployed, as the average period spent unemployed is increasing annually.

Table 4.4 Unemployment by region

			Rate of employment – index for France = 100		
	1987	1988		1987	1988
Alsace	71	68	Languedoc-Roussillon	132	135
Aquitaine	108	108	Limousin	85	83
Auvergne	98	99	Lorraine	102	102
Basse-Normandie	108	101	Midi-Pyrénées	92	95
Bourgogne	97	95	Nord-Pas-de-Calais	133	135
Bretagne	104	101	Pays de la Loire	109	108
Centre	91	89	Picardie	108	109
Champagne-Ardenne	109	108	Poitou-Charentes	109	109
Corse	112	108	Provence-Alpes-Côte d'Azur	117	119
Franche-Comté	95	94	Rhône-Alpes	83	83
Haute-Normandie	123	122	**France Métropolitain**	100	100
Île de France	83	84			

Source: La France et ses Regions, INSEE, 1990

The causes of unemployment in France

First of all, it would appear that although regional disparities do exist, unemployment in France is less of a regional problem than in many comparable economies (see Table 4.4). The low figures for Alsace reflect the ease with which work can be found across the frontiers. The high figures for the Nord-Pas-de-Calais correspond to an area of structural decline and those for Languedoc-Roussillon to the region's failure to provide new jobs for entrants to the labour market.

Whereas the exact level of frictional unemployment is difficult to calculate it is clear that from 1973 onwards it has not represented a significant factor in the growth of overall unemployment. Between 1967 and 1972 the vacancy ratio increased from 0.2% to over 0.9% but fell thereafter until 1984. In 1988 it was just over 0.3%.

An indicator for Keynesian or demand deficiency unemployment is the Okun curve which relates levels of unemployment to capacity utilisation rates in the business sector. According to OECD estimates the adverse effect on demand of the two oil shocks can explain unemployment growth in 1974–75 and in 1980–81. However, the upward shift of the Okun curve outside of these periods suggests a reduction in the importance of Keynesian unemployment (OECD 1988–89, *France*, p. 36). The main reason, then, for the growth in unemployment would seem to be classical, or in other words, rigidities in the labour market leading to a high cost of labour.

To quote from the 1988 OECD report on France (OECD 1989 *op.cit.* p. 36):

> The relative downward rigidity of the cost of labour in the 1970s meant that the business sector had to bear the brunt of the loss of national income due to the two oil shocks. This weighed heavily on production costs and profit margins of firms, thereby eroding their competitiveness, preventing them from expanding their production capacity and ultimately resulting in net job losses up to 1986.

This development can be traced in Table 4.5 indicating the share of added value going to salary payments.

Table 4.5 Share of salary payments as a percentage of value added

Year	Salary remuneration corporate sector
1970	63.5
1976	67.4
1980	68.5
1981	69.0
1985	66.5
1988	61.8
1989	61.4

Source: Comptes de la Nation, 1989

The rigidities in the French labour market stem more from administrative regulation than trade union power. Trade union membership in the private sector is very low in France and employees rely more on the provisions of the *'Code du Travail'* for protection than on unions. Total trade union membership (difficult to assess because the unions are reluctant to provide reliable figures) is probably less than 2 million which is roughly 10% of the total workforce. The three major trade unions, which recruit in all industries, are the communist dominated *Confédération Générale du Travail*, the *Confédération Française Démocratique du Travail* and *Force Ouvrière*.

There are three main sources of difficulty in the French labour market. It is difficult to ascertain their relative importance but their combined role has been implicitly recognised by successive governments in the formulation of policies to reduce unemployment.

First, there is a higher 'tax wedge' on the price of labour than in comparable countries. This is the difference between the salary received by the employee net of income tax and social security contributions and the effective cost of labour to the employer – salary plus employer's social charges. Employers will usually have to pay around 45% of the gross salary in social charges. The determination of salaries is subject to considerable central influence.

Second, there is a high level of direct government influence in the labour market partly aimed at counterbalancing trade union weakness: the guaranteed minimum wage, the *SMIC* has been systematically used to increase low salaries. As a result, whereas in 1979 4% of workers were paid the minimum wage this figure had risen to 9.7% in 1985 before falling back to 7.8% in 1987. In the period 1980–89 the purchasing power of the *SMIC* increased by 20.4% whereas that of the average salary increased by 7%.

The *SMIC* recently (May, June 1990) became a political issue when Mitterand called upon employers to renegotiate low salaries. The government used the threat of a relatively high increase in the *SMIC* to obtain the employers' federation (*CNPF*) agreement to renegotiate the collective agreements which govern salary structures in most branches of industry. These agreements themselves are also subject to influence from the Minister of Labour who can extend their application to all employers within a certain category, even if an employer is not a member of the employers' federation who signed the agreement with the trade unions. In addition, if negotiations between employers' federations and unions result in deadlock, the ministry can insist on compulsory arbitration by a special committee chaired by a ministry official. The *Confedération National du Patronat Français (CNPF),* unsurprisingly, gave a satisfactory response to the Government's appeal and the increase in the *SMIC* was limited to 2.5%.

Negotiations on the revaluation of collective agreements where salaries are particularly low, scheduled to begin before October 1990, are one example of how government pressure can largely compensate for union weakness.

Public sector employment increased from 18.5% in 1974 to a total of 23.1% in 1987. In view of the seniority-related salary structures and the job security in the public sector, this high proportion of public employment tends to inhibit a downward adjustment of salaries. In addition the Minister of Labour has considerable powers to impose centrally agreed collective agreements on large areas of business activity.

Third, there are the limitations imposed on employers in the area of redundancies. Although in July 1986 the right-wing Chirac government abolished the requirement to obtain prior administrative authorisation for redundancies, restrictions still remain. In 1985 a community-wide survey revealed that 81% of French business considered that difficulty of hiring and firing workers was an obstacle to employing more staff. This figure may well be lower in 1990, but it nevertheless remains the case that employing a new worker remains a considerable and potentially long-term investment decision.

Employment policies

Since 1981 a variety of measures have been adopted and tried in the attempt to reduce unemployment, but a major difference exists between the period before and after 1983 with the introduction of the *'politique de rigueur'*.

In 1981 the new socialist government set out to reduce unemployment by general reflation, expanding public emloyment, reductions in the working week and aid to firms and industries which were in difficulties. The problems engendered by the expansionary fiscal policy obliged the Mauroy government to rethink its approach to unemployment. From 1983 onwards it was realised that, although the so-called social treatment of unemployment (training schemes, early retirement etc.) would continue to be important, the creation of plentiful stable employment would be possible only in a growing economy based on profitable enterprises.

The first major stage in this direction was the progressive disindexing of salaries in 1983, but it was not until 1987 that the employment situation showed real improvement.

This improvement at the end of the 1980s was not the result of a successful employment policy, but rather the result of a general improvement in the economy. Nevertheless, it was decided to accompany this upturn by special 'employment plans' in September 1988 and September 1989. These plans involved a number of measures whose general aim was to reduce the social charges for employers hiring their first employee, to emphasise training rather than work experience for young people, and to provide incentives for the employment of the long-term unemployed. Fiscal incentives were concentrated on the small business sector on the assumption that they would be most effective with small employers.

4.2.2 *Output and growth*

Following the Second World War output grew rapidly in France and commentators often refer nostalgically to the period as the *'trente glorieuses'*. From 1969 to 1973 real GDP was growing at around 6% per year. The quadrupling of oil prices in 1973 checked this hectic expansion and coupled with associated anti-inflationary policies brought the rate down to 3.2% in 1974 and 0.2% in 1975. Measures designed to encourage investment and limit unemployment produced a strong recovery (5.2%) but at the cost of external disequilibrium and an

Table 4.6 Contribution to growth at 1980 prices (%)

	1982	1983	1984	1985	1986	1987	1988	1989
Final con- sumption of house- holds	2.1	0.6	0.6	1.4	2.3	1.7	1.9	1.9
of govern- ments	0.7	0.4	0.2	0.4	0.3	0.5	0.5	0.3
Gross fixed investment	−0.3	−0.8	−0.5	0.6	0.9	0.8	1.8	1.3
of which: industrial enterprises	0	−0.5	−0.3	0.4	0.7	0.6	1.2	0.8
Stock varia- tions	1.0	−0.9	0	−0.1	0.9	0.3	−0.2	−0.1
Foreign trade in goods and services	−0.9	1.4	1.0	−0.5	−1.4	−1.1	−0.2	0.3
of which: exports	−0.4	0.8	1.5	0.4	−0.3	0.7	1.9	2.5
imports	−0.6	0.6	−0.6	−1.0	−1.6	−1.8	−2.1	−2.2
GDP	2.5	0.7	1.3	1.9	2.5	2.2	3.9	3.8

Source: Compte de la Nation, 1989

acceleration of inflation. In September 1976 the incoming Prime Minister introduced an austerity policy – the *'Plan Barre'* which restored the external balance and brought down inflation but reduced growth to some 3.4% per year between 1977 and 1979. The second oil shock and the necessary readjustment further reduced growth to 1.6% in 1980 and 1.2% in 1981.

It was after this prolonged period of relatively slow growth, worsening unemployment and restriction that the elections of 1981 produced the Mauroy government with its policy of expansion and economic reorganisation. Unfortunately the measures introduced in June 1981: raising the *SMIC*, increasing social benefits and public sector employment, were not only virtually irreversible, they also came into force when other countries were pursuing restrictive policies. Domestic demand grew by 4% in 1982 and quickly produced a widening trade deficit. Although restrictions were introduced in the summer of 1982, it was not until March 1983 that the government felt able to announce a major change in policy alongside a devaluation of the franc. The new policy, announced to accompany the third franc devaluation since the change of government, aimed mainly at slowing the growth in French domestic demand by cuts in public expenditure and strict budgetary discipline in the period 1984 to 1987. A restrictive monetary policy and low wage norms were introduced and adhered to. Although foreign trade was restored to balance and inflation brought steadily down, the growth rate also suffered considerably. Growth dipped to a low of 0.7% in 1983 and did not pick up until the second half of 1987 (see Statistical Annexe, Table D11).

Whereas the biggest contribution to growth in 1986 came from increased household consumption stimulated by the fall in energy prices, in 1987 and 1988 investment became increasingly important (see Table 4.6). Growth in 1988 and 1989 was 3.7% according to *INSEE*. Of this figure household consumption continued to represent some 2.0% as for the previous five years. Although the contribution of investment fell back to 1.4%, better export performance kept the overall figure up.

A more moderate rate of growth was expected for 1990 at 3–3.5%, principally because of lower foreign demand. Domestic demand and investment is expected to remain buoyant.

4.2.3 *Consumption, savings and investment*

The period of rapid growth following the Second World War was also a period of heavy investment in France. The rate of investment fell considerably as a result of the two oil price shocks and has only recently begun to increase again. According to OECD estimates France was investing 23.3% of GDP in 1963 and 24.3% in 1974. This was considerably higher than the OECD average (1974) of 22.7%.

The first oil shock was marked by a change in this development. From 1973 to 1980 investment rates stagnated and then fell after 1980. Again, on the basis of OECD figures, investment, which had averaged 23% of GDP between 1960 and 1973 slipped back to 22.4 in the period 1973 to 1981, to 18.9% in the period 1981–85 and was 18.9% in 1984. If business investment has improved since its low point of 1984, it has not yet reached the level reached in the early 1970s (see Table 4.7).

The pick-up in productive investment has come about thanks essentially to improvements in business finance and to greater confidence. Earlier investment (1985–86) was devoted principally to improvements in productivity, but since 1987 there has been an increase in investment aimed at expanding capacity. Investment in manufacturing

Table 4.7 Rate of investment and self-financing ratio – corporate sector

Year	Rate of investment (%)	Year	Self-financing ratio (%)
1970	20.6	1970	59.0
1975	16.5	1975	76.7
1980	15.8	1980	58.3
1986	15.3	1986	95.6
1987	16.3	1987	85.1
1988	17.1	1988	87.2
1989	17.6	1989	81.7

Source: Comptes nationaux, 1989

went up by 5.3% in 1986, 7.5% in 1987, 11% in 1988 and was expected to drop to 10% in 1990.

The situation concerning the *'Grandes Entreprises Nationales'*— Charbonnages de France (coal mining), Electricité de France, Gaz de France, SNCF (railways), RATP (urban transport), Air France, Air Inter and the PTT (telecommunication) is somewhat different. This group of major public enterprises is handled separately by INSEE since they are considered as public services rather than competitive firms. If investment was maintained at a high level during the 1970s thanks to the improvements in telecommunications, and the expanding nuclear energy programme, a decline set in after 1980 which was only arrested in 1988 (see Table 4.8). Fleet renewals of the nationalised airlines, and new investment from the EDF were responsible for this slight change. Investment in this area will have continued buoyant through 1990 under the impact of the start of the TGV-Nord programme and infrastructure

Table 4.8 Productive investment of business enterprises – volumes at prices of previous year (% change)

Sector and weighting at 1989 values	1986	1987	1988	1989	1990
GENs 14%	−7.2	−8.5	4.1	4.7	3
Enterprises in competitive sector 86%	9.9	8.3	12.4	7.7	7.5
of which					
agriculture 6%	−7.6	−4.0	13.4	8.3	4
industry 34%	5.3	7.5	11.0	8.1	10
Commerce/services 42%	19.3	11.2	13.2	7.3	7
Building and civil engineering 4%	−4.2	4.8	14.1	7.2	2
All enterprises	6.3	5.3	11.1	7.2	6.5

Source: Note de Conjoncture de l'INSEE, July 1990

improvements associated with the coming winter olympics at Albertville.

Household investment is largely devoted to house construction. As indicated by the non-financial savings ratio of households, the low point was reached in 1985 at 9.2% (% of Gross Disposable Income (GDI)). This figure had improved to only 9.7% in 1989, but expenditure on new construction, as opposed to maintenance, expanded very little and the number of housing starts went up from 327,100 to only 339,000. In 1989 loans granted for new housing construction were even slightly below the 1988 figure.

The personal savings ratio stopped its long-term decline since 1978 after reaching a low in 1987 at 11.1% of GDI. In 1988 this rose to 12.1% and in 1989 to 12.3%. This consumption–savings relationship was not expected to change in 1990. The OECD 1990 report puts forward four possible explanations for this recent increase:

1   the acceleration in the real disposable income growth at the end of 1988;
2   the end of the disinflation process;
3   the desire to reconstitute wealth levels after the stock exchange crash of October 1987;
4   higher real interest rate.

Household consumption represents the largest share of GDP. Although the share grew irregularly through the 1970s from 57.6% in 1970 to 59% in 1981, the figure has oscillated around 60% since then (see Table 4.10). In 1989, 60.2% of GDP was consumed by households which correspond to Ffr3650 bn. This represented a volume increase of 3% compared with 1988. In view of this slightly higher increase in the purchasing power of gross disposable income, this allowed a small increase in the savings ratio. The trends in consumption over the years are given in Table 4.9.

Table 4.9 Consumption by category of goods and services (%)

Goods/services	1970	1975	1980	1985	1988
1 Food, drinks, tobacco	26.0	23.5	21.4	20.7	19.7
2 Clothing and footwear	9.6	8.5	7.3	7.0	6.8
3 Housing, lighting, heating	15.3	15.8	17.5	19.1	18.9
4 Furniture and household goods	10.2	10.4	9.5	8.4	8.2
5 Medical services and health	7.1	7.8	7.7	8.6	9.3
6 Transport and communication	13.4	14.4	16.6	16.9	16.9
7 Leisure, cultural activities	6.9	7.2	7.3	7.1	7.5
8 Other goods and services – personal services, restaurants travel agencies etc.	11.5	12.4	12.6	12.2	12.8

This pattern was confirmed into 1989 with, for example a 5.7% increase in the number of new cars purchased. It is interesting to note that 38% of vehicles sold were imported in 1989. Expenditure on health continued to increase. In general, consumer expenditure in France exhibited similar patterns to those in other EC member states.

Variations around this pattern caused by differences in age, social-professional category and location of domicile can be considerable. Elderly people spend 60–70% of their budget on food and lodging as opposed to 36–45% for singles below 35 years of age.

Table 4.10 Consumption, savings

Household	Consumption as % of GDP	Savings rate as % of GDP
1970	57.6	18.7
1973	57.9	19.1
1974	56.8	19.8
1975	68.6	20.2
1976	59.0	18.2
1978	58.9	20.4
1980	58.5	17.6
1982	61.1	17.3
1983	59.7	15.9
1985	59.9	14.0
1986	60.7	12.9
1987	61.0	11.1
1988	60.6	12.1
1989	60.2	12.3

Source: Comptes nationaux

4.2.4 *Inflation*

France had a tendency to be more inflation-prone than many of her European partners until the mid-1980s (Statistical Annexe, Tables D3 and D17). Although a widespread use of indexation protected the economy from many of the inconveniences of inflation the setting up of the European Monetary System made a reduction of French inflation rates to West German levels absolutely imperative.

Inflation in France has followed a similar pattern to that in other countries. After accelerating in the late 1960s (boosted by the salary concessions of 1968), inflation hit a high level of 15% in 1974 after the first oil shock. Brought down to an annual rate of around 9.5% by the policies of Raymond Barre in the late 1970s, inflation again accelerated from mid-1979 as a result of the second oil shock. Contrary to the deceleration which followed the events of 1973 the situation now worsened partly as a result of the policies of the Mauroy government. Prices continued to rise at over 13% until mid-1982. The price freeze of the summer of 1982 checked the upward trend and heralded a downward movement under the combined impact of a radical change in government policies, salary restraint and subsequently the downward movement in the dollar, oil and raw material prices.

Policies aimed at tackling inflation have been varied, and (until recently) relatively ineffective. From 1945 until late 1986 the Minister of the Economy had wide-ranging powers to control prices. Although the controls were applied with varying severity, it was only in 1978, under Raymond Barre that systematic liberation was applied. The Mauroy government returned to price controls in July 1981, followed a year later by a full wage and price freeze accompanied by a devaluation. Controls remained in force until 1986 when an improved international environment allowed first a loosening and then at the end of the year full abolition of controls. The change of government in March 1986 cannot be seen as marking a change of policy.

Since 1986 the accent has been placed upon providing a competitive environment to justify continued price freedom and upon stringent budgetary policies to avoid any inflationary pressure stemming from central government policies. Other major elements explaining French success have been the fall in raw material and oil prices as well as salary restraint supported by a relatively high level of unemployment.

4.2.5 *Industrial market structure*

Industrial restructuring has taken place under the impetus of the two oil shocks, the integration of world markets and the resulting increase in competition.

The size of firm (see Table 4.11) and degree of concentration depends very much on the nature of the business activity. Small and medium-sized enterprises (SMEs) defined as those with fewer than 500 employees dominate in market services, the building industry, and in commerce. They are less important in financial services, transport and manufacturing. It should be noted, however, that SMEs in manufacturing are bigger and represent the largest group.

In manufacturing the global figure conceals considerable differences. In 1985, for example enterprises with 20–500 workers were responsible for 66% of the production of standard consumer goods, 55% of the production of the food industry, 21% of the consumer durables production and 8% of the motor vehicle industry.

It is interesting to note that in terms of employment the SMEs were

Table 4.11 Percentage of salaried employees in SMEs in each major sector of the economy, January 1987

Sector	Numbers employed					Total employment in the sector
	0–9	10–49	50–499	Total		
Manufacturing	7.4	15.4	29.6	52.4	100	4,630,536
Building–						
Public works	29.4	29.7	22.3	81.4	100	1,175,022
Commerce	31.2	26.1	20.9	78.2	100	1,960,308
Telecommunications	5.3	10.3	13.0	28.6	100	1,223,560
Traded services	29.9	24.4	25.5	79.8	100	1,952,130
Financial services	1.6	2.2	13.7	17.5	100	514,637
Total	17.1	19.1	23.9	60.1	100	11,456,193

Source: INSEE Resultats, système productif, Nos 10–17, Nov. 1989

Table 4.12 Evolution of the financial concentration of the top 20 major industrial sectors from 1980 to 1985

Sector	1980 (%)	1985 (%)	1980–1985
Meat and milk industries	9.9	11.2	1.3
Other food industries	15.6	21.5	5.9
Minerals and ferrous metals	68.9	80.8	11.9
Non-ferrous metals	74.7	69.9	−4.8
Construction materials	21.0	24.3	3.3
Glass	70.4	62.3	−8.1
Base chemicals	40.0	47.1	7.1
Pharmaceuticals	18.3	22.6	4.3
Metals	12.4	12.8	0.4
Mechanicals	12.0	13.2	1.2
Electronic equipment engineering	47.3	48.8	1.5
Household equipment	50.0	48.4	−1.6
Transport materials	70.6	72.9	2.3
Naval construction, aeronautics, and armaments	60.3	71.3	11.0
Clothing and textiles	10.0	11.3	1.3
Oil	19.0	23.6	4.6
Drink	5.5	8.0	2.5
Paper/cartons	22.7	22.1	−0.6
Printing etc.	14.5	15.0	0.5
Rubber, plastics	32.5	30.5	−2.0

Source: 'Les Entreprises à l'Epreuve des Années 80, INSEE, 1989

better able to resist the years of difficulty. In the industrial sector, job losses between 1977 and 1984 amounted to 270,000 in small firms and 550,000 in large ones. As a whole SMEs increased their total share of employment from 63% in 1981 to 66.6% in 1986. This overall improvement is partly due to the number of small firms in the expanding services sector and to the tendency of large firms to 'sub-contract' certain activities. But it is also true that SMEs are quicker to adapt to market changes.

Although the SMEs remain important, the concentration of French industry accelerated after the second oil shock. Between 1980 and 1985 industrial concentration took place in 121 sectors representing 44% of French manufacturing (the share of four leading groups increased from 66% to 72% of turnover). The opposite movement concerned only 16% of industrial activity (see Table 4.12).

4.2.6 *Productivity*

Like most OECD countries, France experienced changes in productivity as a result of the oil price shocks. The disruption caused in 1973 was associated with a slowdown in productivity growth in nearly all countries. The impact of the second oil price shock was more varied. In France a fall in the rate of business investment meant that in the period 1980–89 the stock of capital available increased rather more slowly in France than elsewhere and the average age of capital increased from 12.2 years in 1980 to 13.4 years in 1987. The trend rate of growth in labour productivity (added value divided by number of hours worked per employee) fell from an average of 3.5% in the 1970s to 3% in the early 1980s and is now probably around 2% per year. Recent increases in 1988 and 1989 would seem to be temporary. As employment levels increase, the growth in productivity seems to be disappearing. The productivity of capital had been falling until 1986. It steadied in 1987 and improved slightly in May 1988. According to the 1990 OECD report, the long-term upward trend has been recovered. The OECD estimates that the rate of growth of potential production is around 2.75% per year. In the short run, excess capacity would make it possible for growth to exceed this rate without causing inflationary pressure. In the long run, GDP growth of 3% or more will call for an acceleration in capital formation, if inflationary pressures are to be avoided.

4.3 Government involvement in the French economy

As is the case in other developed economies, the role of the state has expanded in France in recent years. This role remains considerable despite recent policies designed to liberalise major sectors of economic activity.

4.3.1 *Fiscal Policy*

The general policy adopted since 1982 when Mitterand undertook to stabilise and ultimately to reduce the total government imposition in the form of taxes and social security contributions, has been to limit expenditure and reduce taxes. The effects of this change in orientation only became apparent in 1986–87 because of the delayed improvement in economic performance.

Public expenditure has correspondingly been brought down progressively in the recent years even though it remains comparatively high (see Statistical Annexe, Table D 18). This policy of restraint is set to continue in the future. The draft budget for 1991 nevertheless provides for a global increase in expenditure of 5.5% which will allow for a reduction in the budget deficit, but is unlikely to significantly reduce expenditure as a percentage of GDP.

In line with this curb on public expenditure, the trend in tax and social security contributions shows stabilisation followed by a gradual reduction (see Table 4.13).

Table 4.13 Tax and social security contributions as a percentage of GDP

	1982	1983	1984	1985	1986	1987	1988	1989
Tax revenue	24.5	24.7	25.4	25.2	25.1	25.4	25.0	24.6
Social security contributions	18.3	18.9	19.2	19.3	18.8	19.2	19.1	19.3
Total	42.8	43.6	44.6	44.5	44.0	44.6	44.1	43.9

Source: Comptes de la Nation, INSEE, 1989

The policy of reducing tax and social security contributions reflects a two-fold desire to reduce the total share of GDP going to the government and also the necessary process of adapting the French tax system for integration in the single market. This policy, and the parallel reduction in deficits has been made possible by restraining government expenditure. The deficit has been substantially reduced since 1983 (see Statistical Annexe, Table D 19).

The government debt in France is low by international standards although the debt and interest payments have both increased substantially in the 1980s (in 1980 government debt was 16.5% of GDP, in 1988 26.1%). Net of interest payments the budget was in surplus in 1989, and for 1990 the primary surplus is scheduled to exceed the 40 billion francs required to stabilise the debt/GDP ratio. In this way it is hoped that the interest rate differential with regard to Germany can be kept down and that private investment will be encouraged.

Public expenditure continues to favour education and civil research.

The 1991 budget of the *'education nationale'* will increase by 9% as opposed to the global budget increase of 5.5%, and civil research goes up by 7.5%. Other areas of above average expenditure increase are the administration of justice, culture, environmental protection and public-sector housing.

The increase in the debt/GDP ratio which took place rapidly in the early 1980s was due to two factors; on the one hand the accumulation of a series of deficits above 2% and even 3% of GDP, and on the other, the effect of interest rates on the debt and the slowdown in growth. When interest rates are higher than growth, there is an automatic tendency for the debt/GDP ratio to increase and this was the case after 1984 creating a snowball effect. It was to break this vicious circle and to encourage lower interest rates that three objectives in budgetary policy have been followed since 1983.

First, the limitation of the deficit to 3% of GDP, second, a return to a balanced budget before interest and, finally, an annual reduction of the total deficit. This made it possible to reduce the pre-interest deficit substantially between 1983 and 1988 (see Table 4.14).

Table 4.14 Budget balance general government (%), 1980–88

% of GDP	1980	1981	1982	1983	1984	1985	1986	1987	1988
Balance before interest	−0.2	−1.2	−1.4	−1.5	−1.4	−1.5	−1.0	−0.5	−0.3
Interest	0.9	1.4	1.3	1.7	1.9	1.8	1.8	1.8	1.7
Total balance	−1.1	−2.6	−2.7	−3.2	−3.3	−3.3	−2.8	−2.3	−2.0

For details of total government expenditure, government deficit, debt and levels of tax and social security contributions see Tables 35, 36, 37, 38 and 39.
Source: La Croissance retrouvée, INSEE, 1988

Taxation

The tax system in France has a number of particular features that merit attention in addition to the relatively large total tax-take and the high proportion of social-insurance contributions (see Table 4.15).

Personal income tax is highly progressive, takes considerable account of family size and exempts a high proportion of potential tax payers. In fact in 1988 only 54.54% of households paid income tax. Despite reductions in recent years, top rates are among the highest in Europe (57% from 65% in 1986). Payments are consequently highly concentrated, and in 1986 the first 10% of households paid 64% of income tax. On the other hand this effect is compensated by the fact that virtually all households pay social insurance contributions. Consequently, although an average production worker in 1988 paid 7% of his income in income tax, he paid 17% in social insurance.

Taxes on corporate profits have been reduced to replace the tax incentives previously used to encourage investment. Standard corporate income tax was reduced from 50% to 42% and the tax on undistributed profits was reduced in 1990 from 39% to 37%. Special tax credits still exist for business start-ups and for investment in enterprise zones.

VAT is the main tax in France. This situation is likely to remain unchanged even if such a tax is by its very nature regressive. Widespread opposition to any extension of income tax from trade unions and similar pressure groups and considerable administrative difficulties (tax avoidance, an overburdened tax administration, and lack of any structure for collection of income tax at source) combine to make any shift away from VAT and towards income tax a gradual process. The government has reduced the number of VAT rates from five to three and has reduced the top rate from 33.3% to 25%. The standard rate is 18.6%. Excise duties are lower in France than elsewhere.

Local taxation in France is rather complex and varies considerably. There are four local direct taxes. Three are paid by households as occupants and are based on rental value with, as of 1990, a limit of 4% of household income. A business tax produces 45% of local authority revenue.

Table 4.15 Structure of tax and social insurance contributions in 1987 as a percentage of tax revenues

	France	EEC unweighted average
Social security contributions	43.0	29.2
of which:		
employers	27.2	–
employees	12.3	–
self–employed and unemployed	3.5	–
Taxes on income	12.7	26.3
Corporate taxes	5.2	7.4
Payroll taxes	1.9	0.5
Taxes on property	4.7	4.5
Taxes on goods and services	29.3	32.5
of which:		
general taxes	19.5	18.0
taxes on specific goods and services	8.9	13.1
of which:		
excises	6.4	–
Other taxes	3.1	0.4
Total	100	100

Source: OECD, France, 1989

4.3.2 *Regional policy*

Although France is a country with marked cultural and geographical diversities, it has not suffered to the same extent as some of its neighbours from regions afflicted by market and lasting economic difficulties. In 1988, for example, with a national unemployment rate of 10.1% the two worst-hit regions were Languedoc-Roussillon with 13.6% and the Nord-Pas-de-Calais with 13.5%. The most favoured region was Alsace with 6.8% followed by Rhône-Alpes and Limousin with 8.2%.

Since 1963, the *Delegation à l'Aménagement du Territoire (DATAR)* has been responsible for implementing policy designed to deal with two main problem areas; those isolated agricultural regions particularly hit by the exodus from the land and certain areas hit by structural industrial change, particularly the former steel-producing and shipbuilding centres. An example of this kind of activity was the creation of three enterprise zones in 1987 in Dunkerque, La Seyne and La Ciotat to deal with the problems caused by the closure of local shipyards. Businesses starting up in the zones were given a 10-year break from all corporation taxes provided they created sufficient numbers of new jobs.

The main role of *DATAR* has been considerably modified in recent years by two major developments. First, the development since 1975 of the Community regional policy, including the existing aids to agriculture distributed by FEOGA. DATAR co-ordinates the application for and the distribution of aid coming from these and other Community funds. Second, the Law of Decentralisation in 1982 gave considerable new powers to the Regional and the Departmental Councils. These changes led to a series of State–Region planning contracts from 1984. The preparation and negotiation of these *Contrats de Plan* was entrusted to *DATAR*. In the early months of 1989 a second series of 5-year contracts was signed with the regions for a global sum of 52 billion francs. Three main priority themes were picked out for attention: development of the road network, training and research, and economic and social support going to small businesses and rural areas in difficulty.

4.3.3 *Industrial policy*

Successive French governments have not hesitated to implement active industrial policies which have, according to the economic situation of the day, tended to be aimed either at promoting growth and improving competitiveness, or at preserving employment. It is interesting to note that such policies have been based on a wide consensus in political and business circles. The Chirac government, for example, in promoting a policy of privatisation between 1986 and 1988 never intended going as far as the Thatcher government in the UK.

Policies have been varied over the years – sponsoring mixed enterprises, nationalisation, subsidies, advantageous public procurement and so on. One result is certainly that the public–private ownership debate in France is complicated by a question of definition. The dividing line between the two sectors is by no means easy to draw.

Although the state was already involved in production before 1939 the first real expansion of government intervention took place in the period of reconstruction after 1945. The main banks and insurance groups were nationalised along with Renault and the economy expanded rapidly with an active indicative planning system guiding the way. In the 10 years preceding the first oil crisis the government actively encouraged the formation of a number of industrial groups – Thomson, Brandt, Pechiney Usine Kuhlman, BSN, Gervais-Danone, for example. In the period following 1974 up to 1981 considerable aid was given to industry to help enterprises adapt and survive. This was a period of declining profitability and investment linked to rising costs, a worsening salary-profit share and rising interest rates. Most aid, until 1981, was not concentrated on groups with great potential for expansion—main beneficiaries were the iron and steel industry, shipbuilding, aircraft construction and computers. In 1982 state intervention increased considerably. Until 1982 state ownership was limited to the major banks and other companies nationalised after 1945 as well as the so-called *Grandes Entreprises Nationales* (EDF, GDF, Charbonnages de France, SNCF, RATP, Air France, Air Inter and the PTT). The 1982 measures gave complete control over two major financial groups—Suez and the Paribas as well as five leading industrial groups, the two steel producers (already under state control) and gave majority shareholding in Matra, Dassault, CII-Honeywell-Bull, ITT France, and Roussel Uclaf. This meant that some 30% of industrial turnover and 24% of the labour force was now in the public sector.

The total amount of aid given to industry was not out of line with similar policies of support in other EC states. An EC study found that government aid to industry in France between 1982 and 1984 represented 2.8% of 1984 GDP as opposed to 5.8% in Italy, and 2.3% in Germany and the UK. Government procurement represented between 6.3% and 9.3% of GDP in France, 6–8.3% in Italy, 10–14.1% in the UK and 5.4–8% in Germany.

Industrial policy, whether it was aimed at encouraging expansion in strategic high-technology areas or defending the French market from import penetration, does not seem to have been very effective. Indeed aid probably, in the opinion of the OECD, encouraged recipients to avoid making difficult decisions, reduced the incentive to adapt and contributed to 'ossifying the industrial structure'.

From 1985 industrial assistance was considerably reduced and earlier attempts to influence decision-making through government-sponsored sectoral plans were allowed to fall into abeyance.

By 1988 industrial policy had become more neutral. Priority was placed on the provision of an environment favourable to business expansion and to the improvement of profitability. As part of this process competition was to be reinforced, financial deregulation was to be continued and specific aid such as reduced interest rate loans was introduced. As part of this policy, virtually complete price freedom had been reinstalled in 1986, exchange controls dismantled and corporation tax in 1988 was brought down from 45% to 42%. The following year saw the rate further reduced to 39% for non-distributed profits.

The same 'hands-off' policy is being applied equally to the private and the public sector even if the Rocard government was committed to maintaining the public sector intact after the inroads made by his immediate predecessor's privatisation policy.

Privatisation is dealt with separately in section 4.3.4.

4.3.4 *Privatisation and the public sector*

The expansion of the public sector in 1982, in particular the extension of public ownership into competitive industry, was highly controversial. In April 1986, after a victory of the opposition in the legislative elections, a new government was formed by Jacques Chirac who appointed Mr Balladur as Minister of the Economy, Finance and (significantly) of Privatisations. The Chirac government intended to apply a more liberal economic policy than their predecessors and stated their intention to give back to the business sector a 'taste for risk and the determination necessary for enterprise'.

With regard to industry this implied an abrupt change, as it was rapidly announced that the government intended to privatise the major part of the public sector involved in the competitive sector. This covered a number of banks, insurance companies, industrial groups and part of the television network. TF1. Far from being a Thatcherite revolution, privatisation was never intended to involve public enterprises providing so-called public services (largely the *grandes enterprises nationales*).

The arguments in favour of privatisation were similar to those used elsewhere. State ownership stultified enterprise, reduced the freedom of managers to fix an independent strategy, limited their ability to raise capital in a period of budgetary restraint and represented a financial burden on the state's finances. Whether or not these arguments were valid, it is certainly true that the public sector was exceptionally large. France had 16% of industrial employment, 23% of exports, 28% of added value and 36% of business investment in the public sector. It was difficult to justify these levels unless the government had some special claim to business expertise. Since early attempts to influence business decisions had been laid aside, claims to some special quality attaching to public ownership had largely evaporated. Interrupted in their programme by the October 1987 stock exchange crash and their defeat in the 1988 elections, the government nonetheless succeeded in achieving 40% of their programme. Among the enterprises and institutions sold off were TF1, the banks, finance groups, Suez, Paribas, the Société Générale and the CCF and the industrial groups Saint-Gobain, the CGE and Matra.

Criticism of these privatisations concentrated on the decisin to form core groups of stable shareholders, the *'noyau dur'*. The government was accused of using this as a pretext for giving political allies a powerful position in the new enterprises.

In his election manifesto of 1988 Mitterand called for an end to privatisation but refrained from renationalisation. The doctrine of neither privatisation nor nationalisation (*ni . . . ni*) calmed the ideological debate but was to create a subsequent difficulty for the remaining public enterprises. State funding was limited and access to private equity was excluded.

This does not appear to have limited the strategy of the public enterprises since 1988. Of the first 183.4 billion supplied to public sector enterprises over the past two years 34.3 billion came from the financial markets and 85.7 billion from re-invested profits. The rest came from the state in the form of new capital and debt write-offs.

The public sector has been allowed considerable autonomy. The Rhône Poulenc purchase of a pharmaceuticals group in the United States involved complex financing but was accepted. Renault has been transformed into a state-controlled *'société anonyme'* to allow it to link up with Volvo and there has been a major reorganisation in the chemicals industries.

If the Mitterand compromise appears to be working, the basic question of the relevance of state ownership remains. If the state enterprises are to be operated independently of the state why should they not be allowed free access to the stock market with, obviously, the ultimate risk of loss of state control.

4.3.5 *Planning*

One aspect of government intervention in the economy which has attracted much attention and controversy is the system of economic planning which has operated since 1946.

Government attempts to influence the development of industry predate the period of post-war recovery. However, in moving on from the establishment of mixed enterprises to full indicative planning, the French took a major step. In the words of one observer: 'Postwar French planning can be regarded as a device that mobilised a number of instruments of public enterprise, and pressure, which had been lying around for some time, and pointed them all in the same direction' (A Shonfield, *Modern Capitalism*, OUP, 1965). The same author stresses the fact the origins of planning were to be found in habits and attitudes of senior officials and their counterparts in business, saying that planning developed as a 'voluntary collusion' between senior civil servants and the senior managers of big business to the exclusion of politicians. Full governmental commitment to planning did not come before the 1960s and has never been unambiguous.

As introduced into France by Jean Monnet, planning was not ideological: it dealt with the enormous practical problems of an economy devasted by the War. The planning system was also indicative rather than imperative and set out to provide a series of quantified macroeconomic objectives for the period in question. The difficulties of the 1970s made such quantification impossible and in the 8th Plan, Raymond Barre limited the plan to a statement of areas in which effort was necessary, the *'programmes d'action prioritaire'*. In July 1982 a reform of the planning system created two stages. First, a law was to be passed defining the broad strategy and objectives. Second, the means required to achieve these ends would be set aside in a series of *'contrats de plan'* signed by the state and the various regions and major enterprises involved. The preparation of the plan was entrusted to a *Commissariat Général du plan 3* with no powers beyond that of organising debates between the various partners concerned; the detailed work was carried out by commissions and committees who are responsible for a particular problem area. The technical support has become progressively more sophisticated and nowadays various scenarios are examined with the help of computer simulations.

Beginning with the 1st Plan in 1946–50 (prolonged to 1952 to coincide with the Marshall Plan and mainly concerned with providing the necessary capital for the development of basic industries) there were a series of plans, the 8th covering the years 1981 to 1985. This Plan was overtaken, however, by the socialist victory in the 1981 elections. The incoming government insisted on replacing it with an interim Plan for a two-year period awaiting the preparation of a new 9th Plan. The interim Plan, unsurprisingly was adapted to the then current policies of the government. The relationship between plan and economic policy was not entirely clear, particularly, since the appointment of Michel Rocard as Minister responsible for the plan was made with the clear intention of keeping him at arm's length from the day-to-day running of economic affairs.

The main priority of the interim Plan was to stabilise then reduce unemployment, to revitalise the productive apparatus of the economy and to improve national solidarity. These objectives were to be achieved by expanding the public sector, decentralising government power, strengthening workers' rights and reforming the planning system.

Unfortunately, the government was forced to change policy in June 1982 and March 1983 with the result that the priority became one of reducing inflation and the balance of trade deficit.

The 9th Plan (1983–88) was prepared on the basis of the new two-stage procedure. Like the 8th Plan it lacked precise macroeconomic objectives. Contracts were signed in 1983 and 1984 with the enterprises of the public sector and with the regions. But the second stage of the planning procedure and the contracts with publicly owned firms and the regions could not bring about a real renaissance of the planning system. The public enterprises increasingly needed their independence in formulating and applying business strategy and any funds to be made available to the regions depended more on the limitations imposed by budgetary restraint than on the plan.

The whole planning process had fallen into such disfavour with those favouring a liberal approach to the economy that the incoming Chirac government seriously considered abolishing the *Commissariat Général du Plan* altogether. But this did not discourage the Socialist government in 1988 from returning to the planning process. The legislation approving the 10th Plan was duly voted in July 1989. Designed to cover the period 1989/92, the plan had two main priorities. On the one hand the objective was to modernise the French economy in such a way that the country could benefit fully from the construction of the Single Market.

The other main priority was to restore a high level of employment. This improvement was to be brought about by a number of processes. For example, ensuring that, although salary earners were to benefit from economic growth, improved rates of investment should be encouraged so as to provide new jobs. Training and education were to be improved to help the 18–25 age group. Employers' social charges were to be held steady to avoid further increasing the cost of labour and the conditions of employment were to be reorganised in wages favourable to the creation of stable jobs.

The strategy of the 10th Plan was based upon a number of 'construction projects' (*grands chantiers*) or priority areas in which government activity was to concentrate throughout the period of the Plan. In this way even if the 10th Plan, like its immediate predecessors lacks quantitative objectives, it provides a coherent framework for government policy over the medium term and in this respect it fully reflects the Prime Minister's approach to the relationship between Plan and day-to-day economic policy. These projects involve improving education and training, investing in research and raising the competitiveness of French industry, ensuring the maintenance of social solidarity, improving the regional and urban environment and improving the quality and performance of the public services.

4.3.6 *Competition policy*

In the period of reconstruction, France built up a wide range of price controls and it was not until 1977 that the process of dismantling these controls began. In May 1981 the Mauroy government, in order to fight inflation, reimposed those controls which had been lifted, but in December 1986 new legislation abolished virtually all price controls and set up a relatively powerful and independent supervisory authority, the *Conseil de Concurrence*. Areas still coming under administrative or public control include agricultural goods, pharmaceuticals and health services, energy and public transport. Other goods and services are free and can only be fixed by ministerial decree under exceptional circumstances.

To counterbalance this freedom the *Conseil de Concurrence* was given wide powers to investigate and to punish where necessary. A number of restrictive practices are expressly forbidden by the 1986 legislation—refusal to deal, price fixing and retail price maintenance, discriminatory pricing and the use of loss leaders to name but the main ones. Various abuses of dominant positions are also prohibited and the *Conseil* pays particular attention to cases of collusion in the case of public procurement. The *Conseil* can make recommendations, issue orders and impose fines of up to 5% of turnover.

The *Conseil* may be petitioned by companies, the courts, professional and consumer organisations as well as the Minister of Finance. Indeed some 80% of the petitions have come from non-governmental sources. Recent examples of the *Conseil* in action were provided in November 1989 when it imposed fines on 80 major public works contractors amounting to FFr 166 million for conspiring to fix prices on public contracts and in January 1990 when it fined 43 electrical material suppliers for similar offences (*Financial Times* 9/11/90 and 19/2/90).

The *Conseil* cannot independently open investigations into potentially anti-competitive mergers and take-overs. These still come under the authority of the Finance Ministry. However, the law of 1986 extended the discretionary powers of the administration over proposed or actual mergers which met either of the following thresholds:

(a) horizontal or vertical control of more than 25% of the home market
(b) a merger resulting in an annual turnover of FFr 7 billion.

It its report on its 1989 activities, the *Conseil* regretted that the ministry had made little use of those powers to investigate cases of industrial concentration since 1987. The present government, like its predecessors, feels that the industrial restructuring which must take place as French businesses modernise and prepare for 1992, should be given priority.

4.4 The French financial system

The development of the French financial system from the 1960s to the present can be seen in outline as a progressive movement from a system where business finance came essentially from bank- and state-controlled credit to one based on modern financial markets. Until quite recently, the French system featured extensive credit controls, specialised lending circuits, and large-scale use of subsidised credits for favoured sectors. Recent changes towards a more market-directed approach have taken place for several reasons—the government borrowing requirements resulting from the deficits of the early 1980s, the internationalisation of and technical developments in the banking industry, the desire to see Paris play a leading role as an international financial centre, and the prospect of monetary integration in the European Community.

4.4.1 *The French banking system*

Banking in France has undergone a series of major changes, and now includes some of the largest banks in Europe (the Crédit Agricole ranks fourth largest in the world, in terms of capital, Paribas 13th, the BNP 18th, the Crédit Lyonnais 22nd, and the Société Générale 24th according to the Revue Banque).

The *'loi bancaire'* (Bank Act) of 1945, which nationalised the Banque de France as well as the leading clearing banks, provided for three distinct categories of bank:

(a) *'banques de dépôt'* (deposit banks);
(b) *'banques d'affaires'* (merchant or investment banks);
(c) *'banques de crédit à long et moyen terme'* (banks specialising in medium- and long-term credit).

Major reforms were introduced in 1966–67, when it became clear that the investment requirements of rapidly growing French industry called for a less segregated structure. In particular the legal status of the *banques de dépôt* and the *banques d'affaires* were changed so that both categories could compete on the same terrain—the former being allowed to take long-term deposits and thus provide medium- and long-term credit, while the latter were allowed to operate in short-term transactions. A number of technical constraints were relaxed, but the banks continued to make a large proportion of their loans through specialised credit institutions.

The combination of growing competition between banks and the non-bank financial institutions, and between French and non-French institutions, of the problems caused by a series of large-scale internal and external deficits, and the development of large international financial markets meant that in the 1980s a series of reforms and changes were introduced. In addition the Mauroy Government nationalised (1982) the remaining privately owned banks. The major changes in this period can be summarised as involving:

(a) redefining the roles of the various financial institutions;
(b) transformation and integration of the functions of banking;
(c) expansion and integration of the different capital markets;
(d) development of new methods of monetary control.

A new *'loi bancaire'* in 1984 removed the remaining barriers between the various categories of banks—all were henceforth grouped under the title *'établissements de credit'*. Only a limited number of highly special-ised institutions were left outside the single supervisory system and came under the direct control of the authorities.

The Banque de France

Established in 1800 and nationalised in 1946, the Banque de France is the central bank. It has a wide range of functions—it is responsible for the manufacture and supply of bank notes, it manages the foreign exchange reserves and exchange rates, acts as banker to the state (but does not manage the government debt), and supervises the banking system. The central bank also plays an important role in the formulation and implementation of monetary policy even if the policy as such is the responsibility of the Minister of the Economy and the Treasury Depart-ment of the Ministry.

Monetary Policy

In 1986 the former reliance on strictly defined quantitative credit controls (the *'encadrement de credit'*) was given up in favour of the manipulation of interest rates. These rates are decided by the Banque de France. In addition the central bank can use *'réserves obligatoires'* (special deposits) to control credit creation and to influence interest rates.

The general aim of French monetary policy has been to bring down the inflation rate in line with that of the main trading partners, in particular Germany. Two main indicators have been used in the imple-mentation of monetary policy—the value of the franc within the Euro-pean Monetary System, and movements in monetary aggregates (M2).

M2, which in addition to cash and sight deposits, includes a range of savings deposits, was reduced to a target growth of between 3.5% and 5.5% for 1990.

Official targets were met in 1988 and 1989, since the beginning of 1987 the EMS value of the franc has been stable, and the last remaining vestiges of foreign exchange controls were removed in January 1990.

Capital markets: new interest in the Bourse

Until recently the French system was based upon intermediation, meaning that savings were collected by the financial intermediaries, who then made these funds available to enterprises and the state.

In the 1980s this began to change under the impulse of a variety of developments—fiscal changes, the rapid expansion of unit trusts (*Société d'investissement à capital variable – SICAV*) and managed funds (*fonds commun de placement – FCP*), higher real interest rates. Since the early 1980s, then, the Paris market has been characterised by rapid growth and many far-reaching regulatory and technical changes which have made the market intensely competitive in both domestic and international trading. Between the years 1980 and 1986 the capitalisation of French bonds and equities increased 3.5 times. In 1981 new bond issues went from Ffr106 billion to Ffr347 billion in 1986. Issues in 1988 were Ffr346 billion and Ffr329 billion in 1989. Equity issues have also displayed rapid growth going from an average of Ffr30 billion per year in the early 1980s to Ffr73 billion in 1985 and Ffr137 billion in 1986.

There have been several institutional changes. A second market was introduced in 1983 to cater for smaller companies, and a financial futures market, the *Marché à Terme d'Instruments Financiers (MATIF)*, in 1986.

The Money Market

The money market has changed considerably since the reforms of 1985–86 and now consists of an interbank market regulated directly by the Banque de France, and a market for short-term securities open to any individual or company. The main securities dealt with on these markets are commercial paper (*billets de trésorerie*), certificates of deposit (*certificats de dépôt*) and negotiable treasury bills (*bons du Trésor négociables*).

4.5 International relations

The general growth of international commerce and increasing integration into the European Community have ensured a growing importance for exports and imports in the French economy (see Statistical Annexe, Table D 22). In 1989 exports represented 23.3% of French GDP. France is the world's fourth largest exporter, coming well behind Germany, the USA and Japan, and slightly ahead of Italy and the UK.

4.5.1 *Geographical structure of foreign trade*

An overall view of the geographical structure of France's foreign trade can be obtained by consulting Statistical Annexe, Table D 21. From 1958 to 1988 the share of French exports going to EC member states went from 30.9% to 61.6%, and for imports the share went from 28.3% to 65.1%. Trade with the developing world shows a corresponding relative decline, although it is important to note that exports to the developing world remain higher than in most comparable economies at 16.2%, whereas France exports less to Japan, and the USA than do her competitors. This indicates the continuing difficulty faced by French exporters in finding an adequate share of some important industrial markets and a continuing heavy reliance on the slower growing economies.

In 1988 France's four leading customers were Germany, Italy, the UK and Belgium–Luxembourg, and the main sources of imports were Germany, Italy, Belgium–Luxembourg, and the UK in that order.

To some extent France's present difficulties regarding trade in manufactured products arises from a conscious policy to develop exports with the OPEC group of countries, which was laid down in the 7th Plan (1975). Civilian exports to this area expanded until 1982 and exports of armaments until 1984. Since that period, manufactured exports to the region have not met earlier expectations and France has found it difficult, for reasons which are explained below, to redirect export activity towards the industrialised countries.

Table 4.16 indicates trade balances by geographical zone in 1988 and 1989.

Table 4.16 Trade balances of geographical zones

	1988	1989 (Ffrbn)
EEC	−43	−55
(of which manufactured goods)	−83	−100
Other OECD	−39	−55
(manufactured goods)	−36	−50
OPEC	−3	−9
(manufactured goods)	24	30
Other LDCs	5	13
(manufactured goods)	25	33
COMECON	−11	−8
(manufactured goods)	3	4

Source: Douanes, 1989

4.5.2 *Foreign trade by sector*

The French trade position remains vulnerable. Until the first oil crisis the French trade in goods was generally in surplus, but this situation changed fundamentally from 1973. Between 1973 and 1984 the cost of imported oil supplies went up tenfold under the combined impact of oil prices and the dollar. The drop in oil prices and the lower dollar–franc exchange rate have reduced fuel imports from 24% of imports in 1984 to 10% in 1987. The large trade deficit in 1982 was due to the expansion of domestic aggregate demand and was rapidly reduced by the austerity policy introduced in 1982 and 1983.

The structural deficit on energy products was offset by a surplus in manufactures (until 1986), by a surplus in the agro-food sector, and by a growing surplus in services.

In 1988 French trade showed surpluses in the following areas: agricultural goods (export/import ratio 161), food products (111), motor vehicles (114), parachemicals and perfumes (150) and military equipment (surplus of Ffr24 billion). For manufactured goods as a whole the deficit came to Ffr62.6 billion, that of energy products to Ffr66.7 billion and the surplus on agro-food products to Ffr39 billion.

Surpluses in services have largely compensated for the deficit in the balance of trade. In 1989 the surplus on services was Ffr40 billion, which must be added to a, perhaps, exceptional surplus in tourism of Ffr 38 billion (1989 was the bi-centenary of the French Revolution). The total invisible balance was Ffr48 billion after interest and dividend payments. Apart from tourism France continues to earn a substantial surplus in services related to trade and technology, for example processing (nuclear waste), management services (Airbus Industrie), and major public works and technical co-operation projects. A major deficit item continues to be 'patents and royalties' which concerns mainly payments to the USA resulting from the computer trade.

4.5.3 *The balance of trade in manufactured goods*

In 1987 the trade in manufactured goods went into deficit for the first time since 1969. Coming after a period of satisfactory results the 1987 deficit of Ffr10.7 billion was a cause of considerable concern. A number of explanations have been put forward to explain this reversal.

(a) As a result of the first oil shock, French exports to OPEC countries were considerably increased and from 12.8% of the total in 1982 as opposed to 6.8% in 1974. Although this represented a logical response to the trade situation created by the two oil price increases, it left France in a rather vulnerable position when, from 1982 onwards, OPEC countries began reducing their imports.

(b) In this period rates of commercial and other non-physical investment (for example R & D) were allowed to drop, leaving France poorly placed to benefit from the economic recovery when it came. This failure made itself apparent in a fall in French market share in the OECD countries. In 1986 and 1987, for example, French exports to this area grew by 4.7%, whereas local demand grew by 7.9%. The difficulty is not simply one of price. In the period 1980–83 French export price competitiveness improved by 12% but market share grew by only 1%. The problem stems from a lengthy period of underinvestment as compared with France's main trading rivals.

(c) Several French commentators have drawn attention to the fact that French industry has failed to develop sufficient points of specialisation (apart, arguably, from armaments and agro-food products). Only in the field of perfumery and luxury goods can French exporters be considered to have a dominant position.

(d) The OECD attributes a large part of the responsibility to various government policies. Industrial policies in the late 1970s and early 1980s meant that considerable aid went to ailing industries in the hope of preserving employment and reconquering the domestic market, rather than accelerating inevitable readjustment. Export credits may have had the unintended effect of encouraging French exporters to pay too much attention to less solvent markets.

4.5.4 *Foreign investment*

French direct investment abroad increased considerably from 1986 onwards (with the involvement of both private and public enterprises). This investment activity does not represent simply a relocation in search of lower costs of production. In 1988 96% went to the OECD area, and this fact, combined with the high proportion of takeovers and mergers suggests that the motive lies in the external growth strategy of French businesses. The impact of the Single Market can be seen in the geographical structure of the investments. In 1988 70% of French investment went to the EC, instead of 48% in the year before, and in the first half of 1989 as much investment was going to the UK as to the USA.

The rapid rise in rate of investment can be seen in the following figures for the annual total (Ffr bn): 1985 20.1, 1986 36.3, 1987 52.3, 1988 76.1, 1989 52.5 (1st half). (*Source: Balance des Paiements*, B de France.)

Removal of many exchange controls in 1985 (which added around 25% to the cost of foreign acquisitions) and the sounder financial situation of French companies enabled them to become more ambitious abroad from 1986. The public sector was allowed great *de facto* flexibility to allow them to participate.

Regarding inward investment (*DATAR* is the specialist agency responsible for attracting inward investment), new measures were
announced in January 1990 to speed up administrative procedures.
French policy is now to welcome incoming investment, despite a past
reputation for being lukewarm to foreign investors who might compete
with French companies. Most inward industrial investment has gone to
the industrial regions of the Nord-Pas-de-Calais, and Alsace, where
industrial sites and plentiful labour are available. Alsace has the added
attraction of being close to Germany with a largely bilingual population.

4.5.5 *The balance of payments*

The balance-of-payments figures indicated in Statistical Annexe, Table
D 23 provide a typical and comparative view of the French situation. In
the 1980s the French balance of payments have been marked by a
number of particular features.

On current account there has been a persistent deficit. Payments for
goods reached a record deficit of Ffr102 billion in 1982, followed by a
recovery, and then since 1987 a deterioration, as the deficit in manufactured goods began to take effect. This element reached a total of Ffr67
billion in 1989. Also contributing to the current account deficit were the
unilateral transfers which have increased in recent years as net contributions to the EC have increased. Surpluses on services (see above) kept
the overall current deficit in 1989 close to that in the two preceding
years (less than 0.4% of GDP). The trade balance has worsened from a
deficit of 0.6% of GDP in 1986 to one of 1.5% of GDP in 1989.

The period since 1982 (with the exception of 1986) has been one of
regular and large net inflows of long-term capital in the form of purchases
of securities by non-residents. Increasing outward direct investment
since 1987 has reduced the net inflows.

4.6 Special issues

4.6.1 *The French social security system*

Set up in 1945, the French social security system is as extensive in
diversity as it is in complexity. The system in place now in the 1990s, is
highly fragmented, comprising some 500-plus schemes, as reported by
OECD (1990).

Given the publicly stated aim of the Mitterand Government to
reduce its budget deficit to Ffr70 billion over the next two years, the
state now faces the reality that, left unchanged, the social security system
is going to absorb an additional financing requirement estimated to be in

the region of Ffr10 billion per year from now until 1993.

Although the state is the principal partner involved, the system consists of a large number of schemes some of which, particularly the unemployment and supplementary pension schemes, are to a greater or lesser extent under the control of employer and employee associations – the *'partenaires sociaux'*.

The latest OECD survey of France (1990) identifies three main factors for the spiralling costs of the system:

1   demographic changes in France;
2   maturation of retirement schemes;
3   rising expenditure on health/medical care.

Declining fertility rates (from 3 children per woman in 1960s to 1.8 since 1975) and increasing life expectancy (by approximately 3 months a year since the early 1950s), have resulted in an aging of the population. According to the OECD, the population over 60 looks as follows:

Year	Population over 60 years (%)
1984	18
2000	20 (French forecast)
2040	26

Basically this means an increasing financial burden on the working population who will have to finance these pensions.

Adding to this the maturation of existing retirement schemes, and the burden becomes greater. Obviously, there is a blatant need for reform here to balance the costs of the pension scheme, both over the medium and long term.

It is interesting to note that over the period 1970–84, the average pension for retirees over 65 increased by 80% in purchasing power terms, while the average worker's wage rose by 40%. In light of this and the study made of the French social security system, the *'Commission de la Protection Sociale'* recommended a reform of perhaps splitting the burden between those who are working and those who are retired. Reforming the rules for assessing pension rights is another option, as is increasing the number of years required to obtain a full pension.

Finally, the OECD recommends the possibility of raising the retirement age or promoting part-time employment prior to retirement.

A significant factor which must be accounted for is the phenomenal rise in the female participation rate bringing new challenges to a system incorporated in 1945 when this was not a consideration.

France is not alone in the problems it now faces in adapting its social security system to present conditions. The above reforms have already been adopted by other countries facing similar problems (Germany, Japan, USA). However, the final direction the French reforms take must be carefully worked out in the context of the French situation itself.

Health care consumption is the other main area of social security needing reform. In common with other countries, demand for health care has increased significantly, but so also has the cost. However, as Table 4.17 shows, the share of public expenditure on health in value added (6.4%) was higher than in any other major OECD country (OECD Report, 1990).

Table 4.17 Health care expenditure (% of GDP)

Public expenditure on medical care:	1960	1970	1980	1987
France	2.5	4.3	6.2	6.4
Germany	3.2	4.2	6.3	6.3
Canada	2.4	5.1	5.5	6.3
Italy	3.2	4.8	5.6	5.7
USA	1.3	2.8	3.8	6.0
Japan	1.8	3.0	4.6	5.0
UK	3.4	3.9	5.2	5.3

Source: OECD Report, France, 1990, p.77

Reforms have been ongoing since 1983, but much needs to be done. The French social security system is based mainly on the intake of social insurance contributions which in 1988 amounted to 80% of total resources. The social insurance contributions of employers represents a much higher proportion of total tax and social insurance contributions in France than the OECD average (see Table 4.18).

Table 4.18 Social insurance contributions, 1988 (as a percentage of total tax and social insurance contributions)

	Employers	Employees	Self employed/ unemployed	Total
France	27.2	12.3	3.5	43.0
Germany	19.1	16.1	2.1	37.3
Canada	8.5	4.6	0.2	13.5
USA	16.6	11.1	1.1	28.8
Italy	24.1	6.7	3.5	34.3
Japan	14.8	10.2	3.6	28.6
UK	9.4	8.3	0.4	18.1
EC unweighted average				29.2

Source: OECD Report, France, 1989/90

This has had the adverse effect of employers being more inclined to use overtime rather than employing more full-time workers.

As concluded by the OECD, further reforms and control methods are urgent to reduce the pressures of increasing social transfers and spiralling demand and costs of health care. The system as it stands today risks long-term financing problems and is likely to run counter to government budgetary policy, making it difficult to achieve target levels of economic activity.

In short, the 1945 system has served its purpose well over the past five decades, but now is in need of urgent 'reconditioning' to ensure maximum efficiency in the reallocation of social spending and to ensure it can rise to the challenges the 1990s and beyond will undoubtedly pose.

4.6.2 *France's nuclear power industry*

As we have seen, the oil price shocks of the late 1970s and early 1980s succeeded in plunging the French balance of payments into deficit. This, allied to the lack of natural energy resources (coal etc.) acted as a significant spur to France to find an alternative and to decrease its dependence on oil consumption. This policy has been successful in that France's dependence on imported energy has gone down from nearly 80% in 1973 to just under half in 1989.

Now, in the 1990s, France stands as the world's second largest producer of nuclear-powered electricity after the USA. Following 1973, the French Government made the establishment of an independent source of nuclear-based power the key objective of energy policy. In 1989 Electricité de France (EdF) obtained some 80% of its power supplies from nuclear reactors.

The country is now in the enviable position of supplying just over half of her own energy needs and still supplies/produces enough after that to be the EC's largest energy exporter. Britain is the largest customer, followed closely by Switzerland and Italy. So efficient is the operation that French industry enjoys some of the cheapest electricity in the EC. It costs 48% less than British electricity and 54% less than that of Germany.

The French, by using this advantage to the full, have succeeded in attracting many energy based industries to set up location in France.

However, there has been some criticism of France creating over-capacity in the European energy market due to its massive energy surplus, as a result of the major plant building programme of the 1980s. The French are quick to point out, however, that this places them in a significant position of gaining the new market potential emerging in the Eastern European markets. EdF are determined to continue the expan-

sion of their nuclear capacity, and, rather surprisingly, there is no anti-
nuclear lobby of sufficient size to cause any second thoughts.

4.7 Future prospects

In 1990 France's economic situation had improved considerably as
compared to the start of the decade. If this improvement only began to
show through from 1987 (see Statistical Annexe, Table D 11), it was
nonetheless due to policies which had been pursued for some time. To
quote from the latest OECD report: '[France] owes this success not only
to a better external environment but also to the stable and coherent
policy setting in place since 1983.'

On the positive side of the balance can be put a number of points:
relatively low inflation, exchange rate stability, money supply on target,
and interest rates on the way down, an improved rate of growth, higher
rates of investment, healthier business profits, and expanding employment (760,000 new jobs created in the past three years). On the negative
side can be placed the persisting high rate of unemployment, and the
fragility of the foreign trade situation with the continuing deficit in
manufactured goods.

The main problems facing the French economy at the beginning of
the 1990s stem in large part from the social tensions created by
economic policy over the past few years. Several major adjustments are
necessary if France is to maintain its present position in an increasingly
integrated Europe, and it is by no means certain that in the coming years
future governments will be able to count on the same consensus that
marked the 1983–90 period. Radical changes in the taxation system are
necessary to bring France more into line with the EC average. Unfortunately, changes in taxation are regarded with great suspicion in France,
particularly when they concern the social security system and its
organisational structure. Bottlenecks are already apparent in the labour
market, but the national education system clearly finds it difficult to
provide adequate training for industrial manpower. It is unlikely that
sufficient funding can be found, in view of the limitations placed on
public spending, to cater for all France's educational and training needs.
In addition to these points, there is the danger that several years of pay
restraint and improving company profits will lead to industrial unrest or
to inflationary salary pressure.

If some commentators speak of a sense of 'unease' in France in 1990
the origin lies not so much in the economic sphere as in the political one.
Behind France's apparent political stability lies the nationalistic senti-
ments expressed through the National Front party. Although the obvious
explanation for the growth of this movement is the large immigrant

population in certain areas, it is also true that much support comes from those who have been paying the social cost of France's adjustment process in the 1980s, and from those who are concerned by the prospect of French identity being submerged in a Europe in which French influence may well decline.

Official mainstream political sentiment in France is very much in favour of the Single Market, and of Economic and Monetary Union, and so is the majority of public opinion. It is to be hoped that it is this movement of opinion which continues to dominate French decision-making, and that there is no return to the more traditional French reflex of protectionism and nationalism.

4.8 Bibliography and sources of information

Bibliography

Abd-El-Rahaman, K. and J.M. Charpin (1989) 'Le Commerce industrial de la France avec ses partenaires europeéns; advantages comparatifs et performances des enterprises' in *Economie de Statistique*, No. 217–218, pp. 63–70.

Arthaud, L. and D. Cavoud (1989) 'Energie: des chocs au contre-choc' in *Les Enterprises à l'épreuve des annees 80*, INSEE, August, pp. 267–282.

Artus, P. and E. Bleuze (1990) 'Deficit du Commerce Industriel de la France et capacités de production: un examen sectoriel' in *Economie et Statistique*, No. 228, January, pp. 19–29.

Barge, M., L. Bisault and A. Viguier (1989) 'Commerce expansion et modernisation' in *Les Enterprises à l'épreuve des annees 80*, pp. 223–246.

Baslé, J.M. and JJ Boillot *et al* (1989) *L'Economie française Mutations*, 1975–1990.

Cahiers français (1990) 'Les Instruments de la politiqué économique – La politiqué budgétaire au cours des années 80' in *Les Politiques économique*, No. 245, March/April.

Capul, J.Y. (1988) 'La modernisation du systeme financier français' in *Les Cahiers français*, No. 238, October/December.

Capul, J.Y. and D. Meurs (1988) *Les grandes questions de l'économie française*, Nathan Publications, Paris.

Catinat, M. (1989) 'Les Conditions de réussite du marché interieur: concretiser les opportunities' in *Economie et Statistique*, No. 217–8 pp. 97–116.

Cette, G. and D. Szpiro (1989) 'Les enterprises françaises sont-elles bien dimensionnées', in *Economie et Statistique*, No. 217–218, pp. 83–94.

Choffel, P., P. Cuneo and F. Kramarz (1989) 'Des logiques d'enterprise diverses', in *Les enterprises à l'épreuve des annees 80*, pp. 191–205.

Dubois, P. (1989) 'La France dans la perspective du grand marché européen', in *Economie et Statistique*, No. 217–218.

Francq, T. (1990) 'Le rôle des facteurs d'offre dans la baisse des performances à l'exportation: un bilan des années quatre-vingt' in *Economie et Statistique*, No. 228, January, pp. 11–18.

Guillochon, B. (1986) *La France Contemporaine*, Economica.

Holoblat, N., and J.L. Tavernier (1989) 'Entre 1979 et 1986, la France a perdu des parts de marché industriel' in *Economie et Statistique*, No. 217–218, pp. 37–50.

INSEE (1989) 'La France dans la perspective du Grand Marché Européen', No. 217–218, in *Economie et Statistique. Horizon 1993*.

INSEE Résultats (1989) *Comptes et Indicateurs Economiques Rapport sur les comptes de la Nation 1988*.

INSEE (1988) *La Croissance Retrouvée*.

INSEE (1989) *Une Economie plus forte*.

Jeanneney, J-M. (1989) *L'Economie Francaise depuis 1967*, Editions du Seuil – Paris.

Marchand, O. (1989) L'adjustement douloureux de l'emploi' in *Les Enterprises à l'épreuve des années 80*, INSEE, August 1989, pp. 105–120.

OECD: *Economic Surveys France 1980–1990*

Page, J.P. (1981) *Profil économique de la France – au seuil des années 80*, La Documentation Française.

Pollin, J.P. (1988) 'La Politique Monetaire française: historique et perspectives' in *Les Cahiers française*, No. 238, October/December.

Tableaux de l'Economie Française (1989) *La France en Europe et dans le monde*, INSEE.

Turpin, E. (1989) 'Une spécialisation fragile' in *Les Enterprises à l'épreuve
des années 80*, August, INSEE, 1989, pp. 25–35.

Vesperini, J.P. (1985) *L'économie de la France de la crise de mai 1968 aux résultats de l'expérience socialiste*, Economica.

Zaidman, C. (1989) 'Investir sans s'endetter' in *Les Enterprises à l'épreuve des annees 80*, pp. 167–190.

Useful sources of information

Banque de France
   39, rue Croix-des-Petits-Champs, 75001 Paris. Tel: (1) 42 92 42 92
Centre Français du Commerce Extérieur
   10, avenue d'Iéna, 75783 Paris. Tel: (1) 40 73 30 00
Chambre de Commerce et d'Industrie de Paris
   2, rue de Viarmes, 75001 Paris. Tel: (1) 45 08 39 20

INSEE (Institut national de la statistique et des études économiques)

18, boulevard Adolphe-Pinard 75675 Paris Cedex 14. Tel: (1) 45 40 01 12

La Documentation Française

31 quai Voltaire, 75007 Paris. Tel: (1) 40 15 70 00

OECD

2 rue André-Pascal 75775 Paris Cedex 16. Tel: (1) 45 24 82 00

5 *Italy*

Andrea Fineschi

5.1 Institutional and historical context

5.1.1 *Institutional framework*

Parliamentary democracy prevails in Italy, with the government not chosen directly by the electorate, but requiring the support of parliament (the Chamber of Deputies and the Senate). Government stability depends on the electoral system. Italy has adopted the proportional electoral system in one of its purest forms, which explains the continual presence of numerous political parties in parliament. Apart from the legislature (1948–53) immediately following the approval of the constitution, in which one party (the Christian Democratic Party) had an absolute majority in parliament, it has been necessary to form coalition governments for the entire post-war period and these governments have been extremely unstable.

The most important changes in the composition of the power structure occurred at the beginning of the 1960s and during the second half of the 1970s. In the first period the Socialist Party participated for the first time in a coalition government (in which its majority partner was, and continues to be, the Christian Democratic Party). Political scientists have defined the Italian democratic system as a 'locked' democracy, in that it is one of the few systems in the world, at least among industrialised countries, which has not experimented with a system of alternating governments.

The nature of the political system has several economic consequences. We will restrict ourselves to outlining a few of the most important. First, the necessity to form coalition governments from among the major political groupings representing diverse interests in society, and the instability of these coalition governments, have resulted in a preference for monetary policy (carried out by the more stable financial institutions over other measures of economic policy requiring a degree of political homogeneity which is difficult to achieve in governments formed by numerous political parties.

In addition, the Italian administrative structure is characterised by a fragmented system of self-governing local units (regions, provinces and boroughs) whose power is restricted by the fact that finance is controlled by the central government. Furthermore, the members of local administrations with an electorate of over 5,000 inhabitants are elected by means of a pure proportional representation system which means they are also very unstable. This power structure makes both the routine running of the local authorities and the putting into practice of new economic policy measures particularly complex. Furthermore, the presence of a plurality of decision-making centres, and their frequent instability, make the exercise of consistent cyclical economic policy difficult.

Second, economic policy has rarely been used in a 'radical' way (as it was used by other countries after the oil crisis) owing to the excessive fragmentation and instability of the executive power, though it has been used frequently in response to momentary necessities. The motivation for choices in relation to economic policy is often to be found in the attempt to reconcile differing political interests rather than in a rational political line.

The lack of a real possibility of an alternating political leadership of the country and the necessity for governments to be made up of heterogeneous political forces has generated and still generates apparently contradictory policy choices. It was not by chance that, in the early 1950s, there was an economic policy which was clearly orientated towards deregulation of the market and which embodied a refusal to accept Keynesian policies yet, at the same time, there was the creation and development of large-scale state enterprises in several essential sectors of the economy. Nor is it an accident that in recent years, during which the 'return to the free market economy' policy was supported officially, the size of the state enterprise sector has been reduced only marginally and continues to be a major and distinctive characteristic of the Italian economy. These are contradictions with concrete causes.

5.1.2 *Political structure and the trade unions*

The particular political structure of Italian democracy has also had repercussions on the relationships among the workers' organisations and the relationship between the workers' organisations and the government. The organisations which represent the interests of the workers and employers certainly have a strong influence on the economy as is normal in countries with liberal-democratic political structures.

Organised labour in Italy is represented by three main trade unions

(*CGIL, confederazione generale italiana dei lavoratori, CISL, confeder-azione italiana sindacale dei lavoratori* and *UIL, unione italiana lavoratori*) which are organised according to productive sector rather than occupational type. These three trade unions have a high level of membership among workers. However, in recent years, a number of unions have emerged which are occupationally based and independent of the three major unions. The origin of the trade unions can be traced back to the various political parties to which they were linked. For example, the *CGIL* was linked to the Communist and Socialist parties and the *CISL* to the Christian Democratic party. Initially, the Social-Democratic party was the reference point for the *UIL* but in recent years a large number of socialists have joined this union and now control it.

Relationships among the trade unions and between them and the government are naturally influenced by the political relationships that exist between the parties which are the main supporters of the unions. The link between a union and a political party is a complex one and inter-party relationships play an important role.

This, together with the fact that the Communist party is excluded from the government and that its supporters and enrolled members form a majority in the *CGIL* (the largest union), explains the reluctance on the part of the unions to assume a unified position in regard to the economic policy of the government. This is especially true when large-scale social agreements are proposed by the government. In other words, the political origins of the trade unions, and the exclusion of part of the political referents (the Communist party) from the government of the country, are important determinants of the relationship between the government and the trade unions.

The strength of the unions, and their ability to represent the workers, depends to a large extent in Italy (as in all industrialised countries) on various factors: the stage of economic development and thus, the level of related unemployment, the level of structural unemployment, company size and the industrial sectors to which the workers belong.

Other factors influencing the negotiating power of the workers are specifically related to the Italian economy, including whether the company is privately or state-run, the political climate and criteria which influence the employment of large numbers of people in the public administration and, above all, the state of the political relationships between the main unions and the government.

5.1.3 *Social policy*

The principal aspects of social legislation are health care, workers' insurance against industrial accidents and workers' pension schemes.

The national health system provides free assistance for all those

(Italian citizens and foreign residents) who demand its services. Set up during the 1970s, it operates through a system of *USL (Unitá sanitarie locali)*, local health centres, and is financed by transfers from the state to the regions, and then from the regions to each centre.

Pensions are paid on the basis of an assessment of salary over recent working years, through *INPS (Istituto Nazionale per la Previdenza Sociale)*, an institute financed by the obligatory contributions of the workers and employers.

Another institution, *INAIL (Istituto Nazionale Assicurazioni per gli Infortuni sul Lavoro)*, which is also financed by the workers and employers, provides for workers in case of accidents at work.

The state intervention system for workers subject to unemployment acts quite differently from that in the countries of North and Central Europe. There is a hierarchy in workers' assistance. The most protected are generally those who work for large firms, who, because of the social and political importance of mass dismissals, receive the services of the *casa integrazione guadagni* scheme (a wage-related unemployment benefit scheme which pays over 70% of the last salary). It applies both for ordinary cases, such as temporary lay-off, and for much longer periods of unemployment. Workers dismissed by small-scale firms and people looking for their first jobs are given much less protection, and if they are registered as unemployed receive only a small unemployment benefit for a comparatively short period.

5.1.4 *Market regulations*

Recently two laws were passed that were aimed at restricting monopoly power in general, and in the field of information (television and the press) in particular. This 'antitrust' legislation is essentially similar to that of the European Community in that it aims to prevent companies or groups of companies from forming 'dominant positions' which may lead to price-fixing.

In making these laws parliament did not use the classical model of perfect competition because the dominance of companies is evaluated with reference to European and world markets and the assessment as to whether competition rules are infringed is no longer made simply according to company size but rather on the basis of the actual market power that a company or group of companies holds. Thus, even though FIAT produces almost all Italian cars, it is not considered to have a dominant market position unless it acquires this by colluding with foreign companies.

The law limiting firms in the field of information was made to regulate a situation in which the TV market is essentially divided between the State (RAI, Radio Televisione Italiana) and the private corporation Fininvest, and in which the press (mostly daily papers) is controlled by a few big publishing groups, often owned by the important industrial groups. The main characteristic of this law was to consider simultaneously the two kinds of information and then to limit the market power of the companies in the whole information market.

5.1.5 *Historical context*

During the late 1960s and early 1970s Western economies were characterised by a significant level of social conflict both in relation to the distribution of income and industrial relations. Compared with other Western countries, this was a long-lasting and deep-rooted conflict, especially in the 1970s, when a rediscovered sense of trade union unity gave workers' organisations a strong negotiating force.

The prices of raw materials began to increase at the end of the 1960s and these were followed by an unexpected increase in the price of oil (1973–74). These price increases hit the Italian economy when it was in a phase of deep social conflict. The agreement between the trade unions and the major employers' organisation (*Confindustria*) on linking wages to the rate of inflation (the 1975 working agreement on the reform of the *'scala mobile'*), which was later extended to the public administration sector, was considered by the *Confindustria* to be an instrument to lessen the conflict over the distribution of income and to improve industrial relations. It was also encouraged by the trade unions as it automatically protected real wages against sharp price increases (including those of imported goods affected by the constant devaluation of the lira). Even if the agreement did succeed in maintaining the purchasing power of wages in the face of a high rate of inflation, it did not achieve significant success in terms of improving industrial relations until the formation of the national unity government in 1975–76.

Exchange rate depreciation and fiscal policy simply dampened down the bitter social conflict of the 1970s and put the problem off to a later date. During the 1970s public sector savings, the difference between fiscal revenues and current expenditure, which had been in surplus during the preceding period, went into deficit and the debt grew progressively as social security and health legislation caused a sharp increase in public spending in the mid-1970s and because of the loss of potential revenue due to delays in introducing tax reform. A more rigorous fiscal policy would certainly have accentuated the conflict in society. However, the systematic devaluation of the lira meant that the vicious circle of price and salary increases did not halt economic growth and this also helped to reduce social conflict. From 1977, the trade unions became less aggressive (during the period of the National Unity

Government, 1976–79). This, together with a foreign exchange policy which was orientated towards a strong national currency *vis-à-vis* the dollar (the currency in which raw materials and energy supplies were paid for), yet floating in regard to other European currencies, meant that in the late 1970s, there was less inflation, a recovery in investment and an improvement in the foreign trade balance.

The second wave of oil price increases (1979–80) hit Italy when its economy was in a phase of strong growth, which continued until the second part of 1980 thus making it difficult to control inflation and accentuating the trade deficit. The delay in adjusting to the international economic cycle worsened the problem of inflation and foreign debt.

In the late 1970s and early 1980s there were significant changes in Italian monetary, financial and foreign exchange policy, and in the general orientation of economic policy reflecting changes which had occurred in the world economy. In 1979 Italy joined the European Monetary System, which further constrained Italian economic policy and took away a great deal of its discretionary power to influence the value of the currency. Italy, by joining the European Monetary System, suffered a worsening of its foreign commercial accounts as the German mark became, year by year, undervalued in relation to the lira; however, this can also be seen as an anti-inflation policy as it was an indication from the government to the employers and unions that increases in prices would not be accompanied by a policy of devaluation of the lira.

In 1982 the central bank 'divorced from the treasury' with the adoption on the part of the monetary authorities of a measure which relieved the Bank of Italy of the obligation to act as 'buyer of last resort' at the auctions of public debt bonds. This measure was the clearest sign of the change in the policy of financing the public debt, which shifted from financing the debt via the issuing of public debt bonds (outside the market) through the banking system, to financing the debt largely through the market itself. As a consequence both of the divorce between the central bank and the treasury and entry to the European Monetary System, the Italian real interest rates increased sharply in the early 1980s, reaching levels above those of the 1970s and those existing elsewhere in the industrialised world. This elevated real interest rate increased the cost of servicing the public debt and was a major cause of the marked increase in the deficits on the public sector account.

In 1983 parliament passed a measure which changed the method of calculating the link between salaries and the rate of inflation. In itself this measure had only a moderate effect; it was important, however, in that it announced future government policy and showed that the government intended to move towards a hard line in relation to both inflation and the unions (the CGIL was not aligned to government policy).

In the early 1980s the major companies made decisions which

reduced the negotiating power of the trade unions inside the factories such as some dismissals of workers who belonged to extremist organisations, the practice of moving workers from one place to another, and measures to lay off thousands of workers for varying periods of time. In this the companies were helped by the part of the white-collar workforce, whose salaries had been particularly hit owing to the introduction of the *'scala mobile'* (the mechanism which linked salaries to the rate of inflation and which had the effect of levelling out salary differentials). Wage differentials had been hit also by the fiscal drag caused by prolonged and persistent inflation which was not accompanied by variations in the rates of the progressive tax system. Of particular importance was the march of the '40,000 in Turin' (the city of FIAT) organised by the white-collar workers.

During the 1980s there was a sharp reduction in social conflict according to all the indicators of this phenomenon, see for example, Figure 5.1, and this was one of the major reasons for the recovery of the profitability of the major companies, especially those where the trade unions were traditionally the strongest.

At the beginning of the 1980s the economic situation of the major companies was not at all bright. The level of the external debt of the companies was high in relation to their internal financial resources, and the return on investment was low. In 1983–84, however, a new phase of recovery began positively affecting investment and profits. First of all slowly, then gradually more sustained, the recovery has continued uninterruptedly up to the end of the 1980s. While during the first phase investment was largely devoted to the modernisation of capital equip-

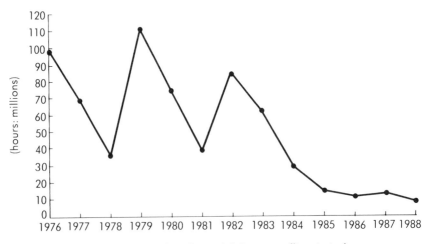

Figure 5.1 Number of hours lost through labour conflicts in industry
Source: ISTAT

ment (a period of company restructuring), in the late 1980s investment has been channelled into the expansion of productive capacity as effective production has approached potential output. The change in the economic behaviour of the major Italian companies was a particularly marked phenomenon of the 1980s. The influence of this phenomenon goes beyond purely economic aspects and extends to the political field owing to the considerable power that the major companies have in forming economic policy.

5.2 Main economic characteristics

5.2.1 *Gross domestic product*

The estimation of the gross domestic product (GDP) is especially difficult in the case of Italy because of the significant quantity of products and services emanating from the 'black economy' which escape measurement by *ISTAT (Istituto Centrale di Statistica)*. Examples include people who have two or three jobs but are only officially registered in one, workers who are employed by a company but are not legally taken on, and workers who work at home and by doing so often avoid paying taxes. Twice in the last 20 years the estimates of national income have been revalued by *ISTAT* to take into consideration black market activity. This means that it is difficult to provide a valid series of figures for the national income in recent years. However, the data for the 1980s can be considered fairly reliable due to the recent estimates of *ISTAT*.

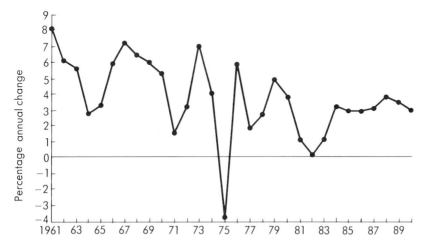

Figure 5.2 GDP: percentage annual rate of change (constant prices)
Source: see Statistical Annexe, Table D 11

From 1984 to 1990, Italy experienced a relatively high growth phase (see Figure 5.2) in comparison with the disappointing results of the early 1980s and is very much in an expansionary cycle.

5.2.2 *Employment and unemployment*

The prolonged upturn in GDP in the most recent period has failed to alleviate the problem of unemployment in Italy as a whole. However, while most of the North and of the Centre of the country has full employment or limited unemployment, the South (the regions south of Rome) and the Islands (Sicily and Sardinia) are suffering from high and rising unemployment.

Since the mid-1970s the Italian working population has grown faster than new jobs have been created which has led to a continual increase in unemployment (see Figure 5.3). However, in the most recent period, data relating to Italy as a whole shows that the increase in official unemployment has not only been halted, but over the last two years has actually shown a slight reduction (see also section 5.6.1 on the different trends of unemployment in the different regions).

The large companies (those with over 500 employees) have shown an almost continuous tendency to reduce their number of employees and if, on the whole, the rate of unemployment has been reduced, this has been due to the activities of small and medium-sized firms.

As in other EC countries, young people, women and less qualified people are the most likely groups to be affected by unemployment.

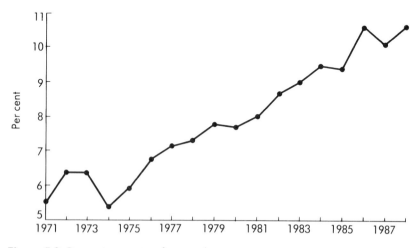

Figure 5.3 Percentage rate of unemployment
Source: see Statistical Annexe, Table D 9

However, in Italy certain areas, especially the South and the Islands (Campania, Basilicata, Calabria, Sicily and Sardinia) have particularly high rates of unemployment among women and young people.

The employment structure in terms of the relative shares of the three traditional productive sectors (agriculture, industry and services) has broadly followed the pattern observed earlier in industrialising economies. Table 5.1 shows the evolution through time of sector employment. This shows the speed with which the structure of the Italian economy has been transformed; from a largely agricultural economy in the early 1950s to a mature industrial economy with (in 1988) less than 10% of its workforce in the primary sector.

It is also interesting to note that the proportion of people employed in industry today is lower than it was at the end of the 1960s when it was at its peak. This reflects a distinct feature of the more recently industrialised economies, which have quickly adopted modern labour-saving techniques. It is also interesting to note that Italy has a lower proportion of industrial workers than a number of countries, in particular Germany and Japan, which have maintained a high proportion of industrial workers owing to an especially good trading performance in manufactures.

Italy still has a high proportion of agricultural workers in comparison with the most industrialised countries, a fact explained on the one hand by the slow process of industrialisation in the South of the country and, on the other, by the labour-intensive nature of agricultural cultivation in Italy.

Table 5.1 Percentage employment by sector

Sectors	1954	1966	1981	1988
Agriculture	39.9	24.9	13.4	9.9
Industry	32.8	40.7	37.5	32.6
Services	27.3	34.4	49.1	57.5
Total	100	100	100	100

Source: ISTAT

5.2.3 *Consumption and savings*

Consumption has been a fairly stable factor in aggregate demand. However, the items consumed have changed notably in the post-war period and especially in the last two decades. There has been a reduction in the amount spent on foodstuffs and an increase in the amount spent on services as a proportion of total consumption expenditure. This phenomenon, as well as changes in the composition and type of products consumed was, in fact, predictable. Italy has followed the same pattern as other countries which experienced industrialisation at an earlier date.

The level of total savings as a proportion of income is particularly high in Italy. Compared with other industrialised countries, Japan is the only country which has a higher savings/income ratio. The explanation is found in the fact that family savings are especially high in comparison with other countries. Italy and Japan are also similar in that they both have a large number of family firms and it is common that the savings of these firms are often counted as family savings, whereas they are really company savings. However, even if the figure for family savings is corrected for this, the level still remains high, and this can probably be explained by the importance of the family in Italian society in comparison with most industrialised countries where the family unit has a shorter life-span and thus a reduced economic role.

Company savings in recent years have once again returned to high levels (and, as a consequence, the generally high levels of self-financing among firms has been restored). This trend has been, to a degree, caused by higher profits. A high rate of company profits has always been the policy of the Central Bank, not only because it is an extremely strong stimulus to investment but also because a high level of company self-financing means that the companies have greater flexibility in decision-making than would be the case if they were financed externally.

5.2.4 *Investment*

In order to evaluate the Italian investment trends in the 1980s, it is necessary to consider the various investment items and leave aside investment in real estate, as trends in the latter depend on very specific factors which are usually dissimilar to the motivations for other types of investment. Investment in plant and machinery is particularly significant in terms of industrial performance. This item has been decidedly positive in the period since 1983, particularly in recent years owing to the growing proportion of investment expenditure devoted to increasing productive capacity.

The data presented in Table 5.2 enables us to fully evaluate the trend in Italian investment on plant and machinery compared to other major industrialised countries. The Italian rate of growth in investment in the 1980s is second to that of the USA, which recorded the fastest rate. The recent company investment trend has been especially impressive and as

Table 5.2 Investment cycles: an international comparison

Countries	Investment								
	Net of buildings			Machinery, plant and vehicles			Constructions net of buildings		
	77–80	81–83	84–87	77–80	81–83	84–87	77–80	81–83	84–87
USA	6.9	−1.6	5.4	6.9	−1.3	8.1	6.9	−2.3	−0.4
Germany	4.7	−2.8	3.2	7.0	−2.0	4.2	2.4	−3.8	1.9
France	2.0	−1.8	3.1	3.1	−1.9	2.8	0.5	−1.6	3.4
UK	−0.1	0.1	5.3	3.5	−1.8	6.6	−4.0	2.9	3.5
Italy	5.2	−4.3	5.6	9.1	−4.1	7.5	−0.7	−4.6	1.7

Source: OECD and *ISTAT*

a proportion of the GDP is a post-war high.

If the proportion of the total investment of the GDP is currently less than it was during the 1950s or the early 1960s, this is largely due to the fact that there is now less investment in the housing sector and by the state.

The total investment trend (excluding investment in real estate) is more in line with other industrialised countries and this is largely due to a relatively low level of investment in the construction sector. If we further distinguish items referring to investment in the construction sector, it is possible to see that investment expenditure by industry in new factories has returned to a high level in the recent period and the modest overall figure is due to trends in the state sector (roads, ports, drains etc.), the level of construction in which has been restricted by financial constraints.

5.2.5 *Inflation*

Inflation in Italy has been closely related to the oil price trend as well as to developments in the negotiating strength of the trade unions. The inflation rate, which was particularly high during the first major hike in oil prices (1972–73), was reduced during the second half of the 1970s and then took off once more at the beginning of the 1980s. After 1988 (see Figure 5.4), it began to decrease and the downward trend subsequently accelerated as a result of the reduction in the price of oil and the sharp fall of the dollar in 1985. When Italy became a member of the European Monetary system (in 1979, see Section 5.5), it was forced to abandon the earlier practice of devaluing the lira and this had a strong influence on the rate of increase in prices.

Price rises were a phenomenon experienced by most countries of the western world, but the level of Italian inflation was one of the most marked in comparison with other industrialised countries. Although price rises have remained relatively high, the inflation rate differentials between Italy and other major economies were significantly reduced during the second half of the 1980s.

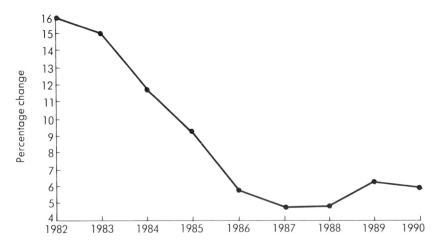

Figure 5.4 Inflation (private consumption price deflator)
Source: see Statistical Annexe, Table D 17

5.2.6 *Market structure*

The Italian productive structure, when analysed according to firm size, presents unusual characteristics for an industrialised economy, because of the presence of a large number of small and very small firms (we shall look more closely at this subject in Section 5.6.2). Nevertheless, the output of 'modern' sectors (i.e. those with a high rate of technological development) has, in recent decades, come to account for an increasing proportion of the total. Moreover, the productive structure is also characterised by the importance of the so-called 'mature' or 'traditional' industrial sectors. These are industries in which technology has reached (or is supposed to have reached) a phase in which the technological improvement is moderate and thus ones which countries at the beginning of their process of industrialisation are supposed to enter quite easily.

The particular role still played by the traditional sectors in the Italian industrial structure (see also Section 5.6.6 on the role of small firms), despite the high labour costs typical of an advanced economy, gives rise to the need for a better definition of the term 'traditional sectors'. On the basis of Italian experience in recent years, it can be observed that product differentiation plays so important a role in a number of 'traditional industries', together with industrial design and the ability to adapt the firm to the changes of the market, that it is not possible to say that the countries with low costs of production are able to be most competitive in these sectors.

5.2.7 *Income distribution*

The pattern of income distribution has changed during the 1980s due mainly to two phenomena (as mentioned in Section 5.1.5), the increase in the profits of major companies and a much reduced rate of increase in wages compared with the preceding decade.

The state has paid a much higher volume of interest on public debt bonds because of the public debt 'demonetisation' policy which has led to the issue of a higher volume of state bills. The higher real rate of interest has also affected the distribution of income. The financial 'rentiers' have taken advantage of the situation and if we consider the fact that most of the financial trading is done by the relatively well-off sections of the population, the variation in public debt financing has redistributed incomes towards the higher income classes. In addition, during the 1980s, from the geographical point of view, there has been an increase in the *per capita* income gap between the South and the Centre-North, a kind of territorial income redistribution (analysed in greater depth in Section 5.6.1).

5.3 Government involvement in the economy

5.3.1 *Expenditure and revenues*

During the last two decades, public expenditure on goods and services has increased at an average annual rate which is above that of the European

Community overall, and above some of the most economically advanced European countries. However, this trend has not been accompanied by the needed improvement in the services offered to the public and industry. There are two principal causes of this phenomenon: poor productivity in the public service sector and the restrictions on increase in expenditure on social services and state investment expenditure in general. Figure 5.5 shows the gross increase in state expenditure and, especially, the sharp increase that occurred in the second half of the 1970s and during the early 1980s.

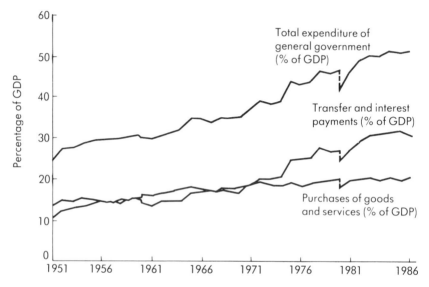

Figure 5.5 Evolution of public expenditure in Italy
Source: ISTAT, ISCO, Ministry of Treasury

As Figure 5.5 shows, the increase in public expenditure has basically been due to transfers to families and firms as well as the payment of interest on the state debt bonds. However, expenditure on social services has been somewhat contained. By glancing at the diagram we can see why the expenditure on collective consumption and investment has increased only marginally: the increase in public expenditure on transfers and the fast growth of the payment of interest on public debt have not left much opportunity for an increase in expenditure on public services and investment.

5.3.2 *Public debt*

The growth in the public debt in the 1970s is explained by the fact that there has been a lag between the increase in expenditure and a corresponding rise in revenues due to a delay in putting into practice tax reforms. The accumulation of an extremely high level of public debt has itself caused an increase in the cost of servicing the debt, something which began to be a problem in the 1970s. The increase in expenditure on debt interest payments rose sharply in the early 1980s due to a change in the way the debt was serviced. As the debt was serviced on the market the rates of interest naturally rose sharply (see Figure 5.6).

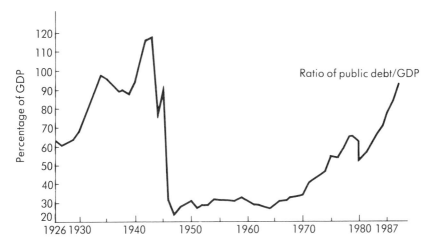

Figure 5.6 Public debt as a percentage of GDP
Source: Ministry of Treasury

In recent years there has been a tendency for the public debt to decrease when calculated net of interest as a percentage of the GDP. This reflects the containment of public spending. However, the total gross public debt is still rising owing to the increasing expenditure needed for interest payments.

5.3.3 *Industrial policy*

During the 1980s Italian industrial policy has concentrated mainly on promoting the process of 'restructuring' among the major industries (see Section 5.5.1), especially those which were the focus of the bitter social conflict of the 1970s.

There were also serious problems with state enterprises (the main state enterprises affected were *IRI, Istituto per la Ricostruzione Industriale, ENI, Ente Nazionale Idrocarburi,* and *EFIM*), which showed continual and serious losses.

The state has influenced the recovery of profits and investment by transferring, in various ways, financial resources to industries (transfers to production, payments for workers suspended from work for short/long periods, contributions for technological innovations, and so on) and these measures eased the social conflict which accompanies a policy of industrial restructuring.

The policy of privatisation, widely practised in other European countries, has only been applied to a limited extent in Italy (the most famous case is the sale of the Alfa Romeo car company by *IRI* to *FIAT*). This reflects the existence of coalition governments in which the different parties could not come to an agreement on privatisation (see also Section 5.1.1). Some important attempts at privatisation, for example, the sale of the wholesale food group SME, have also failed because of political disagreemment.

Even the attempts to find agreement between public and private sector firms, to constitute mixed groups strong enough to be competitive on the European and international market have not been successful. In fact, in the telecommunications sector, an attempt at agreement between *IRI* and *FIAT* failed, and in the chemical sector an agreement between *ENI* and the Montedison group turned out to be largely impracticable. The reasons for these failures can be traced to disagreements between the parties who make up the coalition governments, because such economic choices have significant repercussions on the power of the political parties.

5.4 Financial system

5.4.1 *The general system*

In order to analyse the financial system we need to start by considering the savings patterns in the various sectors of the economy (families, businesses, the state and the foreign sector). Since the beginning of the 1970s, in net terms the household sector has been in credit, industry has been in deficit and the state sector has increasingly been in deficit. The balance on the foreign sector has been much more erratic and more closely linked to market forces.

The structure of the financial institutions in Italy are still basically those which were outlined in the 1936 Banking Laws, even if the current liberalisation of the monetary system and developments at a European scale have influenced, and will increasingly influence, the characteristics of the system. The central aspect of the system, which was essentially designed to avoid collapses of the major banks caused by the bankruptcy of major companies (as happened in the early 1930s), is focused on the separation of banks and companies. Banks cannot own companies and there are no '*banche miste*' as in Germany or France.

In practice, the system has allowed an occasional exception to this separation rule. For example, the *Mediobanca* is a credit institute which operates as a merchant bank for major companies. Recent legislation has, in fact, introduced a few innovations in regard to the running of '*banche d'affari*' in the form of financial firms.

In brief, the financial system operates in the following way. Companies finance themselves directly by means of shares and debentures, indirectly by means of the banks (short-term credit) or by special credit institutions (*Istituti Speciali di Credito*, long- and medium-term credit institutions). The Italian stock exchange has a limited role in the financing of industry owing to the lack of institutional investors and the large proportion of small-sized firms which, by their very nature, do not depend on stock exchange financing.

The main cause of the lack of institutional investors is to be found in the way in which the national insurance system is organised. Until recently, this was almost exclusively state-run and characterised by the fact that payments had to be made on the basis of earnings in the same time period. This explains the modest flow of savings which came onto the stock market. The attempt, in the mid-1980s, to create a financial system which was capable of giving a greater impulse to the stock market with the regularisation of the 'investment funds' though promising in its initial phase due to the then buoyant share prices, eventually proved unsuccessful as there was a lack of important institutional investors.

The state finances its deficit by issuing public debt bonds and by special current account which it holds with the central bank in accordance with strict legal limits. The public debt bonds are bought by the general public, banks and the Central Bank, which, as mentioned above, is no longer obliged to act as a 'buyer of last resort' at the auctions of public debt bonds. Recently the public debt bonds have increasingly been sold to foreign buyers.

Local public administrations have the opportunity of financing their own investment through the '*Cassa depositi e Prestiti*' (Deposits and

Loans Institute), a financial institution that was adapted from the French financial experience and is a section of the Treasury which uses deposits collected by the Italian Post Office. However, its role in financing local authorities has been reduced as savers prefer banks to saving through the Post Office.

The *'istituti speciali di credito'*, whose institutional role is, as mentioned above, that of financing companies in the medium and long term, finance themselves through issuing bonds which are bought by the major banking institutions and by other financial institutions such as insurance and finance companies.

There are also credit institutions specialising in the financing of special economic activities, especially in the medium and long term, such as agriculture, public works and land credit.

5.4.2 *The banking system*

Banks obtain funds from their customers' deposits and pay interest both on deposit and current accounts. Most of the major banks are state-owned, though there is a great variety of legal constitutions. The various types of banks in Italy are categorised according to the way in which they collect funds and by the type of financing in which they are specialised. The evolution of the banking system has, in fact, strongly reduced the operating differences of the various types of banks. A network of banking services in Italy is guaranteed by local credit institutions as the large banks are generally located in the major towns.

Until the European Community Directive comes into force in Italy (1993), banking activities will be controlled by the Bank of Italy. In the future, banking activities, according to the directive, will no longer require the authorisation of the Central Bank and foreign banks will be able to operate freely on Italian territory.

The banks have become the centre of the financial system which was created by the 1936 Banking Law. This characteristic has become gradually more accentuated in the post-war period. The main reasons for this change have been the progressive marginalisation of the Post Office as a means of saving, the increase in the number of banks throughout Italy, the growth of local banks, the progressive growth of the public debt, the increasing placement of bonds and shares in the banks' portfolios (from the state, state organisations and special credit institutes) and the marginal role undertaken by the stock exchange in financing industry.

Between the mid-1960s and the end of the 1970s, due to the indirect pressure such as 'moral suasion' used by the Bank of Italy and/or a 'pegging' policy, or directly because of the administrative measures of the monetary authorities, the banks progressively acquired more state bonds and bonds issued by the special credit institutes. The amount of these bonds they were obliged to have in their portfolio was not less (due to the decisions of the monetary authorities) than a certain proportion of deposits held. On the other hand, the banks, in the same period, were working in a favourable situation as their interest rates on deposits were above those of the other short- and medium-term financial activities, so families preferred bank deposits to other ways of saving. Thus, the banks were, understandably, the centre of the financial system.

This situation was considerably modified at the beginning of the 1980s. The divorce of the Central Bank from the Treasury and the fact that the government intended to finance its deficit through the market, meant that there was a marked change in the role of the banks, with their roles as mediators on the savings market being reduced. This phenomenon was basically caused by the strong competition from public debt bonds with their high net returns.

This process of the weakening of the role of banks can easily be understood in quantitative terms by looking at the composition of family portfolios (the way in which families save their wealth). It is easy to see that the amount of public debt bonds has increased strongly in their portfolios and this has been accompanied by a decrease in the percentage of the family wealth held in bank deposits.

5.4.3 *Monetary policy*

Italian monetary policy during the 1980s can be regarded as both a cause and a consequence of the main economic policy choices made in Italy during the late 1970s and early 1980s: specifically, joining the European Monetary System and the demonetarisation of the public debt. The joining of the European Monetary System involved the imposition of a more rigorous monetary policy in order to maintain the exchange rate fluctuation within internationally fixed limits.

The demonetarisation of the public debt (made possible by the 'divorce' between the Central Bank and the government) allowed a recovery of the autonomy of the Central Bank in controlling the money supply. As a consequence (and, of course, as a result of the lower rate of price increases) the *Banca d'Italia* has been able to follow a more restrictive policy on money creation. This is clear from Figure 5.7 which shows movement in M2, which includes the savings deposits which have, in Italy, a high degree of liquidity.

The higher interest rates caused by the more restrictive monetary policy and the demonetarisation of the public debt have had various effects on the business sector, because the large-scale firms in particular

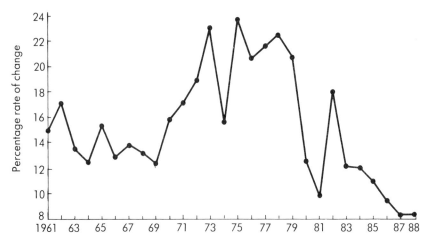

Figure 5.7 Money supply (M₂) annual percentage rate of change
Source: Eurostat

took advantage of the lower level of the 'prime rate' and the ease of access to the international financial markets characterised by lower interest rates.

5.5 International relations

5.5.1 *General remarks*

Throughout the 1980s the balance of trade was in deficit. The trends on the foreign accounts are determined by inherent factors as well as specific measures taken by a country. At the beginning of the 1950s Italy radically changed its international economic policy, transforming itself, in an extremely short time, from a strongly protected to a rather free economy, at least, in regard to trade in products and services. Entry into the Common Market accentuated this process.

The lack of natural resources, the fact that Italy began to industrialise at a later date than many other countries and because its industrialisation has been focused on integration into international markets, has had and still has a dual effect on the economy. These factors have created a strong stimulus for technological innovation by the companies yet, at the same time, have acted as a permanent brake on the expansion of the economy.

As Italy does not have much in the way of natural resources, any expansion in production must, by definition, be accompanied by an increase in the imports of raw materials and energy supplies and, as a consequence, every expansionary phase must be accompanied by an increase in the exports of goods and services or by inflows of capital.

In the first phase of industrialisation after the Second World War exports increased rather more than imports owing to the low level of Italian wages and salaries which was combined with an entrepreneurial ability with respect to the adoption of modern technology in a number of industrial sectors. There was a surplus in the balance of payments including services. Receipts from tourism and the money sent home by emigrants led to a diminished foreign debt. Apart from a brief period (1963–64), this trend continued, in general, until the end of the 1960s.

The first oil crisis worsened the problem of the balance on international accounts but the policy of continually devaluing the lira, which started at the beginning of the 1970s and was pursued until Italy joined the EMS, allowed Italian industrial products to regain competitiveness in the international market.

5.5.2 *Recent trends*

Membership of the European Monetary System involved the ending of the policy which adapted the rate of exchange to internal price rises. If the new policy had positive effects on containing inflation, it also badly influenced the Italian trade balance, most of all in comparison with the German D-Mark area countries.

In the 1980s the balance of trade was continually in deficit and the current account worsened. Recently, besides the items which traditionally feature among Italian imports (raw materials, energy supplies and agricultural products) there has also been a net import of energy produced by neighbouring countries.

The invisible items balance was unable to compensate for the deficit in the balance of trade. Tourism, which in the past contributed in a major way to balancing the current account, is gradually becoming less and less important because the increased *per capita* income in Italy has led more Italians to travel abroad and the higher cost of living in Italy compared to the earlier period has deterred foreign visitors. In the 1980s, the balance of payments became dependent on the net inflow of capital, attracted by the high interest rates in Italy. The rates have been generally above the European and international averages.

The need to have interest rates high enough to rebalance the foreign accounts comes as a direct consequence of the use of exchange rate policy as an instrument to stop inflation (something very close to the policy of the USA).

It seems likely that the balance of trade deficit during the 1980s was largely caused by the worsening of trade with the German D-Mark area and especially Germany itself. The German mark and the currencies with which it is linked are, inside the EMS, undervalued with respect to most

European currencies, including the Italian lira. The rules established within the European Monetary System have largely reduced the room for discretion in exchange rate policy on the part of national governments.

5.6 Special issues

5.6.1 *The economic dualism*

Every European economy has specific characteristics, even if there is a strong tendency with the development of the Common Market for differences to diminish. The territorial dualism and the special role played by the small and medium-sized industries in the production system are two special characteristics of the Italian economy.

Italy is characterised by a marked dualism compared with other advanced industrial countries. The economy has experienced two phases of intense industrialisation; the first at the end of the 19th century and early 20th century and the second in the period since the Second World War. The first phase concerned a small area (almost exclusively the industrial 'triangle': Milan, Turin and Genoa). The second, although more widespread, did not include part of the South of Italy and the Islands. The strong territorial dualism in terms of differences in *per capita* income between the most and the least advanced regions decreased in the period after the Second World War. The difference, nonetheless, still exists and from the mid-1980s relevant statistical data show that the North–South gap is again widening.

The growth of income in the south of the country, *Mezzogiorno,* though continuing, has in recent years been markedly lower than in the North. In particular, it is important to underline the data in regard to *per capita* income in the South as compared to the Centre-North. In the 1980–84 period, the South's *per capita* income was 57.8% of the North's, while in 1987 the proportion had been reduced to 54.9%.

The labour force employed in the South of Italy has fallen during the 1980s. If the proportion of the employed labour force is indexed at 100 in 1980, it averaged 98.4 in the period 1980–84 and by 1987 had fallen to 87.7 There has been a slight reduction in the proportion of the employed workers in the South in comparison with the whole country, but there has been an overall larger increase in the working population in the South. Figure 5.8 clearly shows the unemployment problem in the South in comparison with the Centre-North. While unemployment in the Centre-North has fallen since 1984, it has increased rapidly in the South during the same period. In 1988 the official unemployment figure for the South was 20.6% and female unemployment was 32.7%. It should be noted that the percentage of females available for work was extremely

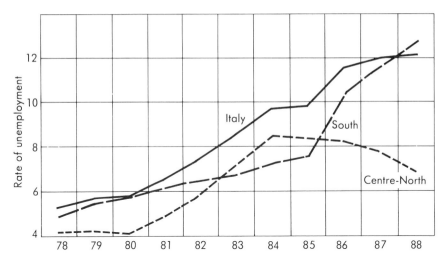

Figure 5.8 Rate of unemployment (number of unemployed persons actively seeking employment)
Source: Bank of Italy

low; only 25% of women in the South are in the labour force.

Unemployment in these areas is considered one of the reasons why there is an extremely high level of organised crime in Campania, Calabria and Sicily, although it would be an overstatement to attribute a direct cause–effect relationship to these variables and it is difficult to establish the direction of the causation.

In many aspects the economic situation of the South is contradictory. Family consumption in the *Mezzogiorno* has increased continuously. If the *per capita* consumption is indexed at 100 in 1980, it reached 113.8 in 1987. The value of investment in the construction sector (excluding housing) has grown absolutely in the South and has, in fact, grown relatively more than in the North. Moreover, investment in machinery has not been less than in the Centre-North. The individual productive sectors are more capital-intensive in the South and by quite a long way; partially due to the presence there of state-owned heavy industry, but also due to the phenomenon known in economic literature as the Leontieff paradox, according to which it is not infrequently observed that there is more capital-intensive production in less developed countries.

Public spending is distributed in Italy largely according to the population distribution and so the *per capita* public spending in the South (both for state investment expenditure and state expenditure for services) continues to be a great deal higher than revenues.

The average rate of growth of the bank deposits, post office savings and bank investments is higher in the South than in the Centre-North. In the South, bank investments have been reduced as a proportion of bank deposits, but this has been due to an increase in bank deposits (the role of the banks in the South has maintained its primary importance) rather than a fall in bank loans.

Figure 5.9, which shows the relationship between the South and the Centre-North in regard to productivity and cost of labour in industry, suggests, to a certain degree, why the position of the South has worsened. The efficiency of industrial production processes in the *Mezzogiorno* is decidedly inferior to those of the Centre-North. Although the cost of labour is lower in the South (by 15% to 20%, according to estimates) and the cost of indebtedness is also lower, due to the more intensive use of credit facilities in the South, these advantages are eroded by lower productivity levels.

Industry in the South is thus less productive and the gap in productivity between the South and the North, which was being reduced has in recent years once more widened. There is no one definitive explanation for this phenomenon and the various theories are often contradictory. Some scholars think that the gap is widening because of the government assistance given to the industries in the South (credit and tax benefits) which allows them to survive, even though they are not really competitive. Other economists believe that the total amount of services offered by the government to the industrial sector (infrastruc-ture and administrative services) is so low that the costs of industries in

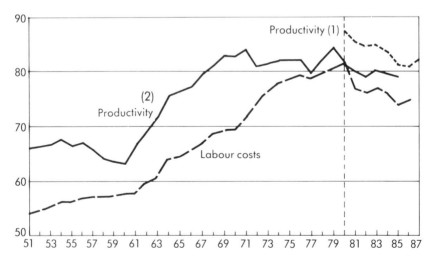

Figure 5.9 Productivity and labour costs in industry: South as a percentage of Centre-North. (1) Revised national accounts; (2) Data corrected according to *Cassa Integrazione* from 1970 on.
Source: Bank of Italy digest of SVIMEZ and INPS data

the South are decidedly higher. Another group of industrial economists believe that there are environmental diseconomies. The industrial sector is not well integrated and lacks important links and this causes high relative costs.

Although the above factors are important, they do not give a complete explanation of the lower productivity in the South. In fact, many other regions of Italy have experienced industrialisation in the last decades and have experienced similar difficulties. Those economists who believe that the problems of the economy in the *Mezzogiorno* are not purely of an economic nature but can be largely attributed to social and political causes would seem to be right.

The lower productivity of some of the firms can be put down to the lack of competition. For example, those firms which operate with state contracts, or where potential competitors are not able to operate due to the unsatisfactory level of 'public order' and/or strong political influences in determining the contracts. In some areas of the South the presence of the public sector in the running of companies producing goods and services means that the management are more concerned with maintaining full employment and with filling the jobs with people of the same political or social background rather than efficient management. Finally, the economic grounds for the running of a company are not the same as in the rest of Italy as many companies are exploited by 'organised criminal groups' and not infrequently controlled by these groups. This discourages potential competition and entrepreneurial activity.

The difficulty of working in the South leads to the phenomenon of 'exit' (as one famous social scientist has called it) of entrepreneurs and managers, as well as of the more skilled workers. This point is a particularly serious factor as those who 'exit' are often the most talented, skilful and enterprising; the people more likely to change the existing state of things.

5.6.2 *The role of small firms*

The second aspect of the Italian economy worth a special mention is the extremely important role that very small and small-sized companies have played and still play in the development of Italian industry. A large number of small and medium-sized industries were created during the Italian industrial boom in the 1950s.

In the 1960s it seemed that the 'natural' development of the industrialisation process would have been linked with an increase in company size as well as a movement from the traditional sector to industries which are, on the basis of historical experience, more typical

of an advanced industrial society. However, the 1970s were characterised not only by a proliferation of small-sized industries (accompanied
by the fact that many large companies ran into difficulty) but also by the
particular vitality of the more traditional industrial sectors (sectors in
which the technology is assumed to be 'mature' and to improve slowly)
especially in the regions characterised by small firms.

The contribution that these companies have given to the development of the Italian economy is multi-faceted, and includes income
generation, employment creation (see Table 5.3) and a significant
contribution to exports. The contribution that they have given to
employment in manufacturing industry can be seen from Table 5.3
which shows the data (taken from the general statistical surveys undertaken by *ISTAT* every ten years) relating to employment. In 1981 the
number of people employed in small-sized firms (both those with less
than 10 employees and those with 10–49) actually exceeded both the
number of people working in large plants (500+ employees) and the
number working in plants with 100 to 499 employees. The increase in
the proportion of the employment found in manufacturing firms with
between 10 and 49 employees was especially marked (see Table 5.3).

Table 5.3 Percentage composition of employment in manufacturing firms by size of plants

Number of employees	1951	1961	1971	1981
Less than 10 employees	29.7	25.3	20.3	22.8
10–49	14.7	19.6	21.9	26.0
50–99	8.3	10.5	10.8	10.1
100–499	21.1	22.5	23.2	21.3
500 and more	26.2	22.1	23.8	19.8
Total	100	100	100	100

Source: ISTAT, ten-year census

From the geographical point of view the industrial triangle has
followed the national trend. In the NEC, North-East-Centre (the 'Third
Italy' as it is often called) the very small and small-sized plants have
developed much faster than the medium- and large-sized plants. The SCI,
Centre-South and Islands, has exhibited an atypical tendency compared
to the nation as a whole, with a reduction in the number of workers
employed in very small-sized companies and an increase in the large
companies.

The phenomenon described above has given rise to a lively and prolonged academic debate. There are two main positions which seem to be contradictory. The first interpretation suggests that the economic development and the particular prominence of small-sized companies can be linked to a single pattern of growth that originates from the regions which have a key role in Italian capitalism and manifests itself in different ways according to the social-geographical conditions that are found in the various areas. This line of thought has two sub-theories.

The first underlines the difficulty of large companies to adapt to conditions of strong instability and change which have affected the national and international markets in the 1970s by decentralising their production to companies characterised by small plants. The second indicates a defensive strategy in which the large companies have reacted to the growth in power of organised labour in the 1970s, and which is based on the decentralisation of the production units into small-sized factories which are, because of their specific characteristics, less union-ised and, therefore, have lower labour costs. Following the reduction in the number of people employed in the large companies the union power, as a whole, has thus been reduced. Both the explanatory positions underline, however, the dominant role of major companies and the dependent one of the small firms.

The second interpretation gives importance to the autonomous role in the development of the small companies. This interpretation includes many differing explanations, the best known is the 'small is beautiful' theory which was linked to the desire for independence of the young generation after 1968. More interesting is the theory which underlines the endogenous elements of strength in the integrated systems of small-sized companies which operate in a restricted industrial area ('industrial districts' in the terminology of Alfred Marshall) and benefit from econ-omies of scale that are external to the single firms but internal to the group of firms which constitute the industrial district.

The existing industrial districts benefited, in the beginning, from a pool of pre-existing skilled craft labour and latent entrepreneurial ability, often related to the types of agriculture traditionally adopted in those areas and in the organisation of the agricultural sector in the period before industrialisation, and created a unique form of industrial develop-ment.

It seems that there is no single adequate explanation of the pheno-menon of the presence of such a high number of very small and small-sized companies in Italian manufacturing industry and all the explana-tions put forward can, in part, help to explain the phenomenon which only at a superficial level seems to be homogeneous. The decentralisa-tion of the production of the large companies into smaller production units, the persistence of small-sized companies in the backward industrial environments and the integrated systems of small companies which have strong internal and (as a whole) external links, are all economic phenomena which are to be found in the Italian economy.

However, it should be pointed out that while the decentralisation of production capacity from large to small-scale units and the persistence of small-sized companies in areas which have experienced a slower process of industrialisation are an international phenomenon, the integrated systems of small companies in delimited industrial districts are a unique Italian phenomenon. This type of organisation of production certainly does not seem to be transitory nor cyclical nor linked to the state of industrial relations in the major companies. Rather it is a special and persistent characteristic in the development of Italian industry, which is able to offer developmental paths, which are, at least in part, different from those experienced by the countries which industrialised at an earlier period. It is this phenomenon which is attracting the interest of foreign scholars of industrial economics.

5.7 Future perspectives

As we have mentioned above, the Italian economy, in the most recent period, has been experiencing a phase of uninterrupted growth. We must ask ourselves if and to what degree this tendency will continue in the future, and what are the main factors likely to influence future performance. As the Italian economy is closely linked to international markets, it is strongly affected by the trends in the other major economies, especially the USA, Japan and Germany. This is not the place to consider the possible development of a world economy, but it is important to consider the possible consequences of the further integration of the Italian economy into Europe in the 1990s.

On the basis of the experience of the continual liberalisation of the economy during the whole of the post-war period (liberalisation in the early 1950s, entry into the Common Market, progressive liberalisation of capital movements with foreign countries and entry into the European Monetary System), one could sustain the argument that the choices in regard to the liberalisation of the Italian economy on the international market have generally brought positive results: stimulating innovation of the production processes and forcing Italian companies to learn how to operate in international markets. We must not undervalue the possible difficulties of adaptation for some sectors (especially credit and finance companies) to the 1993 liberalisation process; however, some sectors which lack competitiveness at present should become more competitive in a freer market environment than in a protected one. There will probably be a marked phase of modernisation as the presence of the state sector in the market – a presence that often cannot be justified and has, in fact, delayed modernisation – is reduced. It is also probable that the co-ordination of the fiscal and monetary policies necessary for European monetary unity will cause the state to act in a very different way than if the market were protected. Internal and external aspects are obviously linked as the process of monetary and fiscal harmonisation needed to integrate the European market will cause a reduction in the margins of discretionality in the management of the national debt and deficits in commercial balances.

One of the most noticeable factors of the present period of development of the Italian economy is certainly the fact that the lira is extremely strong in international markets (due to the high rates of interest) which create inflows of foreign capital, and the seeking of finance on foreign financial markets by Italian operators. The capital account surplus allows the economic system to operate at a high level of activity even though the current account is in deficit. In certain respects the Italian situation reflects, on a reduced scale, the American economy. As we have mentioned above, the high net interest rates are the main cause of the disastrous situation in public sector accounts (a level of public debt which is approximately the same as GDP and a very high deficit in the public sector account, more than 10% of the GDP) and this has caused an unsatisfactory performance in terms of some of the expenditure items, in particular public investment expenditure. So, a reduction in the net rates of interest seems to be indispensable to rebalance the public sector accounts, but at the same time, the net rate of interest must be high enough to guarantee equilibrium in the balance of payments.

Economic policies used to escape from this situation are, at least partially, different according to the international context in which they operate. It seems to be particularly important to assess the future trends in the German economy which are also related to the entire market area. The growth in the German economy in recent years has been slower than the Italian economy as the German authorities have been particularly careful to avoid a new outbreak of high inflation (a policy that can be traced back to the consequences of high inflation in the period immediately after the First World War). German policy and the action of the European Monetary System in maintaining exchange rate stability among European currencies, associated with a higher inflation rate in the Italian economy, has caused a strong deficit for Italy in the trade balance between the two countries. This situation could be rectified by means of either a tighter price control policy in Italy or a higher growth rate in the German economy, or both. It is rather obvious that the second solution would be preferable for the Italian economy as it would rebalance the commercial accounts without having to pay the price of an anti-inflationist policy.

Furthermore, the present exchange rate policy enhances the competitiveness of German industry and the German authorities have shown themselves to be, in various ways, hostile to a change in this policy. The process of the unification of the two Germanies is a new development which will probably cause the West German economy to develop faster than in recent years. If this does happen, the Italian economy will obviously benefit. If there is no rebalancing of the foreign trade accounts, Italian economic policy, especially in regard to the public debt, should become more restrictive as a consequence of the necessity of a more homogeneous European fiscal policy.

The process of European integration could also accentuate difficulties which already exist in the weakest part of the Italian economy, the South of Italy. It is difficult to predict the effect of the process of integration on areas with different levels of economic development. The result of the process of integration depends on the growth potential of the most backward areas and the ability of the most advanced areas to absorb workers from the poorest regions. The present rate of unemployment in a large part of Europe (especially of young people and women) does not allow us to be optimistic about the possibility of absorbing workers from the South of Italy into other Common Market countries and/or in the North of Italy. On the other hand, the type of economic development of the most advanced Italian and European areas requires a specialised workforce that, if it were to come from the South of Italy, would result in a further impoverishment of the South itself as well as a worsening in the prospects for future growth.

We still need to assess if the South of Italy will be able to offer investment opportunities which can be taken by companies from the most advanced areas of Europe when the market is freed and in what measure the southern Italian companies will be affected by the increased integration of the European market.

The answer to the first question involves assessing whether the companies from the advanced European countries will be more able to exploit the development opportunities in the South of Italy than those from the North of Italy have done. The most realistic answer seems to be largely negative, if we reflect upon the comments on the economy of the South of Italy made above. The potential for economic development of a large part of the South is limited by the existing environmental conditions (widespread organised crime and inefficiency in the public administration system) which hampers the development of the entrepreneurial ability which is present in the South, and it is doubtful that the European companies will be able to do better than the entrepreneurs from the South and the North-Centre regions have done up till now. Probably, the ex-Communist Bloc countries of Eastern Europe will offer better investment opportunities than many regions of the South of Italy.

In regard to the second question, it is difficult to see how the process of European integration and the accompanying increase in competition will produce any different results than has been produced by the intense competition during the 1980s. As the latter phenomenon widened the gap between the South and the North, European integration will also probably further increase the gap.

It must be underlined that the possibility of closing the gap between the South and the North and the increase in the productive capacity of the South of Italy is a problem which has to be resolved, above all, by the South of Italy itself, through the removal of the factors which have for so long hindered development. These problems are beyond the scope of economics and their answer can only be found in institutional and political policies.

5.8 Bibliography and sources of information

Banca d'Italia, *Relazione annuale del Governatore alla assemblea generale ordinaria dei partecipanti*, May 1991

Banca d'Italia, '*Il sistema finanziario nel Mezzogiorno*', numero speciale dei *Contributi all'analisi economica*, Rome, 1990.

Confindustria, *Rapporto annuale a cura del Centro Studi Confindustria*, May, 1990.

Commissione CEE, *Le regioni della Comunità allargata.* Terza relazione periodica sulla situazione socio-economica e sullo sviluppo delle Regioni della Comunità, Luxemburg, 1987.

ISTAT, *Annuario di contabilità nazionale*, 1990.

Istituto Nazionale per il Commercio Estero, *Rapporto sul commercio estero*, Rome, 1989.

Ministero del Lavoro e della Previdenza Sociale, *Rapporto 1988. Lavoro e politiche della occupazione in Italia*, Rome, 1989.

Mediocredito Centrale, *Indagine sulle imprese manifatturiere*, Rome, 1989.

SVIMEZ, *Rapporto sul Mezzogiorno*, 1990.

Bagnasco A., *Tre Italie: la problematica territoriale dello sviluppo italiano*, Il Mulino, Bologna, 1977.

Becattini G. (ed), *Mercato e forze locali: il distretto industriale*, Il Mulino, Bologna, 1987.

Cavazzuti F., *Debito pubblico e ricchezza privata*, Il Mulino, Bologna, 1986.

Fineschi A., 'Alcune osservazioni sulla politica monetaria e sul tasso di cambio in Italia negli anni ottanta', *Quaderni di economia, statistica e analisi del territorio*, Messina, 1991.

Fuà G., Zacchia C. (eds.), *Industrializzazione senza fratture*, Il Mulino, Bologna, 1983.

Sylos Labini P., *Le classi sociali negli anni '80*, Laterza, Bari, 1986.

Valli V., *Politica economica. I modelli, gli strumenti, l'economia italiana*, La Nuova Italia Scientifica, Rome, 1988.

6 The UK Economy

Dr Ian Stone

6.1 Historical and institutional context

This chapter is concerned with the structural and institutional characteristics of the economy of the United Kingdom (that is, England, Scotland
and Wales plus Northern Ireland), and its performance over recent years.
Crucial to an understanding of the current UK economy is a recognition
of the role of the Conservative administration led by Margaret Thatcher,
which was in power throughout the 1980s. The high degree of centralisa-
tion of power and control within the UK, allied to an essentially two-
party electoral system which gives the party obtaining an overall
majority very large powers to introduce whatever legislation it wishes,
made it possible for the Thatcher government to make sweeping changes
in respect of economic policy and institutions. Prior to the Thatcher
period there was a general post-war consensus between the two main
political parties (Conservative and Labour) over economic policy, with
both adhering to the notion of a mixed economy of private and public
enterprises, with regulation of markets, the use of Keynesian demand-
management policies, and the maintenance of the welfare state. The
1980s has seen a marked departure from this well-established pattern.

This has, primarily, come about as a result of the relative failure of
the UK economy in the post-war period. The economy had functioned
poorly in comparison with other OECD countries during the 1960s,
lagging behind in terms of the main performance indicators. It also
suffered from 'stop-go' cycles, whereby attempts to expand demand, and
thus increase output and employment, repeatedly led to a rush of
imports and balance of payments difficulties followed by the inevitable
deflationary measures. The problems of the 1970s were appreciably
worse. Although it retained (through the Commonwealth) a special
association with its former colonies, the focus of British post-war

economic interests moved increasingly towards Europe – in particular the EC – and the country eventually took the decision to join the Community in 1973. This move not only opened the economy to increased competition, but the years following entry were especially difficult in terms of inflation, unemployment, and serious balance of payments problems. The interventionist policies deployed with apparent effectiveness during much of the post-war period – aggregate demand management mainly through fiscal adjustments, backed up by some form of prices and incomes policy – became less effective in the face of important structural changes taking place in the international economy. After a period when intervention in the economy was intensified (during the Labour administration of the second half of the 1970s) the electorate opted for what, in terms of UK post-war experience, was a radical alternative approach to economic management.

Although it was subsequently to modify its stance, the Thatcher government set out determinedly to apply Monetarism, with its underlying emphasis upon markets and rejection of the notion that the government should act as a prime mover in the economy. Medium- and long-term strategies were preferred to the short-term 'fine-tuning' of demand management via fiscal policy. Controlling the rate of money supply growth was the main instrument, and reducing inflation the principal macroeconomic objective. Other aspects of the approach involved allowing the currency to find its own level (a view which was subsequently modified), balance between government expenditure and revenue, and a much reduced role for the public sector in decisions on consumption and resource allocation.

The economic strategy has also consistently embodied an attempt to improve the output responsiveness of the economy. This 'supply-side' emphasis, which contrasts with the demand-focus of the previously dominant Keynesian approach, is exemplified by the policies introduced in relation to the labour market. Personal income tax cuts for higher-rate payers – permitted by restraints on government spending – have been used in an attempt to stimulate work effort; successive social security reforms have sought to reduce the disincentive effect of benefits on the willingness of people to accept low-paid jobs; and legislation has been passed to limit the activities of trade unions and thus their power to increase real wages. Other supply-side policies include: tax reductions on business; the 'liberalisation' of markets through the abolition of controls (e.g. on pay, capital export, prices and bank lending); the reduction in subsidies to industry; measures to increase competition in the economy (including deregulation); and the transfer of nationalised industries and public corporations to the private sector.

6.2 Main economic characteristics

6.2.1 *Population and labour force*

In common with other EC countries, the rate of population growth in the UK has fallen markedly over the post-war period. While total numbers increased from 50.3 to 55.9 million in the two decades to 1971, a further rise of only one million (to 57 million) had occurred by 1988 (Statistical Annexe, Table D 6). Despite this, however, there has been a substantial increase in the size of the UK labour force. Fewer retirements (due to a low birth rate during the First World War) and the enhanced inflow of people joining the labour market (due to the high birth rates of the 1960s) has, since 1971, caused a rise in the population of working age (16–60 for females and 16–64 for males) amounting to more than one million for each of the sexes.

The civilian working population – those willing and able to work, excluding the armed forces – is relatively high in the UK. In 1988 it stood at 28.2 million, or 49.5% of the total population. With the notable exception of Denmark, this is the highest proportion in the EC, the average for which is 43% (Statistical Annexe, Table D 7). In fact, since 1971, the UK civilian labour force has been rising at an even faster rate than the population of working age. This is largely a reflection of the increasing activity rate among women. Male activity rates have been falling for a long time, partly due to the rising numbers staying on in education, but also because of the increase in early retirements over the last decade, and the 'discouraged workers' who have dropped out of the labour force on losing hopes of finding employment. The male activity rate, which stood at 81% in 1971, was down to 74% in 1988. In contrast, female participation rates have risen, from 44% to 51% over the same period. Smaller families, labour-saving household devices, the structural shift within the economy away from manufacturing towards services, and a change in social attitudes have all contributed to this trend.

The rise in both the number and proportion of females in the labour force has been accompanied by a significant increase in part-time working. Almost a quarter of all jobs fall into this category. Figures for the mid-1980s show that 42.2% of female workers are part-time, compared with 6.6% among males. The particularly rapid growth of service sector employment in the UK over the 1980s has been a major factor in this development, since it is in this sector (notable in distribution, hotels and catering) that so many of the part-time job opportunities have arisen. In the five years to 1988, the increase in the number of part-time jobs in the UK (1.4 million) was almost twice the number of full-time jobs created (0.8 million).

6.2.2 *Employment structure*

In terms of labour demand, the main feature of the period since 1971 has been the dramatic fall in manufacturing employment. Employment (including the self-employed) in this sector has fallen over the period by almost 3 million, from 8.2 to 5.3 million in 1988. A substantial proportion of this fall was concentrated in the period 1979–81, when the effects of world recession were intensified in the UK by tight monetary and fiscal policies, contributing to a reduction of over a million, or 13.3%, in manufacturing employment over just two years. The contraction in manufacturing has been more than balanced in aggregate terms by the expansion in the number of service sector employees. Overall, employment in the sector grew over the 1971–88 period by around 4.3 million, from 12.8 to 17.1 million. While the main sub-sectors of manufacturing have experienced similar falls in the number of jobs, there is considerable variation among the different activities within the service sector. The male-dominated transport and communications sub-sector has contracted over the period, while the other sub-sectors – distribution, hotels and catering; banking, finance, insurance and business services; and 'other services' – have all shown significant growth. Proportionately large falls have occurred in the number of people engaged in agriculture and in the energy and water supply industries, though in absolute terms the contraction is small alongside the scale of changes in manufacturing and services. Agriculture, as Table D 8 in the Statistical Annexe shows, accounts for only 2.2% of the civilian employment in the UK, the lowest in the EC.

6.2.3 *Unemployment*

In the UK, as in the EC in general, the average rate of unemployment during the 1980s has been more than double that of the 1970s. OECD figures are given in the Statistical Annexe, Table D 9. These count as unemployed those seeking work in the last four weeks and who have not done any work during that period, expressed as a percentage of the 'working population'. The table shows an average unemployment rate which has risen from the 1960s level of under 2% to 3.9% in the 1970s, and 9.8% in the last decade (Table D 9). This latter figure is the same as for the EUR12, though above the figure for the USA and nearly four times the level in Japan. Unemployment in the UK rose rapidly in the early 1980s; from 1.1 million (4.7%) in 1979, it increased to 2.2 million (9.1%) in 1981, and continued upwards until 1986, when 3.1 million people (11.5%) were registered as unemployed. With restructuring and steady recovery of output, the rate has since come down, reaching 6.8%

in 1989. This is below the figure of 9% for the EUR12, and close to the rate in West Germany, which pursued less contractionary policies in the early 1980s and thus avoided the sharp rise in unemployment experienced in the UK.

The official rate of unemployment is normally substantially higher for men (9.5% in 1988) than for women (5.5%). The figures are distorted, however, by the fact that the unemployment count includes only those who are claiming unemployment benefit, and married women make up a significant proportion of the estimated 870,000 people seeking work but not eligible for benefit. Moreover, comparisons of unemployment rates over time are misleading due to several changes in the official definition of unemployment during the 1980s. According to estimates made by the Employment Department, the jobless total in 1986, when unemployment peaked, was around half a million under the figure which would have applied had the changes not been introduced.

6.2.4 *Output and growth*

The UK GDP (factor cost, 1985 prices) stood at £336 billion in 1988, up from £277 billion in 1980. The 1980s growth performance was noticeably better than that achieved in the 1970s which, following the expansionary boom of the 1970–73 period, subsequently averaged less than 1% per annum. During the 1980s the average real rate of GDP growth was 2.4%. If the recession years 1980–81 – when output fell by 2.0% and 1.1% respectively – are left out, the rate is considerably higher. Indeed, the average of 3.4% growth in real terms over 1983–88 represents the highest sustained rate of increase in output since 1949–54.

Outwardly this constitutes a dramatic turnaround in the performance of the UK economy. It has gone from being the nation with by far the lowest real rate of growth among the EUR12 in both the 1960s (EUR12 average 4.8%, UK 2.8%) and the generally more difficult 1970–80 period (EUR12 average 2.9%, UK 2.0%), to being among the best performing of the EC industrial economies (see Statistical Annexe, Table D 11). In fact, between 1981 and 1987, average real *per capita* output growth in the UK (2.9%) was significantly ahead of *all* OECD countries bar Japan, which was only slightly better. The appearance of excess demand pressure since 1988 led to a slowing of growth relative to other European nations, and for the 1980s overall, UK average growth (2.4%) is only fractionally ahead of that for the EUR12 (2.3%) which, in turn, has been behind that of the USA (3%) and Japan (4.1%) (Statistical Annexe, Table D 11). The improved record has thus not been sufficient to alter significantly the UK's relative position in terms of *per capita* GDP. As

Table D 12 in the Statistical Annexe shows, in 1988 it was significantly behind not only the USA (to which it was second in 1966) and Japan, but also the other major economies of West Germany and France; while being scarcely ahead of Italy with its underdeveloped South.

The contribution of individual sectors to overall growth in output has changed as the economy has evolved structurally. The largest change involves the contraction of the share of output coming from manufacturing, down by 7 percentage points over the 1972–88 period to stand at less than a quarter of GDP, and the corresponding rise in the share contributed by services, from 55% to 63% (Table 6.1). Finance-related activity has been the main contributor to the expansion in the service sector, with an output (including net interest receipts) of £77 billion in 1988. Agriculture has continued its relative decline, while the figures for Energy in the table reflect the development of North Sea oil and gas, including the fall in oil prices between 1985 and 1988. Sectoral growth rates combined with the relative importance of each industrial grouping determine the contribution of each sector to the UK output growth in the 1980s. No less than two-thirds of the total growth came from services, followed in importance by manufacturing, which contributed one-sixth of the increase.

Table 6.1 Contribution to UK GDP by industry (%)

Industry	1972	1975	1980	1985	1988
Agriculture	2.7	2.6	2.0	1.7	1.4
Energy and water supply	4.8	4.9	9.3	10.1	5.6
Manufacturing	30.7	28.1	25.4	22.6	23.7
Construction	6.9	6.9	5.8	5.6	6.5
Services	55.0	57.6	57.5	60.0	62.8

Source: UK National Accounts 'Blue Book', CSO, various years

6.2.5 *Market structure*

Of nearly 130,000 manufacturing enterprises in 1986, 95% employed less than 100 workers. These – largely single establishment independent companies – account for less than a fifth of total manufacturing output. Enterprises with 100 to 3,000 employees – making up less than 5% of the total number – contribute roughly 40% of output, while the remaining 40% is produced by just 114 giant enterprises with 5,000+ workers. The 20 largest enterprises alone have, between them, 1,300 establishments which together produce one-fifth of UK manufacturing output. In employment terms, firms with under 100 workers account for just below a quarter of the total for manufacturing, while the largest 114 firms alone employ 35%.

During the 1960s and 70s large enterprises were favoured by government and formal attempts were made in the late 1960s to promote mergers through the Industrial Reorganisation Corporation, in the interests of achieving scale economies. The neglect shown towards small businesses has since been reversed, and the present government has placed great emphasis on promoting the formation and growth of small firms. A range of support measures have been introduced, from payments to the unemployed who start their own business (the Enterprise Allowance Scheme), a Loans Guarantee Scheme improving access to finance, and special tax relief on sums invested in small firms (the Business Expansion Scheme). Partly as a result of such policies, there has been a rise of around 40,000 in the number of small businesses over the past decade, and the share of employment in firms with less than 100 workers increased from 17.4% to 24% during 1978–86. The measures have also stimulated a rise in the number of self-employed – from 2 million at the end of the 1970s to 3 million in 1988 – though in keeping with broader structural trends, the vast majority of these are engaged in services and construction, rather than manufacturing.

The large enterprises do not necessarily possess great market power, since a company can grow via diversification and operate in a number of different markets. Indeed, many of the industrial giants are multi-product conglomerate businesses. The degree of concentration (as measured by the share of the largest five enterprises in the total sales by industry) shows that there are a number of sectors where the net output of these firms is in excess of 75% of the total. These sectors include aerospace equipment, iron and steel, cement, motor vehicles, man-made fibres, and tobacco. However, while the evidence suggests that there was an increase in sectoral concentration ratios during the 1950s and 60s, concentration ratios adjusted for foreign trade actually declined during the period 1970–84. A similar conclusion can be drawn regarding overall concentration: the share of the largest 100 firms in net manufacturing output, which rose from 22% in 1949 to 41% in 1968, stabilised during the 1970s, and actually fell slightly in the 1980s.

Finally, it should be noted that most large firms operating in the UK are multinational enterprises, with extensive activities overseas. Indeed, among the 100 largest manufacturing firms (in output terms), 20 are foreign-owned. Altogether, in the mid-1980s, 1,500 of the manufacturing enterprises – just over 1% of the total, but accounting for no less than one-fifth of total sales and 14% of employment – were in foreign ownership. In 1987, over half of the foreign sector's manufacturing employment, and two-thirds of its output, were American, though the balance has shifted to some extent in recent years with expanded direct investment by Japan (one-third of its investment in the EC has come to the UK) and the Far East, and by EFTA countries concerned with access to the EC market after 1992. Foreign interests tend to be concentrated in the medium and high research-intensive sectors, with proportionately high representation in chemicals, mechanical engineering, electrical and electronic engineering, motor vehicles, instruments and office machinery. New foreign investment was much encouraged by the Thatcher government, partly as a means of introducing into the economy new work practices and manufacturing techniques. Combined with acquisition activity it has caused the foreign sector to grow rapidly in recent years, leading to a forecast that by the mid-1990s around 40% of UK manufacturing capacity will be foreign controlled.

6.2.6 *Productivity*

The productivity performance of the UK economy, which was especially poor in the 1970s, showed significant improvement during the 1980s. This is perhaps not surprising, given the emphasis by government on supply-side policies. Since 1960 all OECD countries have suffered a decline in productivity growth as represented by increases in real output (all sectors) per employed worker (Table 6.2). In the 1960s, when the average percentage increase in productivity among the large industrial (G7) economies was 3.5% per annum, the UK rate of 2.4% was well behind that of Germany, Italy, and France. OECD figures for the 1970s similarly show the UK rate (1.3%) running at less than half the annual averages in the other three large EC economies. However, the increase in the UK rate during the period 1980–88 – to an average of 2.5% per annum – is very much against the downward trend affecting virtually all

Table 6.2 Output per person employed in the major industrialised countries (average annual % change)

| | Manufacturing | | | Whole Economy | | |
	1960–70	1970–80	1980–90	1960–70	1970–80	1980–90
UK	3.0	1.6	5.2	2.4	1.3	2.5
USA	3.5	3.0	4.0	2.0	0.4	1.2
Japan	8.8	5.3	3.1	8.9	3.8	2.9
FRG	4.1	2.9	2.2	4.4	2.8	1.8
France	5.4	3.2	3.1	4.6	2.8	2.0
Italy	5.4	3.0	3.5	6.3	2.6	2.0
Canada	3.4	3.0	3.6	2.4	1.5	1.4
G7 Av.	4.5	3.3	3.6	3.5	1.7	1.8

Source: HM Treasury, Economic Progress Report, No. 201, April 1989

OECD countries, and is comfortably above the average for the largest seven industrial economies (1.8%). Only Japan (2.9%) performed better than this.

In manufacturing alone, as Table 6.2 shows, the UK's average annual rise in output per person employed, at 5.2%, is easily above the next highest figure (USA 4%) for the major industrial economies, the average for which was 3.6%. Around one-third of this rise in productivity has been attributed to the increased capital per worker resulting from the exceptional labour shedding which occurred in UK manufacturing during 1979–81. The rest can be ascribed to factors such as technological progress, education, and more efficient use of capital stock. Economic growth depends on the growth of capital and labour, and the efficiency with which they are used. The latter – called 'total factor productivity' – has been growing at over 3% per annum in the UK. This is faster than at any time during the last three decades, and largely accounts for the improved performance since 1980.

The turnaround in productivity has had a limited effect in terms of enhancing the international competitiveness of the economy, due to the continuing high level of British wage and salary increases. The UK economy has long been characterised by ongoing rises in wages and salary costs, and the trend has been steeper in the 1980s than the 1970s. From 1982 onwards the growth of average annual earnings was steady at 7%–9%, little influenced, it would seem, by variations in either the inflation rate or the state of the labour market. The effect of this enormous rise in costs per worker is offset by increases in labour productivity. While in the 1970s, when productivity growth was low, unit labour costs tracked the path of wages and salaries quite closely (and rose by 230% between 1971 and 1980), in the 1980s higher productivity has caused a sharp divergence between wage costs and unit labour costs. However, although unit labour costs in the period 1980–86 grew by only around a quarter, the equivalent figure for trading partners shows a slight *fall* over the same period. The UK has thus only been able to narrow the gap in competitiveness through a relative fall in the exchange value of sterling. In fact, the actual depreciation has been less than that required to maintain international equality of unit labour costs.

6.2.7 *Consumption, savings and investment*

Consumer spending is by far the largest component of total expenditure within the economy. As a proportion of GDP (market prices), it has throughout the 1980s been in excess of 60%. The buoyancy of this element of spending is the principal source of increased demand on which recovery from the recession of the early 1980s was based. Public spending on goods and services has been tightly constrained during the decade, and has steadily fallen back from around 22% of GDP in 1980 to 19% in 1989, though, as a source of overall growth in the economy, in real terms it rose by 9% over the period. Consumers' expenditure, however, increased by no less than 35% in real terms over 1980–89, rising from 60% of GDP to almost 66%.

The growth in consumer spending is in part explained by the growth in personal sector incomes. The largest component of this is wages and salaries, which, as has already been noted, have been rising steadily in recent years due to the buoyant labour market and overtime working. Aided by reductions in rates of income tax – an element of the government's supply-side strategy – the average annual rate of growth in the post-tax personal incomes has been roughly 7% to 8% over the decade, with the real rate of post-tax income growth reaching as high as 5% by 1988.

The proportional rise in consumer spending is also related to the steady fall in the personal savings ratios (saving as a percentage of personal disposable income) from 13.5% (£31 billion at 1985 prices) in 1980, down to 4% (£13 billion) in 1989. The expansion of credit as monetary restrictions were relaxed in the mid-1980s has, through making it easier for households to borrow, contributed to the fall in savings. The trend has also been ascribed to the 'wealth effect', whereby, as property prices and the value of shares have risen faster than inflation over the 1980s, people with such assets have felt wealthier and been less inclined to convert income into wealth through saving.

National saving is, of course, the sum of private (personal and company) saving and public saving, and the decline in personal saving has been offset by an increase in company saving and a steady fall in the level of dis-saving by the public sector (e.g. it recorded a positive level of savings in 1988). Thus, *total* savings as a percentage of GDP at factor cost, either in terms of current prices or adjusted for inflation, show a relatively stable proportion over the 1980s, at around 7%.

Investment (gross domestic fixed capital formation, or GDFCF) has increased proportionately more over the 1980s (45%) than consumer spending, though it is less important as a component of demand, amounting to only a quarter to one-third the level of consumer expenditure. From its 1980 figure of £53 billion (1985 prices), investment in the UK fell back in the following year to £48 billion, before rising to £77 billion in 1989. From 16% of GDP in 1981, the proportion rose steadily to 19% at the end of the 1980s (Statistical Annexe, Table D 16).

Total business investment (i.e. by the trading sector of the economy, including nationalised industries), which was generally static in real terms between 1973 and 1979, fell sharply in the early 1980s, but has increased markedly since 1982. Between 1982 and 1987 the annual average real rate of growth was 5%. Manufacturing is a relatively small part of total business investment, accounting in 1987 for 26% of business investment (16% of GDFCF) compared to 34% in 1970. Investment in this sector was relatively static in the 1980s, with the result that its share of business investment has continued to fall even as the total has risen, reflecting ongoing structural changes within the economy. Another important feature is the noticeable shift in favour of the private sector which has occurred since the early 1980s in the pattern of investment expenditure. Private sector investment as a proportion of GDP has increased from 11% in 1977 to 16% in 1988. The share of General Government Investment and Public Corporation Investment as a proportion of GDP contracted over the period 1977–88 from a combined total of 6% to 2.6%. This partly reflects privatisation, but is in line with the government's aim of reducing public spending and moving away from demand management policies.

6.2.8 *Income distribution*

How has the considerable rise in UK National Income over the last decade been distributed among the population? Income in capitalist societies is generally unevenly distributed, and it takes a combination of progressive income taxes and welfare benefits to reduce the inequality. In practice, the experience of the last four decades indicates that redistribution of post-tax incomes via direct taxes has tended to be more from the top towards the middle income groups, rather than towards the bottom; it is effectively left to the welfare benefits to affect an improvement in post-tax position of the poorer groups. Personal income (after tax) has, in fact, become more unevenly distributed in the 1980s, as the share of the top 10% of the distribution rose after steadily declining since 1950. This is partly because of the attempt by successive Conservative governments since 1979 to reform taxation and reduce the burden of direct taxation in line with its supply-side strategy. This has been done by a combination of increased tax thresholds and cuts in marginal tax rates. By 1988, the standard rate of income tax had been cut from 33% to 25%, and the maximum rate on earned income from over 80% down to 40%. Such changes are of little assistance, however, to those either below the tax threshold or paying little tax; while being of considerable benefit to the better-off groups previously in high tax brackets.

Recognising that governments influence the pattern of income and consumption by means other than income taxation, it is possible to encapsulate that activity and its impact on income distribution by obtaining a measure for 'final income'. This is disposable income (original income from earnings, pensions, annuities and investment – all net of income tax and national insurance contributions – plus cash benefits) *minus* indirect taxes and benefits in kind (including health, education, housing subsidies, etc). The dispersion between income groups is much less marked in final than in original income. Table 6.3 shows that the respective 1986 figures for the top 20% are 41.7% and 50.7%, as against 0.3% and 5.9% for the bottom 20% (and 6% and 17.3% for the bottom 40%). It is also the case that the dispersion between the different groups was higher in 1986 than in 1976, with the share of the top 20% rising from 37.9% to 41.7%, and that of the bottom 40% falling from 20.1% to 17.3%. Thus, both in terms of the distribution of original income, and in the distribution of incomes after adjustments for taxes and benefits, there has been a trend towards greater income inequality since the mid-1970s.

Table 6.3 Cumulative distribution of original and final household income in the UK, 1976 and 1986

Quantile group	Original income		Final income	
	1976	1986	1976	1986
Top 20%	44.4	50.7	37.9	41.7
Top 40%	71.0	77.6	61.9	65.6
Top 60%	89.8	94.0	79.9	82.6
Bottom 40%	10.2	6.0	20.1	17.3
Bottom 20%	0.8	0.3	7.4	5.9

Source: CSO, Social Trends, 19 (1989)

6.2.9 *Inflation*

The UK economy suffered relatively high rates of inflation during the 1970s in comparison with its trading partners, and although the situation improved in the 1980s, by the end of the decade the problem was once more a cause for concern. The annual increase in retail prices of below 4% in the 1960s (the same as the average for the EUR12 given in the Statistical Annexe, Table D 17), was accelerating in the early 1970s even before the first OPEC oil shock – and high import prices in general – helped push the rate up to 24% in 1975. The rate fell back to 9% by 1978, giving an average for the 1971–80 period of 13.3%, which was above the EUR12 average (10.8%), and substantially higher than that for West Germany and France, though not Italy (which since 1970 has generally performed worse than the UK in terms of inflation).

The second oil price hike, relaxed monetary controls, and the increase in VAT from 8% to 15%, were all behind the sharp rise in the UK inflation rate at the end of the 1970s. The rate climbed to 18% (as measured by the UK Retail Price Index (RPI)) in 1980. 'Eliminating' inflation was declared the principal aim of the incoming Conservative Government in 1979 and the chief weapon for achieving this objective was control of money supply growth. Tight monetary policies were enforced in the early years of the decade, and these certainly contributed to the fall in inflation to 5% by 1984. They were also instrumental in bringing about the deep recession of the early 1980s, which itself had the effect of reducing inflationary expectations, while rising unemployment and trade union reform weakened the power of labour. These circumstances combined to bring UK inflation rates down to levels near to those of its main trading partners during the mid-decade period (see Statistical Annexe, Table D 17).

Since then the rate has begun to increase once more, reaching 8% in 1989 and the RPI rose to over 10% in late 1990. While to some economists this is the inevitable outcome of the relaxation of monetary control when the government, on getting the inflation rate down, switched to the exchange rate as its policy target; to others, this is simply a reflection of excess demand and changing labour market conditions. In technical terms, the recent official inflation figure has been affected by interest rates, which have been raised to protect the value of the pound. This affects the RPI via interest paid on mortgage loans for house purchase. With a large owner-occupier sector in the UK, this can have a significant impact upon the RPI (compare, for instance, the standardised 1988 figure used in Table D 17 with the RPI level of 8%) and the government has recently begun to issue statistics on inflation which exclude the cost of mortgages. The official argument for this is that such interest-induced changes are unrepresentative of the 'true' rate of inflation; opponents say that to exclude the cost of home ownership from the measure of cost of living makes the latter unrepresentative, because the mortgage repayment takes a large proportion of many incomes.

6.3 Government involvement in the economy

6.3.1 *Public expenditure*

The 1970s saw public spending rise as a proportion of GDP, with general government spending (central and local government spending, including grants and net lending to public corporations) reaching 44% of output in the mid-1970s (see Statistical Annexe, Table D 18). Although this was a trend widely shared among industrial nations (the UK figure being the same as the EUR9 average), in the context of a poor domestic economic performance, there were many who supported the incoming Thatcher government's aim of 'rolling back the frontiers of the state'. The public sector was regarded by the Tory government as a burden on private sector business and a restriction on the consumer's freedom to choose. Policies were introduced designed to lighten the burden of taxation, reduce intervention in favour of more reliance upon market forces, and progressively cut back the share of the GDP taken up by government spending.

A number of measures have been deployed to bring about a reduction in the size of the state sector. Government involvement in industry was curtailed through a programme of privatisation; greater efficiency in the public sector was sought via such methods as insistence upon the 'contracting-out' (through tender) of certain public services to the private sector; and tight controls on public expenditure were implemented. During the 1980s the Medium Term Financial Strategy (MTFS) – the preparation, on an annual basis, of cash expenditure plans covering a three year period – has been used as a weapon to force public spending proportionately onto a downward path. Since 1976, expenditure plans have been made in terms of cash rather than volume, on the grounds that when planning was done in terms of goods and services provision this simply resulted in higher expenditure whenever inflation was above the anticipated rate. Around 60% of public expenditure is 'cash-limited'; the rest is 'demand-led' and spending in these areas is determined by take-up rates for benefits and services. Cash limits for individual departments have also had the effect of keeping downward pressure on public sector wages and reducing the number of public employees.

In spite of persistent government attempts to reduce public expenditure, the state sector has proved stubbornly resistant to such attempts at pruning. In 1988–89, general government expenditure (at £181 billion) still accounted for over 38% of GDP; down only a little on the figure of 41% for 1978–79. The public sector still employed 6.25 million people, which is around a quarter of the UK workforce. Indeed, over the period 1979–83, public spending – both proportionately and in absolute terms – increased, reflecting mainly the rise in unemployment-related payments with the onset of recession. Only in 1987–88 i.e. *after* economic recovery – did the ratio of general government spending to GDP fall below its level at the time the Thatcher government took office. Final government consumption of goods and services as a percentage of GDP, which reflects the extent of government's call on national resources, did not fall at all over the period, remaining at almost exactly 20% of GDP (current prices). Of the other half of government spending, there has been a marginal fall in transfers (mainly comprising social security benefits, debt interest payments, and subsidies) from 19.3% to 18.6% of GDP, and a proportionally large decline in public spending directed at capital projects, in particular roads and public transport, down from 3% to 1.2% over the period. Although the latter figures are distorted by considerable capital receipts (treated as negative capital expenditure) from sales of council houses and other government assets, which increased substantially over the decade, the proportion of government capital spending as a proportion of GDP fell noticeably.

There has been a significant change in the composition of public spending over the decade, with the largest government departments increasing their share of the total budget. Social Security spending, accounting for 31% of public expenditure (mainly transfers) in 1988–89, grew by over a third in real terms during the decade, as did that of Health, which accounts for 17%. Both of these sectors are in areas of expenditure influenced by the rising number of elderly in the population. Of the other departments, Defence (21% of total spending and up by 18% in real terms) and Education & Science (14%, up by 9%) have both increased their share of expenditure, while spending on Law & Order, though relatively small, has grown faster than any other department or function. Of the other smaller departments together constituting 20% of total expenditure, the budgets of Trade & Industry, Transport, Housing and Energy have all been cut in real terms, reflecting reduced state subsidies to industry and the shift of public assets (including nationalised industries and council houses) into private hands.

6.3.2 *Revenue sources*

In spite of the avowed intention of the Thatcher governments to reduce the burden of taxation, it remains persistently above that prevailing in 1979. This is substantially due to 'fiscal drag', whereby the rate of income growth exceeds that of prices, by which tax rates are adjusted. The burden is, however, relatively modest by international standards: with tax revenues at 45% of GDP in 1986, the UK was some way behind France (over 50%), and considerably behind the Scandinavian countries, particularly Denmark and Sweden (with figures of over 60%). The UK is out of line with other OECD countries in that income tax as a share of GDP fell rather than rose over the three decades to 1986. This is in part a reflection of the government's wish to shift tax from a direct to an indirect basis. Income tax, which is equivalent to 12% of GDP, is nonetheless the largest component of government revenue, accounting for 23% of the total. Top tax rates have been substantially reduced since 1979, and in the late 1980s were lower than those in all major economies other than the USA, though the top rate applies at a comparatively low income in the UK. Other features are that the standard tax rate in the UK is relatively high by international standards, while the tax threshold is low in comparison.

The reduction in the higher rates of tax and the relative shift away from direct taxation is part of a programme of tax reform, a principal aim of which is to stimulate work effort and entrepreneurial activity. It is thus not surprising that in terms of equity the changes are regressive. The changes also reflect the fact that the punitive high tax rates of the 1970s actually caused the tax base to shrink, as people were encouraged to seek ways of avoiding tax, and there was a large increase in tax-relieved perks.

The same problem afflicted corporation tax in the 1970s, when high marginal tax rates and extensive deductible investment allowances encouraged large companies to manipulate balance sheets, so that many large companies paid very little tax in the UK. In common with other taxes, this has been simplified, with the phasing out of many of the allowances. A reduction in the tax rate, in stages, from 52% to 35% (and even lower rates for companies earning less than £100,000 per annum) has been carried through since 1979. UK company taxation is now attractively low in comparison with other countries, though the phasing out of capital allowances has made the 35% figure a deceptively modest one. In 1988–89, corporation tax contributed £129 billion to the Treasury (11% of total revenue).

In common with other countries, the UK has placed increased emphasis upon National Insurance (NI) contributions as a source of revenue. Although this is technically not a tax, it has the same effect upon disposable income as income tax. The contribution of NI is noticeably smaller as a proportion of the UK GDP than its equivalents in either the Scandinavian countries or France and West Germany, but it still accounts for over 16% government revenue. Indirect taxes have increased in their importance. VAT – the rate of which was raised to 15% in 1979 – currently contributes over 14% of public revenue. Excise duties (levied on petrol and fuel oils, tobacco, alcohol, betting and gambling), and principally aimed at raising revenue, contribute a further 10% to revenue; leaving aside Denmark and Eire, this represents a high proportion in comparison with other European countries. The only other item of significance involves local authority rates, which bring in over £20 billion, or 10% of total revenues.

6.3.3 *The PSBR and the National Debt*

The Public Sector Borrowing Requirement (PSBR), or difference between revenue and expenditure (including borrowing by public corporations from the money markets and overseas), which rose precipitously during the early 1970s from less than 2% of GDP to almost 10% in 1975–76, has shown a clear downward trend since that time. Table D 19 in the Statistical Annexe, which relates only to general government net borrowing and lending, shows that, while the average annual net borrowing figure in the UK during 1971–80 (3%) was identical to that of the EUR9, in the 1980s it has been substantially below the EUR9 average (1.5% compared with 4.3%). Indeed, aided by privatisation proceeds (counted as 'negative spending' by the government) and unexpectedly high tax receipts, the PSBR itself became negative in 1987–88. This was the first time this had occurred since 1971, and it meant that the PSBR was converted to the PSDR, or Public Sector Debt Repayment. The PSDR, which was equivalent overall to over 2% of the GDP (£14 billion) in 1988–89, has been used to reduce the National Debt, which stood at less than £200 billion at the end of 1988. The notion that the Debt could disappear altogether within 20 years has subsequently receded, however, as the PSDR has rapidly evaporated in the face of the enhanced expenditure necessitated by rising inflation.

6.3.4 *Industrial policy*

Radical changes have occurred since the 1970s in UK policy towards industry. The Labour government of 1974–79 placed emphasis upon interventionism in the form of an industrial strategy which extended the 1960s attempt to bring together employers, the unions and government to plan for industrial growth. Specifically, it involved the setting-up of a National Enterprise Board, extending state ownership through national-isation, entering into planning agreements with industry, seeking to develop industrial democracy, and introducing a range of financial subsidies for firms, sectors, and problem regions. The interventionist approach was replaced in the 1980s by a policy of increased reliance upon the market. Supply-side policies, aimed at reducing the level of dependence upon the state and encouraging an 'enterprise culture', have involved the following: a general contraction of the public sector; denationalisation of publicly-owned industries through an extensive programme of privatisation; deregulation (removal of restrictions under which firms can supply particular goods and services) and introduction of more competition in the economy; contracting-out of public services to private firms; reductions in the range and levels of sectoral and regional subsidies to industry; and support for new and small businesses.

Before considering other aspects of government industrial policy (relating to privatisation, the regions and competition) it is worth setting out the overall position in relation to state aid to industry. During the 1960s and 70s, UK expenditure on subsidies increased substantially. Whereas in 1965 it amounted to 2% of GDP and 4% of government expenditure, by 1975 the respective figures had risen to 4% and 8%. Since 1979 the annual level of real spending on subsidies to industry has fallen, and in 1986–87 was equivalent to just 1.5% of GDP and 4.2% of public expenditure. During the 1981–86 period, an annual average of £7 billion in subsidies was awarded to UK industry by government (that is in addition to around £2 billion per year from EC funds), in a variety of forms, from straight subsidy payments to grants, soft loans, and tax concessions. The coal industry absorbed 22% of the total value of subsidies; among other sectors, shipbuilding and steel received 12%, agriculture and fisheries 13%, rail transport 16%, broad industry 17% and regional aid 15%. While within the EC, the UK (9.4 billion ECU) was the fourth highest provider of state aid over 1981–86, behind Italy (annual average 27.7 billion ECU), West Germany (19.1 billion ECU), and France (16.7 billion ECU), as a proportion of GDP, the UK was well down the list in eighth place. Italian state aid as a proportion of GDP during 1981–86 (5.6%) was three times the level in the UK (1.8%).

6.3.5 *Privatisation*

In 1979, the state sector of industry, the public corporations, accounted for 11.5% of GDP. While the major programme of nationalisation occurred in the early post-war years, when coal mining, railways, gas and electricity were taken into public ownership, further (less systematic) nationalisation took place in the 1960s and 70s, largely involving industries in long-term decline (steel, shipbuilding) and individual firms facing bankruptcy, such as British Leyland and Rolls-Royce. Since 1979, the trend has been put into reverse, with ownership of many of these industries reverting to the private sector. The first phase of privatisation involved firms whose assets have been acquired through the National Enterprise Board, followed quickly by a shift in the denationalisation focus towards the public utilities, British Telecom, British Gas, and water companies. By the end of 1988, 19 major public corporations (involving 750,000 employees) has been returned to the private sector, and the state sector as a proportion of GDP was down to half its size in 1979.

Although the state assets were, for the most part, put on sale at prices which were significantly below their market value, cumulative proceeds by the late 1980s were, nonetheless, around £25 billion and the privatisation programme has had a significant impact upon government finances and contributed to the trend improvement in the PSBR. The government has also realised – in some degree, at least – one of its privatisation aims, namely to widen the private shareholding base within the country. It is estimated that the proportion of the adult population holding shares rose over 1979–88 from 7% to 20%. The privatisation programme has been criticised, however, for transferring utilities to the private sector as single units with a considerable degree of monopoly power, rather than breaking them down into smaller competing entities.

Apart from the practical difficulties of achieving the latter situation, it was recognised by government that monopoly companies are attractive to buyers, and the successful denationalisation of these industries took precedence over the pursuit of competitive markets. The result is that regulatory machinery has had to be developed to monitor (quality) and control (prices) the denationalised public utilities, notably in relation to British Gas (regulatory agency OFGAS) and British Telecom (OFTEL). In addition, the government has retained an ability to exert influence over some of the privatised corporations by retaining either a major share-holding interest, or a single ('golden') share to which is attached the right to vet 'undesirable' takeover bids from (particularly foreign) predator companies.

Other types of privatisation can be identified. One is 'contracting-out', whereby provision to public bodies (e.g. local authorities, central government departments, publicly-owned schools and hospitals) of certain goods and services is switched from the public bodies themselves to private firms. The other involves the removal of restrictions on competition, termed 'deregulation'. The ending of legal monopolies granted to suppliers of particular services – for example, the legislation limiting competition in the provision of bus and coach passenger transport – has been seen as an aspect of privatisation in the 1980s.

6.3.6 *Regional policy*

This was largely pioneered in the UK, and grew in importance over the 1960s and 1970s to become a large component of industry policy aid. In terms of its proportion of public expenditure, spending on regional policy during the late 1970s was twice as high as in most other European countries. Regional aid was principally directed at the peripheral regions – Scotland, Wales, Northern England and Northern Ireland – where the traditional industries of coalmining, shipbuilding, steel and textiles were in decline. With the 'new' industries concentrated in the Midlands and the South, post-war regional policy was designed essentially to encourage large companies to establish factories in 'Development Areas' (DAs), through offering investment grants, subsidies and tax concessions. In addition, until the late 1970s, the process was supported by refusing expanding companies development permission in the South and Midlands.

The policy was justified in times of full employment in that it worked to reduce pressure on the labour market in areas of excess demand, and avoided the private and social costs involved in inter-regional migration. It is estimated that the policy-induced diversion of growth from the 'successful' regions led to the creation of half a million jobs in the DAs between 1955 and the late 1970s. It was criticised, however, for not being effective in terms of cost per job, for being insufficiently selective (in particular, supporting investments which would have occurred anyway), for its relative neglect of services and indigenous enterprise, and for encouraging the establishment of 'branch plant economies', largely restricted to assembly activities and prone to closure during company rationalisations.

A succession of changes to regional policy during the 1980s have transformed this aspect of government involvement in the economy. Automatic investment grants to companies in DAs have been phased out. Regional Selective Assistance – available on a discretionary basis – has been retained and is now the main source of regional industrial assistance (£90 million 1988–89 at 1980 prices). This assistance is provided for projects which maintain employment or create additional jobs, the aim being to provide the minimum grant needed for the project to proceed in an assisted area. The policy has also moved towards giving more help to the 'indigenous sector', that is, local small and medium-sized firms, through special investment grants and innovation support for product and process development, and to subsidising the use of consultancy services in relation to marketing, design and manufacturing systems. There has also been a revival of interest (largely cost-driven) in relocating government offices out of London.

The overall defined area eligible for regional assistance has been pared back considerably since the 1970s when 45% of the population lived in such zones; the current figure is 15%. With the exception of Northern Ireland (for which there are special provisions covering the whole province), the policies relate to sub-regional areas centred on major conurbations in the North and West, plus underdeveloped rural areas such as the Scottish Highlands & Islands. A substantial proportion of assisted areas have 'intermediate' status, and do not qualify for the full range of assistance, though they do have the advantage of qualifying for the European (ERDF) aid. The spending has been reduced sharply from its peak in 1975–76 of £1.25 billion to £300 million in 1988–89 (all figures at 1980 prices), reflecting, in part, the diversion of spatially-defined assistance towards the inner areas of the major cities.

Overall, while the new policy has been designed to give greater encouragement to enterprise in the regions than the previous support measures, it is increasingly insignificant in terms of resource commitment, and thus even weaker in its capacity to make a significant impact on regional differences. During 1975–88 the unemployment rate increased by 3 percentage points in the South (South-east, East Anglia and South-west), compared with an average of over twice that figure in Scotland, Wales, the North and Northern Ireland). There is considerable debate in the UK about the 'North–South Divide', and whether it has increased since a more market-oriented approach to regional issues was adopted by the present government. The problem is that the manufacturing decline has mainly hit the areas of the North (reaching right down as far as the West Midlands, centre of the motor industry), while the services-based expansion of the 1980s has been located disproportionately in the South, and particularly around London. The regions of the 'North' suffer from outmigration (a net loss of 316,000 people during 1979–86), and in 1989 had unemployment rates in the 7.5% to 9.8% range, compared to 3.3% to 4.7% in the 'South'. Regional incomes (GDP per head) vary less than unemployment rates, but still reveal the advantage of the South-east. Index figures for 1986 show that, within Great Britain, Wales has the lowest regional GDP per head at 86 (UK= 100), compared to 116 in the South-east; Northern Ireland, with 15.5% unemployment in 1989 and a GDP per head index figure of 69, is by far the worst-off UK region. In overall terms, the 'North-South divide' is yet another dimension to the issue of manufacturing decline.

6.3.7 *Competition policy*

Legislation relating to UK competition policy dates from 1956 in the case of restrictive practices and 1948 for monopoly and mergers. Current policy on the latter is based on the Fair Trading Act (1973) and Competition Act (1980). Usually a monopoly is defined as one firm (or group of firms acting in concert) accounting for 25% or more of the relevant regional or national market. These may be referred for investigation to the Monopolies and Mergers Commission (MMC) by the Office of Fair Trading or Minister for Trade and Industry. Mergers can be subjected to similar investigation where they involve 25% or more of market share, or the takeover of assets valued at £30 million or above. The latter criteria allows investigation of vertical and conglomerate mergers.

It is the purpose of the MMC, an independent body, to determine whether the referred monopoly or proposed merger operates (or is likely to operate) against the public interest, and to make recommendations for appropriate action to the Minister. 'Public interest' is defined to include not only the maintenance and promotion of competition and consumer interests relating to price, quality and choice, but also the promotion of technical progress and international competitiveness. In fact, the MMC is free to take into account any factors it considers relevant. In contrast to practice in the USA and elsewhere, UK policy is not based on the presumption that monopoly is undesirable; it recognises that there are potential benefits (such as scale economies and technical progress) to set against the costs of reduced competition, and accordingly it examines each case on its merits using a cost–benefit approach.

An additional dimension was given to this area of competition policy in 1980, when the Competition Act recognised that the 'anti-competitive practices' of individual firms can 'restrict, distort or prevent competition', through, for example, predatory pricing, price discrimination, and the tying of the sales of one product to those of another. This act also made it possible for nationalised industries and other public sector bodies to be referred for investigation by the MMC.

Critics of UK monopoly policy insist that it is slow and ineffective: they point out that investigations can take up to three years, and that governments have been reluctant to take remedial action, usually preferring to accept voluntary assurances from the companies involved, rather than formally imposing conditions. This, plus the fact that relatively few monopoly and oligopoly industries have actually been subjected to investigation, leads to the conclusion that the policy has not modified significantly either the structure or the conduct of these industries.

Similar conclusions apply in the case of mergers. During the 1980s merger boom, very few takeovers were referred to the MMC. Indeed, since the legislation was introduced, a very small proportion of mergers have actually been subject to investigation, though the possibility of referral has undoubtedly modified behaviour, particularly in relation to horizontal mergers. The current view of government is that the capital markets function generally in an efficient manner, moving assets into the hands of the companies and management best equipped to make use of them, and that merger decisions are thus best left to the market, the vast majority of takeovers raising no competition or other objections. Following a number of highly politicised merger references involving, in particular, foreign takeovers of British companies, a public statement was made in 1984 to the effect that, henceforth, merger references would be based predominantly on the possible effect of a merger on competition. The refusal of the Minister to refer the 1988 Nestlé bid for Rowntree to the MMC is consistent with this approach. There was considerable pressure to refer this Swiss bid on nationalistic grounds, especially since the comparatively efficient capital market in the UK makes it easier for continental European firms to acquire British firms than for the latter to take over companies in Europe.

Current policy towards restrictive practices is defined by the 1976 Restrictive Practices and Resale Prices Acts. It is operated by the Restrictive Practices Court (part of the judiciary), and is concerned with price agreements and market sharing arrangements. By law, restrictive agreements have to be registered, and are presumed to be against the public interest unless a case can be made before the court for exemption. This is acquired via passing through at least one of eight 'gateways', e.g.

that the restrictive agreement provides substantial benefits to consumers, or that its removal would result in unemployment or a fall in exports. While this legislation has been effective in removing restrictive agreements which were the basis for the extensive system of cartels existing in the 1950s, by the 1980s the effectiveness of the legislation in detecting and tackling such behaviour was called seriously into question. The Restrictive Practices Court can also grant exemption from the provisions of the Retail Prices Act (1964), which prohibited producers from fixing minimum retail prices for their goods. This legislation proved particularly effective. With the exception of books and medicines (together accounting for less than 2% of consumer expenditure), fixed prices for goods in all UK shops have virtually disappeared.

Following an official review of competition policy in 1988, major changes are planned to restrictive practices legislation, involving a new competition authority, with stronger enforcement powers, to administer legal penalties for any agreement with anti-competitive effects. To deal with mergers, it has been proposed that a system of pre-notification of mergers be introduced, with the granting of conditional permission for mergers (in exchange for statutory undertakings) without full reference to the MMC. The national policy on competition is increasingly influenced by EC policy. The Community policy relating to cross-border mergers, which came into force in 1990, means that large mergers will increasingly fall within the ambit of European competition policy (Article 85). Already the Commission and UK merger policy have come into conflict, for example over the takeover by British Airways of British Caledonian. Although the deal was previously granted approval by the MMC, the Commission insisted that, in the interests of European competition, conditions (the selling-off of particular routes) should be attached to the takeover. The Commission also intervened recently to bring about a reduction in the amount of state aid offered as part of the deal by which British Aerospace took over the Rover Group.

6.4 Financial system

6.4.1 *Financial institutions and markets*

The UK financial sector comprises banks (as defined by the 1979 and 1987 Banking Acts) and 'other financial institutions'. The financial system has undergone radical structural change over the last decade or so, being subject to processes of concentration (via mergers), functional 'despecialisation', and internationalisation, resulting in more competition between institutions over a wider range of financial activities.

The banking sector

This sector consists of all recognised banks and licensed deposit takers, together with the National Girobank, Trustee Savings Bank, the banking department of the Bank of England, and those institutions in the Channel Islands and Isle of Man which operate according to the 1979 Banking Act. The Bank of England, a public sector body since 1946, is central to the financial system. Its Banking Department functions as banker to the Government and to banks in general. In its role as the government's banker it implements monetary policy through influencing interest rates in the bill market, using direct controls and restricting bank credit; it also regulates the issues of notes and coins, manages the issue of government stock, and intervenes on behalf of government in the foreign exchange market. It generally supervises the banking system and acts as 'lender of last resort' to banks. Its supervisory role has been strengthened by the recent Banking Acts, as a result of which it acts to ensure adequacy of banks' capital reserves, that an acceptable ratio of primary liquid assets to deposit liabilities is maintained, and that each bank's exposure to risk of loss on foreign exchange markets is in line with its capital base.

The banking sector is dominated in terms of lending and depositing in sterling by the 'commercial banks'. These are the London clearing banks – dominated by the 'Big Four' (Barclays, Lloyds, the Midland and NatWest) – and those with extensive branch networks, such as the Scottish and Northern Ireland clearing banks, and National Girobank. They mainly deal in individually small transactions, and accounted for £187 billion out of £363 billion in sterling liabilities for the banking sector as a whole in September 1988. The rest was accounted for by banks which concentrate on large sums (wholesale transactions), such as merchant banks, overseas-owned banks, and consortium banks (UK registered institutions owned by banks or financial institutions). Merchant banks have diversified their activities away from their former role as acceptance houses (guaranteeing repayment of commercial bills), towards provision of advice for companies on matters such as mergers and takeover, financial reconstructions, underwriting of new share issues and portfolio management. The separation of deposit banking and investment banking has now virtually ended, since all the large British and overseas deposit banks have either acquired an existing merchant bank, or themselves built up a facility in this field.

Taking the banking system overall, it is clear that foreign currency business dominates, with bank foreign currency denominated liabilities totalling £593 billion in 1988, compared with the £363 billion in sterling accounts. The growth of foreign currency business (up from £85 billion in 1979) has been located mainly in the wholesale banking sector, and, within that, has been very much related to the activities of Japanese banks (liabilities up from £12 billion to £234 billion over

1979–88). The latter have grown much faster than the more numerous US banks, and now command almost 40% of the foreign currency market (three times the US share). The Japanese sector now has total deposit liabilities virtually equal to those of the retail banks, and is well placed to further increase its share given its possession of electronic banking technology and the asset backing from its parent companies. The rise in the number of foreign banks in London – to around 450 in 1988 – is a reflection of the growth of the Eurocurrency market and financial deregulation in the UK. In terms of combined sterling and foreign currency liabilities, the foreign element of the monetary sector has around 60% of the market, and the position of London as a major financial centre (with 24% of international bank lending in 1987), depends in substantial part on the contribution of overseas banks.

Other financial institutions (OFIs)

These include pension funds, building societies, unit and investment trusts, and insurance companies. They fulfil a range of specialist functions and lend mainly through the acquisition of assets, rather than through direct loans and advances. The largest category of non-bank OFIs is the building societies, the total sterling deposits of which were comparable in 1987 to those of the banks. Their prime purpose is to take deposits and lend money for house purchase (via mortgages). In the 1970s, the societies, with the advantage of tax concessions available to mutual societies, and no need to build a profit margin into interest rates charged, faced little competition from the banks, and operated an interest rate cartel. The situation has changed markedly, however. The 1986 Building Societies Act freed them from many of the restrictions on their activities, and allowed them to offer a greater range of financial services (e.g. insurance, pension fund management, and investment). Societies now offer chequing accounts, credit cards, and other facilities previously associated with banks. The distinction between banks and building societies has been narrowed from the banks' side also, as the latter have increasingly moved into the provision of loans for house purchase. There is now keen competition between them for deposits and business.

Insurance companies are important within the OFI sector because of the vast sums – particularly in relation to life insurance – accumulated over long periods and invested in ways which can meet claims and earn profits. In 1988, estimated funds were put at £160 billion. While in the 1970s insurance companies showed a preference for (fixed interest) government securities, the balance in the 1980s has been in favour of commercial and industrial shares, both UK and overseas, which now make up half the assets. The improvement in the UK equity returns is a factor in this development, together with the abolition of capital controls in 1979. Pension funds have increased at an even faster rate than insurance over the period since the 1960s, and accumulated funds in 1987 amounted to £200 billion. Most of this total (two-thirds) is held in the form of ordinary shares, including a significant increase in overseas company shares since the ending of exchange control. Insurance and pension funds have built up a considerable stake in the ownership of UK industry. With merchant banks, the OFIs owned in 1986 three-quarters of ordinary shares by value, compared to under 40% in 1963, when the majority of shares were held by individuals. The portfolio decisions of the OFIs thus affect considerably the share prices, and on balance add to their volatility.

The financial market can be divided into two components, the money market and the capital market. *The money market* is where financial institutions come together to borrow and lend wholesale funds for varying periods up to one year. The primary money market, the discount market, is centred upon the activities of nine discount houses, the principal role of which is to discount Treasury bills of exchange (financial instruments redeemable at a particular date, issued by the Bank of England on government instructions to meet short-term financial needs), the weekly issue of which they underwrite. They purchase the bills by taking surplus funds on a short-term basis from the banking sector. These funds, obtained at low rates of interest, are available to the banks 'at call' should they be required for liquidity purposes. Discount houses also provide short-term finance for companies by discounting commercial bills, which have recently been used increasingly for this purpose. In addition to its role in maintaining liquidity in the banking system, the discount market plays an important part in the conduct of monetary policy, since it is through buying and selling bills in this market that the Bank of England can influence the amount of cash in the system and therefore short-term interest rates.

In addition to the discount market, there are a number of other sterling money markets, known collectively as parallel markets. The largest is the inter-bank market, in which banks lend directly to each other. Similarly, large companies lend to each other in the inter-companies market. Among other such markets, the building society market has developed recently as a reflection of the changing role of these institutions and their growing need for access to wholesale money markets.

The capital market

The capital market is where new long-term finance is raised by the private and public sector via the sale of securities (also known as stock or bonds, and – in the case of government securities – 'gilt-edged' stock) and new share issues; it is also where the trading of existing stock and equity (ordinary shares) is conducted. This activity is centred upon the

International (formerly London) Stock Exchange (SE). Existing companies can raise funds on the Stock Exchange by becoming a 'public' company and obtaining a full SE quotation. This involves complying with certain rules and offering a minimum proportion of shares to the general public. It is a costly process and smaller/new companies find it easier to gain admittance to the Unlisted Securities Market, which has less exacting rules.

Until 1986, there were two main groups of SE participants: stockbrokers, who acted on behalf of individual and institutional clients to buy and sell stocks and shares on a commission basis; and jobbers, who held stocks and shares on their own account and dealt with the brokers according to the market. Stock Exchange rules maintained this separation of functions, as well as restricting Stock Exchange membership. The system had its defects: in particular, the fixed scale of commissions paid to brokers (which penalised large institutional and small individual investors alike), and the limits on the scope of member firms to increase their capital resources. With the amount of share trading which bypassed the Stock Exchange (through direct dealing) increasing, cheaper international trading available in the New York stock market (due to the effect on commissions of deregulation and computerised dealing), and the threat of a Restrictive Practices investigation into its commission rates, deregulation was a logical development. 'Big Bang', as the October 1986 deregulation of the Stock Exchange was dubbed, introduced negotiable commissions, reduced restrictions on outside ownership (and capital resources) of member firms, replaced the system of brokers and jobbers with broker-dealers who deal directly with the public, largely replaced the partnerships with corporate members, and computerised the dealing through the Stock Exchange Automated Quotations system (which has decentralised the process, and led to a virtual desertion of the trading floor). Capital market deregulation has necessitated an increase in investor protection, introduced in the Financial Services Act (1986) and exercised through the Securities & Investment Board.

As a result of Big Bang, large financial corporations have moved into the stock market – several of them international firms – resulting in half London's brokers being foreign-owned. The market has become more competitive, with much lower commissions on large deals. The new technology has enabled London to participate fully in the trading on global securities, and the merger of the Stock Exchange and the International Securities Regulatory Organisation in 1986 (to produce the International Stock Exchange), has resulted in a unified market for dealing in international shares. This has been important in maintaining London's position, alongside New York and Japan, in the 'Golden Triangle' of security dealing.

6.4.2 *Banks and industrial finance*

It is a long-standing criticism of the UK banking sector that it has failed to provide adequate finance for industry. In the bank-based financial systems of France and West Germany, the banking sector does play a major part in the financing of industry, while the securities market is poorly developed and plays a relatively minor role. Bank-based systems foster close relations between banks and their large customers; the former often have a substantial equity stake in the company and are well-placed to provide financial support for new products and expansion. The UK financial system, like that of the US, is basically a market-based one; its securities market is active and provides a major part of the finance for industry, while the banking sector role is less prominent. UK banks do not generally buy shares in companies, and it is the institutional investors which are the major holders of industrial equities. UK companies thus meet their long-term capital needs mainly by selling shares, or through the sale of fixed interest securities to individuals or non-bank financial institutions such as pension funds. UK banks finance firms via loans and overdrafts, providing mainly short-term (working) capital. Thus, one survey has shown that the average original maturity of long-term loans in the UK were only one-third of the 7–8 years average in France and West Germany.

There are a number of implications arising out of the way in which finance is provided in the UK. Reliance on the equity and securities market for long-term finance results in a preoccupation, on the part of companies, with short-term profit and dividend goals. This is because poor performance can lead to a fall in the share price (and thus value) of the company, making it vulnerable to takeover by predators. The encouragement to short-term over long-term decision-making can undermine a company's development. Moreover, while institutional shareholders have been criticised for not using their influence to ensure firms are managed efficiently and enterprisingly, industrial restructuring within the bank-based system is often initiated and orchestrated by the banks, and 'constructive' mergers are more common as a result.

A trend towards closer links between banks and industry is under-way in the UK, with greater use of industrial experts by banks, and greater willingness to take equity in promising companies. The growing influence of foreign banks has been important in this process, as has the integration of banking and the securities business. The gaps in the UK market in the provision of funds for risky ventures and smaller firms have to some extent been filled in recent years by developments such as the Unlisted Securities Market, the Third Market, the Business Expansion Scheme, and the emergence of a number of institutions specialising in the provision of venture capital.

6.4.3 *The money supply*

The Medium Term Financial Strategy (MTFS), introduced by the Thatcher government in 1980, has provided the framework for monetary policy over the last decade. It was the belief of the authorities that excessive monetary growth (i.e. growth in money stock which exceeds that of real output) was the primary cause of inflation and the MTFS aimed at controlling the rate of growth of the money supply over a four-year period, so as to keep it broadly in line with the growth in nominal output and income. Interest rates and PSBR were used to control monetary growth as measured by $£M_3$ (stock of cash and sterling bank deposits – interest bearing and non-interest bearing – held by UK residents). Higher interest rates were aimed at both restraining private sector lending and making it possible to fund the PSBR by selling government debt to the non-bank public. The idea behind the latter was to prevent the banks increasing their holdings of public sector assets, on the basis of which they would be able to create deposits and thus expand the money stock. Reductions in the PSBR (via fiscal means) were necessary because of its direct impact on the growth of $£M_3$.

The 1980 MTFS set targets for $£M_3$ of 7%–11% in 1980–81, falling progressively to 4%–8% in 1983–84. However, the government failed to keep the money stock within the set ranges, and the problem of overshooting led eventually to the abandonment of the practice of announcing targets. Indeed, the nature of the target itself was subject to considerable change. Up to 1982, government used $£M_3$ as its target measure, then widened it to include other measures. During 1984–87 M_0 (notes and coin held by banks and the public) and $£M_3$ were the chosen targets. In 1987, M_3 was abandoned, leaving just M_0.

Nonetheless, although the actual MTFS targets were exceeded, the percentage growth in money supply in the UK was similar to that in France and Italy (though twice as high as that in West Germany) during much of the first half of the 1980s. The period 1985–88, however, has seen a rapid increase to around 20%, which is double the EUR12 rate, and between two and three times the rate in Germany, France, Italy and Spain. This substantially reflects the fact that interest rates, which were a principal weapon for the control of the money supply, have since the mid-1980s been used increasingly to influence the exchange rate.

Why did the authorities find it so hard to achieve monetary targets? Partly it was due to the existence of a range of substitutable monetary assets, so that control over one form of 'money' led institutions and individuals to make increased use of forms which were not subject to control. It was also due to structural changes occurring within the financial sector; for example, the reduction of differences between banks and building societies, and the competition between them, resulting in increased holdings of assets in interest-bearing deposit accounts. Changes in behaviour also had an impact, in particular the increased insensitivity of private sector borrowing to interest rates. With these difficulties, it is not surprising that the government opted to control the economy through adjustments to the exchange rate, which is more easily influenced than the money supply.

6.5 External economic relations

6.5.1 *The current account*

For its size, the UK is a relatively open economy, with exports of goods and services during the 1980s averaging 26.6% of GDP (market prices). While this is below the figure of 28.5% for the EUR12, apart from West Germany (30%) it is the highest among the large EC economies (France 22.6%, Italy 21.4%, and Spain 20.3%) (Statistical Annexe, Table D 22). Over the post-war period, an increasing proportion of UK output has been traded overseas, with a particularly sharp rise occurring in the years immediately following entry to the EEC in 1973.

Geographically, UK trade has in recent decades reversed its historical dependence upon sales in developing countries (the share of which fell from 38% to 11% over the period 1955–88) and the former major Commonwealth nations (Australia, New Zealand and Canada), in favour of trade with advanced non-Commonwealth industrialised economies, and especially those of the EC. Thus, while the general trend within the EC has been for intra-community trade to take up an increasing share of the total imports and exports of member states, this is most dramatic in the case of the UK. In 1958 only 22% of UK trade was with countries currently making up the EUR12; the figure for 1988 was 50%, although this is still (with Denmark's) the lowest proportion of all EC countries (EUR12 figure 59%) (Statistical Annexe, Table D 21). In terms of the UK's relative share of EC trade, in 1988, UK goods and services accounted for 6.4% of total imports by EC countries – some way behind the respective market shares of West Germany (15.5%), France (9.3%) and the Netherlands (8.1%), though in line with those of Italy and Belgium/Luxembourg. As a market, the UK took 8.1% of Community exports, which made it the third most important market after West Germany (12.3%) and France (11%). West Germany, accounting for nearly 16% of UK imports, has become easily the country's most important supplier of foreign goods and services (Statistical Annexe, Table D 21).

Another perspective on the transformation of UK trade can be gained from an examination of changes in the commodity composition of exports and imports. In the 1950s the UK was essentially an importer of primary products (77% of all imports in 1955) and an exporter of manufactures (80% of the total in 1955). A massive deterioration in the non-manufacturing side of the balance of payments resulting from the Second World War meant that it was necessary for the UK to run a substantial manufacturing trade surplus (equivalent to 11% of GDP in 1951). Since the 1950s the non-manufacturing sector has steadily improved its position.

Table 6.4 UK visible trade balances by main categories (% of GDP)

	Manufactures	Food, drink, tobacco	Basic materials	Fuels	Total	Visible balance
1951–60	+8.4	−5.6	−4.6	−0.7	−10.8	−2.4
1961–70	+5.6	−3.4	−2.0	−1.0	−6.4	−0.8
1971–80	+3.4	−2.2	−1.5	−1.8	−5.4	−2.1
1981–85	−0.2	−1.1	−0.9	+1.9	−0.1	−0.2
1986	−1.7	−1.2	−0.7	+0.8	−1.1	−2.7
1987	−2.1	−1.1	−0.7	+0.8	−1.0	−3.0
1988	−3.8	−1.1	−0.8	+0.3	−1.6	−5.3

Source: Derived from Table 19, NIESR, *The UK Economy* (1990)

The non-manufacturing visibles balance (foodstuffs, raw materials and oil) moved from a deficit in the early 1950s equal to over 13% of GDP, to a position of virtual trade balance in the 1981−85 period (Table 6.4). This transformation reflects a number of developments, including a fall in the real cost of food and raw material imports, increased domestic food production due to technical advances and subsidies, the switch from natural to synthetic production materials, and changing output composition in the economy as a whole. Nonetheless, though falling as a proportion of GDP, foodstuffs and raw materials have remained in overall deficit, and, as Table 6.4 shows, it is the exploitation of North Sea oil which has done most to improve the non-manufacturing visible account, mainly through the conversion of the £4 billion oil trade deficit in the mid-1970s into a surplus of £8 billion in 1985.

In addition to oil, UK's invisible trade has contributed a substantial and rising surplus to the overall current account. Indeed, since 1985, surpluses on services and on interest, profit and dividend payments (IPD) have both been larger than the surplus on the oil account. In 1987, for example, the oil surplus was £4.1 billion, compared to £5.3 billion and £5.5 billion respectively for IPD and services. The contribution of IPD has been growing due to the accumulation of overseas assets by UK residents, while the services surplus is largely in trade related to banking, insurance and financial services. Rising transfers (such as the contribution to the European Community Budget), on which there was a deficit of £3.5 billion in 1987, have offset somewhat the trend among invisibles.

The improvement of the non-manufacturing part of the current account has been accompanied by important changes in UK trade in manufactures. In terms of commodities, while the share of finished and semi-finished manufactures in total exports (by value) has remained at around its 1955 level of 80%, the share of these goods in imports has increased from 24% to 79%. UK trade is now characterised by the exchange of manufacturing goods and services with other advanced industrial nations. This means that the economy is more exposed than previously to overseas competition, and this has been linked to the other major trend, namely the gradual disappearance of the manufacturing surplus. From the massive surpluses of the 1950s, the trade surplus as a proportion of GDP fell to an average of 5.6% in the 1960s, and 3.4% in the 1970s before it vanished altogether in 1982. By 1988, the deficit on manufacturing trade was over £14 billion, equivalent to 3.8% of GDP (Table 6.4). From producing 17% of world manufacturing exports in 1960 (similar to West Germany with 19%, but well above France, 10% and Italy 5%), the UK in 1986 accounted for just 8% (compared to West Germany 21%, France 9% and Italy 8%).

The UK has traditionally had a current account surplus, with the positive balance on invisible items being more than sufficient to offset deficits on the trade in visible goods. The period since 1970 has seen a departure from this pattern. Poor export performance in the early 1970s combined with OPEC price rises to push the current balance into deficit during 1973–77. When North Sea oil came on stream in the late 1970s, the current account moved sharply back into surplus, reaching £6.9 billion in 1981; even the visible balance was positive during 1980–84. Since then the situation has been reversed. With a growing manufacturing deficit, and a fall in the oil surplus, a domestic consumer boom (at a time when the considerably diminished UK manufacturing sector was operating at near full capacity) made matters worse by sucking in imports. In 1987, the visible trade deficit was £10 billion, and this figure had doubled by 1988, when it reached £21 billion. The surplus on invisibles has been insufficient since 1986 to cover the visibles deficit, and in 1988 – after allowing for the invisibles surplus of nearly £6 billion – the current account was still £14.7 billion in the red. The trade deficit, which has continued to be in this order of magnitude, is a matter of some concern. Table D 23 in the Statistical Annexe shows it to be by far the highest among EC economies in 1988; higher in fact – as a proportion of GDP – than the 'crisis' US trade deficit of 1987.

6.5.2 *The exchange rate*

Since the abandonment of the fixed rate in favour of a 'managed' float in 1972, the general trend in the value of the pound has been downwards, with periods of depreciation being followed by only partial recovery. In spite of its possession of oil, and the currently high interest rates, the UK exchange rate compared with its value in 1970, has depreciated by more than all but one of the long-standing members of the Community. The Dutch, Belgium/Luxembourg, and West German currencies appreciated against the ECU over the period 1970–89, while those which depreciated – the currencies of France and Denmark – did so to a smaller extent than sterling. Leaving aside the newer and less developed entrants to the EC, including Spain, only Italy has experienced a greater fall in the value of its currency since 1970. A relatively poor UK trade performance, together with the country's generally higher inflation rates, has been behind this pattern.

Most of the pound's fall since 1970 occurred during the first half of the period. Its value (in currency units per ECU) dropped by around 55% between 1970 and 1978. There was then a period of recovery by sterling, reflecting the move back into current account surplus, the build-up of North Sea oil production, relatively high interest rates and a favourable reassessment by speculators of prospects for sterling given a Monetarist government and petro-currency status. Coinciding as it did, however, with a rise in the prices of UK goods relative to foreign goods, this increase in the pound's value was accompanied by a serious loss of UK competitiveness, resulting in recession and a sharp rise in unemployment. In contrast, as Table D 24 in the Statistical Annexe shows, EC competitors experienced a *fall* in their currency values in the early 1980s. Since that time sterling's value has once more moved downwards, from an index value of 116.7 in 1981 (1980=100) to 91.5 in 1987, before slowly improving to 97.1 in 1989. Plainly, the UK derives little benefit in terms of competitiveness from the 1989 exchange rate compared to that of 1979. The value of sterling was down only marginally over that period, compared with much sharper depreciations affecting the peseta, franc and lira (see Statistical Annexe, Table D 24 and Figure D 1).

Since the abolition of UK capital controls in 1979, interest policy has played an increasing role in exchange rate management, with the adjustment of short-term rates being used to influence the net flow of speculative funds ('hot money') into the country and thus demand for the currency. Even so, for almost a decade following 1976, interest rates were adjusted principally with reference to domestic monetary conditions. The high exchange rate of the early 1980s, through making imports cheaper in terms of pounds, helped in the fight against inflation.

However, since the mid-1980s at least, when inflation was considered to be under control, the government has made use of short-term interest rates – backed up by intervention on the currency markets (buying and selling sterling) – to keep the pound steady at a lower level. The impact of this was to give an expansionary boost to the domestic economy. The fall in oil prices from 1986 was expected to act as a counterweight to the inflationary effects of currency depreciation. Problems have, nonetheless, arisen due to the fact that the main lever for influencing both domestic money supply and the value of the exchange rate is the interest rate. Thus in 1988, when interest rates were raised to curtail excessive monetary growth, the resulting influx of short-term funds from abroad put upward pressure on the pound at a time of serious current account deficit. The selling of pounds on the international money markets was not sufficient to prevent a rise in the value of sterling and a loss of international competitiveness.

6.5.3 *The value of the pound and UK manufacturing*

A major influence over the UK exchange rate has been the production of oil from the North Sea. It is this which, more than any other factor, dramatically improved the current account in the late 1970s and so exerted strong upward pressures on the value of sterling. In so doing it reduced the competitiveness of the non-oil tradeable sector, principally manufacturing, causing it to decline seriously.

There has been much debate over the significance of this development and the related deficit in the manufacturing trade balance. To one body of economists, the worsening manufacturing balance reflects simply a shift in the UK's comparative advantage: other sectors – agriculture, services and oil – have all become relatively more important within the economy and manufacturing less central. The shift in the manufacturing trade balance is, according to this argument, simply a response to market forces working through the exchange rate mechanism, as UK manufactures are priced out of some markets by the higher value of the pound. The process, which has taken place over a long period, was simply accelerated in the first half of the 1980s. The appropriate response to oil-induced exchange rate appreciation, it has been argued, is to allow oil proceeds to be used to build up assets overseas via portfolio and direct foreign investment. This was facilitated in the case of the UK by the abolition of exchange controls in 1979, which gave rise to an increase in outward portfolio investment by banks and non-bank intermediaries (pension funds, unit trusts, and insurance companies) from an average of £400 million in the second half of the 1970s to one of over £10 billion per year during 1981–86. With UK outward direct investment overseas over that period around double the level of investment in the UK, the country became one of the largest net creditor nations in the world, with net external assets valued at £100 billion in 1988 (lower than the totals for West Germany and Japan, but higher than both in terms of percentage of GNP). This stock of assets is expected to provide a continuing source of income as the oil surplus declines, while the currency depreciation accompanying the loss of oil revenue will provide an opportunity for other sectors – such as services, but possibly a leaner and fitter manufacturing sector also – to expand their exporting role.

On the other hand, there are those who contend that the manufacturing trade performance reflects government neglect of the sector, particularly during the 1979–82 period, when high interest rates and an overvalued pound compounded the problems of producers already facing a world recession. Proponents of this view argue that the contraction forced upon manufacturing was inappropriate given an oil surplus known to be temporary in nature. They argue that it is unrealistic to expect to be able to switch in and out of manufacturing, and are sceptical that invisibles will be able to compensate for the falling oil surplus and manufacturing decline. They would appear to have a point, given that many traded services are linked to manufacturing, only 20% of services are traded internationally (compared to 50% for manufactures), and the fact that many UK service sectors are actually in deficit (e.g. travel and tourism, sea transport, and civil aviation). This group of economists argue that the proceeds of oil should have been directed towards a programme of industrial regeneration, or – given the lack of profitability in manufacturing at the time – into investments in infrastructure (roads, education and training), with positive long-term effects on industrial competitiveness as oil production declines.

6.6 Special issues

6.6.1 *Investment in Research and Development*

One such area crucially affecting future industrial competitiveness is Research and Development (R&D). For some time it has been clear that the UK has been falling behind its trading partners in terms of its investment in relevant R&D. This is reflected in the fact that, almost regardless of industry, the UK has tended increasingly to export lower value, less R&D-intensive products ('mature' technology), and to import high value new technology items. Its exports are thus in areas where world demand is growing relatively slowly, as well as being more open to competition from newly industrialising countries.

A recent OECD study of firm-funded industrial R&D showed that the volume of activity in West Germany was more than double that of the UK, and that the real rate of growth of R&D expenditure over the 1967–83 period was 1.1% in the UK, compared to 5.6% in Germany and over 5% in most major European countries. Taking R&D expenditure from all sources, as a share of GDP, the UK is at the same level as in 1963 (2.25%), when it was second only to the USA. By the mid-1980s, Germany, Japan and Sweden had all overtaken the UK. The situation is not helped by the relatively high concentration of R&D effort on defence industries. While the total government-funded R&D spending (as a share of GDP) was in 1987 higher than in some EC countries and virtually identical to that in Germany, a relatively large proportion (around one-half) goes on defence-related projects. This is a similar proportion of GDP (0.5%) to that going on defence-related R&D in France, but it is far higher than the equivalent figure for Italy, Germany and Sweden. The spin-off to the wider industrial economy from this expenditure is limited, due to the specialised nature of defence products, and security-related restrictions on the diffusion of resulting technological developments. Continuing weakness in the area of R&D will restrict UK participation in the growth of trade in high technology products.

6.6.2 *Education and training*

The tendency to concentrate on lower technology products is linked to the comparatively poor UK performance in terms of education and training. R&D is unlikely to be fully exploited unless management and workforce have the appropriate skills. The fact that in a recent report the UK was placed 22nd out of 23 industrialised countries in respect of the overall quality of its workforce, gives some credence to the view of economists who argue that the UK is caught in a low skill/low technology vicious circle. In the 1980s, compared to most other advanced industrial nations, Britain produced fewer graduates overall, had a smaller stock of scientists relative to the population, and a lower output of engineers and technologists. Recent research has shown that UK school children show a lower level of achievement in science than children of the same age in 17 other countries studied. The UK is the only major nation where the majority of pupils leave full-time education or training at the age of 16, with the result that a larger proportion of the UK labour force have less upper-secondary education than in other major economies.

The low level of educational attainment is not offset by higher levels of work-based training. A recent EC survey showed that only 38% of the UK workforce has experienced training, compared to 50% in Portugal and 80% in France. UK firms devote on average just 0.15% of turnover to training compared to 1%–2% in Japan, West Germany and France. Despite this, government initiatives on training place great reliance on the role of the private sector, and are widely criticised for the relatively low level of public financial support, which seems unlikely to offer sufficient incentive to bring about the major expansion in private training required. At a time when it would seem to be appropriate for government to be expanding its real expenditure on training, the already inadequate level is due to be reduced further in coming years.

6.6.3 *Transport*

Another important area of weakness involves transport infrastructure. With 1992 looming, efficient transport links are vital in overcoming cost disadvantages for the UK in general and the peripheral regions in particular. Although the construction of the Channel Tunnel is well underway, the UK is failing to put in place the supporting infrastructure. Increasing congestion on roads – itself a reflection of a relative lack of investment (Germany and France both spending considerably more than the UK on road infrastructure) – is making rail links of potentially great importance in a relatively compact Europe, particularly if nineteenth-century infrastructure can be adapted to technological developments permitting high speed rail transport. An integrated high speed rail network is taking shape on the continent, and the UK is lagging well behind on this. The government has just refused to commit funds to a high-speed rail link between London and the Chunnel, making it possible that such a line will not be built. Even if it were to go ahead, the link would not now be in operation until the turn of the century. Further such links to elsewhere in the country – perhaps connecting with the west-coast ports – are even further away.

Given the time lag before such schemes can come to fruition, it is unfortunate that severe curbs placed by government on public spending during the 1980s prevented strategic investments in transport infrastructure offering real cost savings over the long term. Similar long-term benefits might have derived from higher investment in education, training and civil R&D. For reasons largely of dogma, the 1980s have been characterised by a preference for private market-based decisions over collectivist solutions. This has limited spending in a number of areas where competitor states have been prepared to commit public resources towards the achievement of long-term strategic advantage. Free marketeers would argue that 'government failure' can lead to misplaced investment which is wasteful of resources. But what about market failure? In the longer term, it may be the case that the UK government's insistence upon reliance on the market in key areas of resource allocation caused too short-term a view to be taken, resulting in the loss of long-term opportunities for growth and development.

6.7 Assessment and future prospects

The end of a decade of 'Thatcherism' has been the occasion for assessing the government's achievements, and the prospects for the economy in the 1990s. The previous sections have pointed to a number of positive developments – including output and productivity growth, a budget surplus, rising living standards and falling unemployment – which the government would ascribe to the freeing of markets and a new spirit of enterprise engendered by supply-side policies of cuts in marginal tax rates, deregulation, privatisation and a 'new realism' among labour buttressed by trade union reform. There is another view, however, which questions both the 'achievements' of the 1980s and the notion that the UK's long-run economic trajectory has been dramatically altered.

Taking the achievement claims first, comparison with 1979 shows that current (mid-1990) unemployment, at over 1.6 million, is still considerably above the figure the Thatcher government inherited from the last Labour government. This can only rise given the deflationary measures currently in use to reduce inflationary pressures and the trade deficit. Inflation itself – the government's principal target – is very similar (measured by the RPI) to the mid-1979 level (10.3%), as well as being above that in other industrial economies. The trade deficit is the worst in UK history, and proportionally the largest among industrial nations. With the oil bonanza almost at an end, some observers insist that the UK is returning to the old 'stop-go' pattern of the 1960s and 70s. This argument is based on the fact that the prolonged expansion of the economy has been sustained by, first of all, the contribution of North Sea oil, and secondly, since 1987, by a massive inflow of foreign savings (attracted in by high interest rates to cover the current account deficit). Whereas previously the high propensity of the UK to import has seen domestic booms quickly brought to a halt by balance of payments problems, in the 1980s North Sea oil and the vastly increased supply of footloose funds on the international market permitted the UK to enjoy a more sustained boom.

For critics, the worrying aspect to this development is the fact that much of the output and employment growth has been concentrated upon the (internationally) non-traded sector, principally within services. The poor performance in terms of output growth in traded goods and services, has meant that increased domestic spending on these items has involved more imports and a rising trade deficit. The manufacturing sector may have shown impressive rates of productivity growth, but actual output growth has been comparatively small (the UK is placed eighteenth among OECD countries in terms of manufacturing output growth over the period 1979–88), and the sector has failed to recover the losses which it incurred in the early 1980s. Production by the sector is now arguably *too small* in relation to the economy's requirements, particularly for the achievement of full employment.

While UK citizens have been benefiting from a consumer boom, insufficient resources have been put aside for investment purposes, particularly in those areas where international competitiveness is important. Domestic savings have been run down in favour of private consumption, and only a proportion of foreign savings coming in to cover the external deficit has been directed towards investment. The government has contributed to this through its restrictive attitude towards public investment and its preference for personal income tax reductions.

The real test of the Thatcher policy experiment is now taking place, as the government reins back private expenditure and seeks to correct the trade imbalance. This will involve a response from the sectors of the economy exposed to international competition, since their output – and particular that of manufacturing – will have to grow rapidly in the next few years. Without this, a very sharp cutback in consumer expenditure will be required, with knock-on effects in the non-traded sector of the economy and a sharp fall in employment.

Industry is undoubtedly leaner and fitter as a result of recession-induced restructuring and the supply-side measures of the 1980s, and there are signs of a response by the sector to the new circumstances. Sterling's loss of petro-currency status has resulted in the pound falling from its highly uncompetitive level of the first half of the 1980s, and this has been accompanied by a rise in manufacturing output of nearly 20% in the 2½ years to 1989, and a jump in manufacturing investment from £9.6 billion (1986) to £12 billion in 1989 (1985 prices). Changes during the 1980s in the legislation relating to trade unions have significantly curtailed the power of labour to strike or take other industrial action, and this, plus the fall-off in union membership (to below 50% of employees in employment in 1986), has allowed managers to introduce new work practices.

There is, nonetheless, concern about the potential for continued rapid growth of the manufacturing sector. The UK is recognised as having some strong sectors, such as chemicals and pharmaceuticals, but fundamental structural weaknesses exist in that its industrial resources are too thinly spread without strength in depth; in contrast to West Germany and Japan, hardly any of Britain's industries have high world market shares. Among other things, this reflects UK corporate strategies which have increasingly opted for specialised product lines aimed at niche markets, rather than standardised products for mass markets. While 'British firms have undone some past sins', wrote one analyst recently, 'most have yet to create the basis for future growth'. Nor is their competitive position strengthened as a result of the government's recent decision to enter the European Exchange Rate Mechanism at a comparatively high sterling exchange rate.

6.8 Bibliography and sources of information

UK Government/Official Publications
Bank of England Quarterly Bulletin
Central Statistical Office, *Annual Abstract of Statistics,* HMSO
Central Statistical Office, *Economic Trends,* HMSO (monthly plus annual supplement)
Central Statistical Office, *United Kingdom National Accounts* (the 'Blue Book'), HMSO (annual)
Central Statistical Office, *Regional Trends*, HMSO (annual)
HM Treasury, *Economic Briefing* (Available free from COI, Hercules Road, London, SE1 7DU) (three editions per year)
HM Treasury, *Treasury Bulletin*, HMSO
House of Lords, *Report from the Select Committee on Overseas Trade,* HL 238 (HMSO 1985)

General Textbooks on the UK Economy

Artis, M.J. (ed.), (1989) *Prest & Coppock's The UK Economy: a manual of applied economics,* 12th Edition, Weidenfeld & Nicolson Ltd, London.
Curwen, P. (ed.) (1990) *Understanding the UK Economy,* Macmillan Education Ltd, Basingstoke.
Harbury, C. & Lipsey, R.G. (1989) *An Introduction to the UK Economy*, 3rd Edition, Pitman Publishing, London.
National Institute of Economic & Social Research (NIESR) (1990) *The UK Economy*, Studies in the UK Economy, Heinemann Educational, Oxford.

Part C

International comparisons

7 International Comparisons

Dr Frans Somers

7.1 Introduction

This last chapter deals with international comparisons, examining similarities as well as differences in the developments in the five major European countries. The role of government has diminished in all five countries in favour of more market-oriented policies. This movement is obviously consistent with the overall market orientation of the Community policies. There are differences too, however. Changes in Italy have not been as profound as in the degree to which this has occurred with for instance the UK, leaving the other countries somewhere in between. This subject is discussed in Section 7.1, where the possibility of disparities in policies within the framework of the emerging economic and monetary union are also reviewed. Sections 7.2 and 7.3 deal with output, growth and international competitiveness of the five countries. It will be shown that Germany is in a strong position to take advantage of the internal market, while perspectives for the French economy look promising as well. The benefits for the other economies are more uncertain in the short run. Marked differences in the financial systems still exist within the EC, especially in relation to the financing of firms. The UK holds a rather unique position in this area. This is covered in Section 7.4, where the differences in monetary policies are also discussed.

In Section 7.5 a speculative attempt is made to identify possible fields of national specialisation within the framework of the coming reallocation of factors of production within the Community. Section 7.6 draws some final conclusions, one of which is that, despite some shift in favour of the importance of regions vis-à-vis nation states in the future European Community, the significance of national states will, nevertheless, for the greater part be unimpaired.

7.2 The reduced role of government

7.2.1 *The return of free-market ideologies*

The economic crisis of the 1970s and the early 1980s marked a turning point in views on the role of government in the mixed economies of the Western World. The general consensus on state interventionist policies in the Keynesian welfare state broke down.

After the Second World War social tensions in Europe were reduced considerably by the settlement of a kind of 'historical compromise' between labour and business management. Private enterprise and the freedom of the market were accepted by labour, in return for collective bargaining, social security, income and full employment policies and demand management. For business management this arrangement meant reasonably harmonious labour relations, political stability, assured demand and motivated workers. The welfare state enjoyed wide political support from both conservative and progressive parties. Naturally, there were differences in political opinions and aims, but in most West European countries these differences tended to be fairly small. Parties on both the extreme left and extreme right generally attracted a limited number of voters. Only in France and Italy did the communist parties remain significant; though even in these countries they were unable to gain power. The main exceptions were Spain and Portugal, both ruled by right-wing dictatorships, and both with highly regulated, centralised and autarchical economies with protected interests for vested business groups.

Income and production in Western Europe increased very rapidly in the decades following the Second World War. Average GDP real growth rates amounted to about 5% and unemployment was reduced to low percentage levels. The Keynesian welfare state seemed to enjoy a measure of success in generating prosperity, employment, social security and harmonious industrial relations. Among theorists, a certain degree of consensus emerged; with a majority believing that a regulated market economy would lead to optimal results.

Within this framework of a 'mixed economy', the degree of regulation, however, remained a subject of extensive debate. In Germany, for instance, the idea of planning in any form was widely rejected. France on the other hand adopted a system of 'indicative planning', intended to establish a state controlled framework for the market economy. There remained also differences of opinion on the issues of nationalisation of key industries, the extension of social security systems and the size of the public sector in the various West European countries. But the extremes on the one hand, a free market economy and on the other hand a centrally planned economy, were almost completely abandoned as realistic options; instead a convergence of economic policies along the lines of Keynesian theories took place.

There were two main causes for the breakdown of the general post-war consensus on economic policies which took place from the early 1970s: (a) the economic crisis and (b) the internationalisation of the economy.

(a) *The economic crisis* is generally dated from the early 1970s. The rapid economic growth of the post-war decades had started to slow down, mainly because of increasing labour costs, saturation of output markets, surplus capacity and environmental constraints. The economy experienced serious difficulties after the first oil shock in 1973; and after some recovery, further serious problems accompanied the second oil price hike in 1979. Both oil shocks resulted in very rapidly increasing input prices for industry, putting a very strong upward pressure on inflation. This process was reinforced by a rapid expansion of the money supply, resulting in a situation of 'stagflation': a situation of inflation and stagnation combined. The welfare state proved unable to deal with mass unemployment and stagnating economic growth, because these phenomena put heavy pressure on government expenditure while reducing revenue simultaneously. The social safety net of the welfare state was built for individual cases, not for mass unemployment. Thus, the 1970s was marked by increasing government expenditure, deficits and rising taxes, adding an increased tax burden to already depressed business profitability. Reduced profits meant a deepening of the crisis and gave rise to a vicious circle via lower investment and shut-down of firms. Keynesian demand policies were generally not effective in face of this crisis, because the problems were essentially located on the supply side: rising costs of inputs of energy and labour.

(b) *The internationalisation of the economy* resulted, among other things, in an intensification of competition. Domestic industries became more exposed to the world economy. Companies were forced to lower costs to compete in world markets, demanding improvement of efficiency and putting downward pressure on wages and labour.

In order to support their industries, governments were inclined to decrease taxes and reduce social security contributions and to relax labour protection.

Another consequence of the increasing internationalisation was the reduced ability of national governments to implement stabilisation policies. To be effective, such policies should be carried out more and more on a global scale, via supranational authority, as yet not in existence.

The above developments paved the way for what could be called a new paradigm in economic theory and practice. Many economists and politicians blame the problems of the 1970s and early 1980s on government involvement in the economy. The welfare state, it is argued, created too heavy a burden for business and resulted in rigidities in many markets, particularly the labour market. Prices were distorted by taxes and subsidies, resulting in misallocation of production factors; profits were squeezed. And on top of that, governments were inclined to cover their deficits by monetary financing, fuelling inflation in the process. This is not the place to discuss the relative merits of these arguments. Indeed, some can be inverted: the welfare state did not cause high levels of government expenditure and the consequent economic crises, rather economic crisis resulted in high levels of government expenditure. Similarly, deficits (e.g. the US deficit) can be seen as acting as a locomotive for the stagnating world economy instead of slowing it down.

The point here is that from the 1970s on there has been a strong preference among economists and most governments of the Western World in favour of a return to the principles of the free market. This tendency has been reinforced by the events in Eastern Europe, where the failure of the planned economy became manifest.

In practice, free market principles have not been wholly dominant. It can be argued that an undoubted advocate of the free market like Ronald Reagan, President of the United States from 1980 to 1988, combined supply-side measures with Keynesian demand policies. In Europe, pollution and other urgent environmental problems called for new regulations. But the general tendency of the last decade is clear. Most Western governments, whether led by Christian or Social Democrats, by Socialists, Liberals or others, have been in favour of 'more market and less state' ideologies. To a certain degree that is in line with the Community policies in Europe which, as we have seen in Part A, are largely founded on free market principles. But substantial differences nevertheless exist in the approach to the role of government by the various countries in the EC. These distinctions could become important barriers to further economic integration, particularly to the Economic and Monetary Union (EMU).

7.2.2 *Policy shifts in the major EC countries*

United Kingdom: sweeping reforms

Arguably it is the *United Kingdom* that has made the most pronounced changes towards creating a more liberal economy. These changes were set in motion when the Thatcher administration came to power in 1979. What has been said above about breaking an existing consensus is especially applicable to the UK. 'Thatcherism' stands for the abandonment of Keynesian demand management, deregulation of labour and capital markets, denationalisation of state enterprises, withdrawal of subsidies to industries, dismantling of labour union power, reduction of government expenditure and taxes and the eradication of the budget deficit. The only goal which has eluded the government has been that of controlling the money supply.

The Thatcher government was able to carry out such a sweeping shift in policy because the British political system normally guarantees that one party will be in power.

Federal Republic of Germany: moderate changes

In comparison with the UK, reforms in the Federal Republic of *Germany* have been moderate. In Germany, too, tax reforms, reductions in the growth of government expenditure, elimination of the budget deficit, deregulation and some privatisation have been carried through. But, alongside the UK, changes since the beginning of the 1980s have been more gradual. A tight monetary policy and an anti-inflationary stance have been consistent factors in German political attitudes ever since the War. The *Bundesrepublik* never experimented with forms of economic planning and established few large state enterprises. Public sector ownership is mainly limited to the holding of private sector company assets or shares by the federal government or the states.

Arguably, the biggest change has been the shift from short-run stabilisation and full-employment to long-run growth policies. Demand management was renounced in favour of supply-side policies. These policies included measures to decrease labour and other costs (for instance by reducing the tax burden), deregulation (e.g. in the field of telecommunications, transport and housing) and privatisation (in the form of selling of government assets).

France: role of government still significant

The last decade has also witnessed a remarkable policy shift in *France*. Though France can be considered as a market economy, it has a long tradition of state intervention, which goes back as far as the mercantilist policies of the 17th-century statesman Colbert (see Chapter 3). Changes took place only after a fruitless attempt during the early 1980s to combat the crisis with intensified state intervention. After 1982, which can be considered as a watershed year in French politics, the ruling Socialist government became converted to supply-side politics. To a certain extent it was forced to do so, because the French membership of the EMS effectively prevented the depreciation of the French franc in order to restore competitiveness and reduce the trade deficit. The free market principles of the Community influenced an individual member state to act according to common principles in relation to a matter which could be considered as a one of national sovereignty.

A whole range of measures to strengthen the supply-side were implemented, from austerity policies to denationalisation and deregulation. The famous French system of 'indicative planning' was partly dismantled and the rigid French financial markets liberalised (in 1984). Industrial policy shifted from supporting specific industries and enterprises to provision of a favourable overall business environment. Nevertheless, state intervention has not altogether vanished in France. The role of government remains significant when compared with most other Community countries. Privatisation has been limited in extent and large state enterprises still exist. In 1990 state-owned companies still accounted for about one-third of the French GDP and state-owned manufacturing and banks alone employed 1 million persons or so.

After an attempt by the right-wing Chirac government in the second half of the 1980s to abolish the planning process completely, the new Socialist government, which came into power in 1988, came up with a new Plan. This 10th Plan (the 10th since the War), designed for the period 1989–92, defines a range of targets, some of which require a substantial government involvement. Government-financed education and civil research, for example, will get high priority, and the level of social security will be maintained. This approach is noticeably different from the British one, and also, to a lesser extent, from the German one.

Spain: liberalisation led by the State

For different reasons *Spain* is also moving in the direction of a freer market economy. This is mainly caused by Spain's efforts to integrate in the world economy in general and the European economy in particular. This integration represents a distinct break with the practices of the Franco era. The early Franco period was characterised by extensive and wide-ranging public intervention, the existence of large dominant industrial groups, the complete absence of social concertation and high external trade barriers. The year 1959 marked the initial turning point. Spain became a member of the OEEC (the predecessor of the OECD) in that year and started a liberalisation process by removing controls and relaxing import restrictions. This development gathered momentum after Franco's death in 1975 and particularly after Spain's entry into the European Community in 1986.

The Civil War and the first period of Franco's dictatorship (1939–59) are crucial to understanding why Spain still lags so far behind in Western Europe. The international isolation, monopolistic structure and the rigid state intervention were responsible for a long period of stagnation in the Spanish economy. That is why Spain has been liberalising its highly centralised economy since 1959 and is aiming to convert it eventually into a market-dominated system. But before the Spanish economy can be fully exposed to international competition (planned for the end of 1992), its industry needs to be modernised, competitiveness enhanced and productivity increased. It is quite remarkable, however, to observe that the restructuring of the Spanish economy along market lines has not only been performed by relaxation of controls and regulations, but also in large measure by state intervention. The state has sought, for instance, to revitalise traditional manufacturing sectors, to stimulate technological innovation, to build a social security system and to remove rigidities in the labour market.

The restructuring measures have met with considerable success since Spain is catching-up very rapidly. Compared with other advanced market economies, however, the involvement of the Spanish government in industry is still very large. Total financial support for the business sector in the middle of the reconstruction process (in the mid-1980s) rose to over 5% of GDP, which is the highest percentage within the EC next to Italy. A large part of these transfers and subsidies went to public enterprises. They have been only partly reduced since, preventing the market-determined structural adjustments. Despite a vigorous privatisation programme in the 1980s, Spanish state-owned businesses still accounted for 9% of GDP by the end of the decade. On the other hand, the provision of public services (e.g. health care services, public education and transportation) is still underdeveloped. This could become an important constraint for continuing growth. Generally, a sufficient level of these services is considered to be a necessary condition for the functioning of the market; that is why the Spanish government, despite a tight budget policy, is intending to give public investment a high priority in the near future.

Italy: still a high degree of state intervention
Of the five countries covered, *Italy* is probably least effected by the reinvigorated neo-liberal free market ideology of the 1980s. Like France it has a long tradition of state intervention. General government was responsible for more than a quarter of total investment in Italy in the second half of the 1980s; direct investment by the public sector in a broad sense (including state enterprises and public and semi-public enterprises in which the State has a large stake) accounted for 6.5% of GDP in the period 1980–87 according to OECD figures. Italy devoted a larger part of its GDP to aiding industry than any other major European country in the early 1980s. A substantial proportion of this aid was destined for (not especially successful) development programmes for the South of Italy and for the support of ailing industries. Public expenditure, too, increased considerably in the last decade, mainly due to transfers to families and companies and payments to service the rising national debt.

Nevertheless, in Italy, too, a movement towards the free market can be observed. There has been a shift in industrial policy towards favouring the more advanced and strategic sectors, encouraging R&D expenditure and stimulating export performance. The financial system has been deregulated and capital can move more freely, especially since Italy accepted the Community Directive on this which came into force in July 1990.

A beginning has also been made on a programme of privatising of State enterprises. The main aims of this policy are the reduction of the public debt and the strengthening of the role of the market in the economy. Public enterprises and the public service sector in general in Italy are notorious for their inefficiency; the discipline of the market is expected to reduce costs and to increase productivity.

As yet, however, this denationalisation process has not gone as far as in the UK, or even France. A large State enterprise sector remains a distinctive characteristic of the Italian economy, accounting for about one-third of GDP (as in France). The three major state companies (IRI, ENI and EFIM) employ 550,000 people.

One of the main reasons why major policy shifts in Italy have not been carried out thus far is to be found in the Italian political system. Radical political solutions and economic measures are ruled out by the fragmented political power and the necessity to form coalition governments, as Fineschi points out in Chapter 4. This is a major contrast to the situation in for instance the UK, where the political system facilitated significant changes.

7.2.3 *European integration and government involvement in the economy*

Does the completion of the internal market and the coming of the EMU require a further convergence in economic policies, e.g. in the field of fiscal policies? To a certain extent it surely does. Large inflation, wage and productivity differentials between EC countries cannot be offset any more by national use of the exchange rate mechanism. Large and sustained budget deficits can result in inflationary pressures, which in turn can threaten the common monetary policy of the Community (to be implemented by the future European Central Bank). Fiscal discipline is therefore supposed to be a crucial component of EMU.

With regard to fiscal policies, (more) convergence for indirect taxation and capital income taxation is certainly needed, because these taxes relate to free-moving goods and capital. According to an EC report of 1990 on the EMU, however, there is no case for an overall harmonisation of the tax systems; member states would remain free to choose their tax and spending levels. Tax differentials, especially of income taxes and social security contributions, do not necessarily cause individual citizens to move if higher tax levels are matched by higher public welfare provisions and vice versa. This raises the question of the cost of public goods and services. First, there is the issue of efficiency. An inefficient public sector, like in Italy, will result in higher costs, to be financed by higher taxes. Second, countries with high debts have to devote a relatively large proportion of their budget to servicing their debts. This means that (as in Italy) their public goods provisions will be low compared with their tax levels.

So, a mismatch of taxing and levels of public provisions can be a reason for citizens moving from one country to another in order to maximise their benefits and minimise spending.

Apart from this mismatch, moreover, benefits and costs of public goods can spill over from one country to another. This applies for instance to transportation and telecommunication provision and a clean environment.

Finally, divergent redistributive policies can cause spill-over effects if persons with higher incomes are allowed to migrate to countries with low tax regimes and if those entitled to social benefits also have some freedom of choice in selecting a country in which to reside (e.g. after leaving the workforce).

It may be that a complete harmonisation of fiscal policies is not needed. But there are clear limits to the extent to which disparities may occur. In the emerging Common Market, the level of taxation and public goods will be prominent elements in the increasing rivalry between national states. Governments want to offer favourable conditions for business; hence it is most likely that there will be a downward pressure on taxes.

For public goods and services the question is more complicated. On the one hand, a high level of public provision will strengthen national competitiveness; on the other hand, financial constraints (because of higher taxes) and the possibility of cross-frontier spill-over effects will have a negative impact on government spending.

This inclination to lower public provision may be offset partly by common regulations, which will involve long and complicated negotiations. The fact remains, however, that the intensified competition in the Common Market, together with the loss of national autonomy, tend to result in a further reduction in the role of government in the EC. This tendency may be reinforced if competition increases due to an economic recession. The traditional instrument of protection cannot now be used; hence governments will be inclined to reduce tax burdens in order to enhance competitiveness.

State aid to industry is also under threat. This aid distorts free competition and is one of the barriers to be (at least partly) removed in order to achieve a barrier-free internal market after 1992. It is likely therefore that despite vigorous opposition from countries like France and Italy, EC limits to state aid will be tightened in the near future.

For all these reasons it seems likely that the trend towards a free market economy, which started in the 1970s, will be furthered by the process of the European unification.

7.3 Output and growth

The period 1984–90 constitutes a period of considerable growth for the European Community, with an average real growth rate of almost 3% (Eur12). This period was preceded by a deep recession, with average real Eur12 GDP growth slackening to 0.2% in 1981. The recovery of the European economy has been remarkable. Nevertheless, recent European real growth rates have still lagged quite far behind the US and Japanese figures. The USA achieved in the same seven prosperous years, a real growth rate of 3.9%, and Japan 4.5% (see Table 7.1.). The major European countries together grew 2.9%; though there were quite noticeable differences in economic performances within the group.

Table 7.1 Real GDP growth rates of the five major European countries, the USA and Japan, 1960–90

	Germany*	Spain	France	Italy	UK	USA	Japan
1970–79	3.1	3.8	3.7	3.2	2.4	2.7	5.2
1980–83	0.6	1.0	1.5	1.6	0.5	0.9	3.6
1984–90	2.9	3.4	2.5	3.2	2.7	3.9	4.5
1960–90	3.1	4.6	3.7	3.9	2.4	3.2	6.4

*Federal Republic

Spain: highest growth rates

The highest rates of growth were recorded by Spain and Italy. Apart from short cyclical disturbances, *Spain* has shown high growth rates ever since it began to liberalise its economy by the end of the 1950s. The average real growth rate over the last 30 years is about 4.6%; the highest (after Greece) of the twelve countries of present EC. For all that, Spain has been confronted by very serious imbalances, in respect of high unemployment and inflation rates, large trade deficits and substantial regional disparities. Its infrastructure and social security system are still underdeveloped. Despite the progress made, Spain's *per capita* income is still only three-quarters of EC12 average.

For Spain in particular, with its economy still on an intermediate level, it will be of vital importance to increase productivity while controlling labour costs. The key factor for the Spanish economy is to enhance competitiveness and to keep real unit labour costs at an acceptable level in order to withstand European competition after 1992.

Italy: impressive

For *Italy*, too, growth in the last 30 years has been impressive. With an average rate of 3.9%, it is comfortably above the EC12 average and surpasses most other European countries, including Germany. But like Spain, growth lacked balance in a number of respects.

First, there is an immense regional problem, with marked disparities between Centre-North and the South (*Mezzogiorno*). It can be argued that these disparities constitute an impediment to the further development of the more prosperous parts of Italy. Support for local industries, development plans and unemployment benefits put large claims on the budget already in deficit. A substantial part of the trade deficit is also attributable to the stagnation in the South. Second, servicing the rising national debt and transfers to families and companies are crowding-out urgently required public investments in infrastructure and public services. Third, public services in Italy are very inefficient and ill-suited to an advanced economy like the (North and Central) Italian economy. Public education, too, should be upgraded to meet the growing demand for well-trained management. Fourth, wage increases and inflation rates are both too high, resulting in a deterioration of competitiveness and a persistent balance of trade deficit.

Many of the above disequilibria are interrelated and call for (sometimes radical) political solutions. Not an easy task if the fragmented Italian political system is taken into consideration. On the positive side, the private sector, especially the small and medium-sized industrial enterprises, has proved itself a strong feature of the Italian economy, and has shown itself capable of adapting to changing conditions. Italian entrepreneurship has proved to be very vibrant and innovative. A substantial reduction of the disequilibria would strongly improve the effectiveness and the overall performance of the Italian economy.

Germany: moderate, but solid and stable growth

Growth of the *Federal Republic of Germany* has been very moderate; in the 1984–90 period it occupied a middling position with a real GDP growth rate of 2.9%. From 1960 to 1990 its growth rate of 3.1% put it, not only behind Spain and Italy, but also behind France. The German expansion, however, has been very solid and stable and it has been achieved without many imbalances. Inflation rates and the budget deficit have been very modest. Unemployment, however, though relatively low if compared with other European countries, is considered as too high in Germany, especially in the last decade. Another notable disequilibrium consists of the persistent current account surpluses. Nevertheless, in sum, Germany's economy seems to be 'shock-proof' more than any other, mainly because of its solid character and its basically sound structure.

However, there are three major concerns for the German economy. The first is the high level of labour costs. This level can only be maintained if Germany manages to achieve a sustained increase in productivity. The competitive advantage of the German economy lies in its ability to develop quality products with a high-tech content, not in its labour costs. If it wants to keep up with its main rivals the USA and Japan, it needs to continue to devote a large proportion of its GDP to investment and research and development. The second concern is fear of loss of German dynamism. The growth of capital formation is rather low for a innovation-driven economy. There are some signs of changing attitudes towards risk-taking and entrepreneurship. New business formation is stagnating and there is a tendency among big firms to co-operate; both factors may be attributed to a decline in domestic competition. Rigidities in the labour and capital markets and a high degree of industry regulation in the field of working and closing hours, entrance requirements and competition rules also undermine flexibility, dynamism and ultimately international competitiveness. The third concern is related to German unification, which took place in October 1990. The integration of the former GDR will put a heavy burden on Germany as a whole, resulting in inflationary pressures in the short-term, large-scale bankruptcies and increasing unemployment in the eastern part of the country, a rising budget deficit, environmental problems, etc. Forecasts for the short-term of the five leading German Economic Research Institutes indicate a decrease of 10% or so in production and income in East Germany, slowing down the overall German growth rate by some 1% next year. This problem comes at a time when growth rates are already dropping off, mainly due to cyclical factors, the Gulf crisis and, to a lesser extent, environmental problems. The German economy, however, seems sufficiently strong to cope with these problems; after the initial effects, a successful integration may possibly raise the German long-term growth trend. Because of a catching-up process, East German growth could take off at a later stage and then eventually surpass West German growth, increasing the combined German figure. Together with the challenge of the emerging Internal Market, the unification process may also contribute to a revival of German entrepreneurship and dynamism.

United Kingdom: recovery not founded on a firm base yet

Long-term growth in the *United Kingdom* has been the lowest of the five countries under consideration: only 2.4% during 1960–90. This is basically due to the poor performance of the UK economy in the period preceding the last upswing in the international economy in the 1980s. Since then, the country succeeded in keeping pace with the average trend within Europe. The Thatcher government claimed the credit for this recovery, ascribing it to the return to the market and supply-side policies. The British service industry – and especially the financial sector – have expanded sharply in the last seven years. However, the present British economy still exhibits important structural weaknesses.

First, the recent growth has been accompanied by growing inbalances within the economy. Inflation is, despite vigorous attempts to fight it, rather persistent, saving and investment (especially in R&D) remain comparatively low; and regional disparities have increased. Since 1986 the current account has deteriorated and there is now a large deficit. Underlying the latter is the lack of competitiveness of British industry, manufacturing in particular. There is a tendency for UK manufacturing to concentrate on lower value products, as Stone explains in Chapter 6. A positive element, however, is the high level of direct foreign investment in the UK, Japanese in particular. This development could contribute substantially to a revitalisation and modernisation of British manufacturing, for example in the field of (electrical) engineering, office machines and vehicles. Second, the example of the UK clearly highlights the negative aspects of rigorously implemented supply-side and other-market oriented policies. Public investment in infrastructure has been neglected, with serious consequences for public transport, education, training and the level of R&D. A satisfying level of public provision is arguably a necessary condition for a flourishing private sector. The current insufficient level of provision of public goods is one of the explanations for the deterioration of the competitiveness of British industry. To conclude; although there clearly have been positive developments in the UK economy in the last decade, future prospects for the UK economy do not seem to be especially bright. The recovery of the British economy is not founded upon a particularly firm base as yet. Some policy adjustments in order to secure long-term growth would seem to be necessary.

France: strong improvements

The *French economy* has strongly expanded in the mid-1980s, after a deep recession in the beginning of this decade. It appears that it is returning to its long-term growth path characterised by a comfortable overall real GDP growth rate of 3.7% on average over the last 30 years. Generally the French recovery has been attributed in large part to the successful adjustment policies implemented by consecutive governments since 1983. There has been an impressive increase in exports and investment, which has restored the growth momentum. Still, France also has its problems. The sluggish expansion of production capacity is becoming a major constraint for further economic growth. Gross investment has contributed little to capacity expansion hitherto, because of simultaneous large withdrawals of obsolete capital equipment.

This capital-deepening trend is narrowly related to another problem of the French economy: unemployment. After reaching a peak in the middle of the 1980s of well over 10%, unemployment has proved to be rather persistent, even in times of output expansion. Rigidities on the labour market seem to be the major reason for this development, which also explains – at least partly – the capital-deepening trend.

Another cause for concern is the vulnerable external position. Although the current account is normally approximately in balance, the trade balance (visible trade) is not. This is mainly due to a severe deterioration of the manufacturing trade balance in the 1980s, brought about by the lack of specialisation of French industry and, to a lesser extent, the unfavourable geographical orientation of French exports. Further modernisation of French industry, a shift away from the traditional areas in French-speaking Africa and the Middle-East, and a continuing reduction of market rigidities (especially on the labour market) would appear to be required. Investment, education and – last but not least – European unification should play a significant role here. In general terms, however, the overall picture for France looks rather sound. Apart from the effects of international business cycles the French economy should be capable to maintain the upward long-term trend.

In this section we focused mainly on long-term growth perspectives. The last seven years (1983–90) constituted a very favourable period for the world economy. The year 1990, however, marked a turning point in the business cycle; it is to be expected that the world economy will slide into a recession in the early 1990s. Overheating, rising inflation, interest rates and oil prices, slowing growth rates and political problems around the Gulf are the precursors to this development. It is not expected, however, that this recession will be as severe as the one in the early 1980s. The economic basis of business, as well as the public sector in most EC countries is much sounder than it was a decade ago. Moreover, there are also positive aspects, notably the political détente, the developments in Eastern Europe and the European integration process.

With regard to the European integration, it would be reasonable to conclude that, in terms of economic structure, growth potential and competitiveness, Germany seems to be best prepared to benefit from the coming common internal market after 1992, followed by France. For Italy, 1992 will offer many new opportunities but also many new problems with which it will have to deal. For Spain the crucial question will be whether it can succeed in completing its restructuring and catching up process before the end of 1992. Finally, the position of the UK in the proposed EMU may be quite vulnerable in the short run. Some sectors (services and financial services in particular) will clearly benefit while others are not really prepared yet to face full exposure of European competition. The manufacturing sector, for instance, will be confronted with sweeping adjustments; these adjustments will probably be aided by the high level of inflow of foreign investment from the Far East in particular. Infrastructure, for instance in the fields of education, transport and research is underdeveloped, mainly because of the low current level of public provision. In the long-run, however, Britain's reluctance to participate fully in progress towards EMU may prove disadvantageous. Integration in a large economic entity such as the EC is of vital importance for the British economy. Britain's future, too, lies within a united Europe.

With this preliminary conclusion in mind, it is not surprising that Germany and France in particular are strong supporters of the integration process, while the UK, in certain respects, is hesitant. Apart from political reasons, like the fear of loss of sovereignty, there are also a number of economic arguments affecting the attitudes of the present European governments towards 'Europe'.

7.4 Productivity and competitiveness

7.4.1 *The overall picture*

National competitiveness is affected by inflation, unit labour costs and productivity growth in relation to exchange rates. It is usual to consider these factors as they relate to tradeable goods and services. The competitiveness of the European economy as a whole improved strongly in the 1980s, even relative to Japan and the USA. In the case of Japan, this is largely explained by the appreciation of the yen over the decade. By the middle of the 1980s the dollar too increased very strongly in value, which has a very negative impact on the US competitiveness. In the second half of the 1990s the dollar depreciated dramatically to reach in 1990 an even lower level than a decade earlier. This fall has, nevertheless, only partly offset the acquired competitive advantage of the European economy during the 1990s vis-à-vis the USA.

Considerable progress has thus been made, mainly due to very moderate wage increases and sharp rises in productivity. The modest wage rises can be attributed (at least partly) to a Phillips curve effect: unemployment and the unfavourable economic conditions of the beginning of the 1980s considerably reduced the bargaining power of the trade unions and hence resulted in limited wage demands. Labour productivity rose because of the lay-off of workers in company rationalisation measures and the capital-deepening investment policies implemented by employers in response to the economic crisis in the early 1980s. As a result, the real unit labour costs of the total European

economy decreased by 7% between 1980 and 1989, while they stabilised in the USA and fell by only 3.7% in Japan. The real labour cost
reduction contributed significantly to the improvement in company
profits.

More relevant for the degree of competitiveness, however, are the
unit labour costs of exported goods and services. If we take the double-
weighted* nominal unit labour costs of the total economy in a common
currency (relative to 19 industrial countries) as a standard, then the
competitiveness of the EUR12 countries as a whole rose by 22.6% between
1980 and 1989, while the American and the Japanese competitiveness
fell by 8% and 38% respectively (see Statistical Annexe, Table D 15).

7.4.2 *The major European countries*

For individual European countries their national degree of competitiveness is much more important, however, especially since over 50% of
their exports goes to other member states of the Community. If we look
at the figures of the five major European countries, striking differences
can be observed (see Figure 7.1). Competitiveness in Germany and

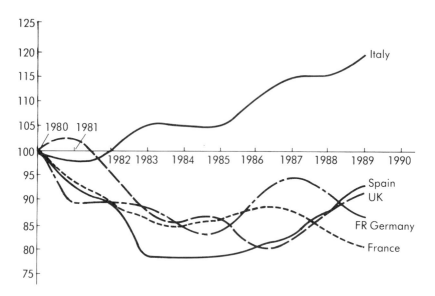

Figure 7.1 National unit labour costs in a common currency (USD): total
economy. Relative to 19 industrial countries; double export weights,
1980–89

*Weighted for geographical orientation and basket composition.

France clearly improved in the 1980s. This can be explained by sharp increases in productivity and moderate wage rises. Spain and the UK made an impressive start in the first half of the decade, but fell back in the second half mainly due to inflationary pressures. The growth of annual earnings has been quite considerable in the UK and has not been compensated by productivity growth. The deterioration of competitiveness by the end of the 1980s was somewhat slowed by the depreciation of sterling, but the upward trend is, nevertheless, clear. Again it explains Britain's hesitation in the past to join the EMS (and the European integration process in general), because the UK's membership will largely rule out use of the exchange rate mechanism. So the entry of the UK in the ERM in October 1990 may even worsen Britain's competitive position in the short run. Inflationary pressures in Spain were mainly caused on the demand side. Buoyant demand in an economy operating near capacity resulted in a gradual overheating and a tendency for inflation to rise. This tendency can be reinforced in 1990 by cost-push factors, such as increasing energy prices, which are of particular relevance for the import-dependent Spanish economy. Wage rises tend to accelerate from 1989, among others due to a breakdown of the social dialogue and the absence of *social concertation* in general.

Italy's experience is quite different. Its steep deterioration in competitiveness in the 1980s compared to other European countries seems to be dramatic; but this is a too black and white a conclusion. Admittedly, for the Italian economy as a whole, wage increases are higher than improvements of productivity. After a marked diminution of pay rises in the beginning of the decade, provoked by the unfavourable economic circumstances, wage inflation picked up again in the second half of the 1980s. This can be explained by the regained strength of trade unions, the continuing rise of social security transfers and the generally high level of inflation in Italy.

The problem, however, is that Italy should perhaps, in this respect, not be treated as one country. While wage negotiations are centralised and on a national level, productivity improvements are certainly not. There are marked disparities between the Northern and Central parts on the one hand and the South on the other. So the increase in labour unit costs in the South has been much more dramatic than in the Centre-North. These nuances notwithstanding, concern over Italian competitiveness is justified. Italian industry has lost some market share recently; a situation which will possibly be aggravated because Italian industry is not particularly strong in those sectors which will benefit most from the completion of the internal market (i.e. the advanced sectors). The removal of internal barriers will also sharpen rivalry in the more mature and labour-intensive sectors which are still of great importance for Italy. Decentralisation of wage negotiations, an industrial policy encouraging

R&D expenditure and the promotion of education and skills might be the main spearheads in a medium-term policy to reverse the negative trend in Italian competitiveness.

This brief discussion of competitiveness confirms the conclusion stated at the end of Section 7.3: Germany and France seem to be best placed to benefit from an united Europe, at least in the near future. For (parts of) Italy and the UK the situation is less propitious, while Spain might be seen to occupy a position somewhere in between.

7.5 Financial system

7.5.1 *The European financial markets*

Financial markets and financial intermediation play an important role in the economy. They provide, for instance, the following services:

- gathering financial surpluses (savings) and channelling these funds to investment opportunities (real and financial);
- allocation of financial resources to the most efficient users;
- spread of risks.

The financial sector is also quite important in terms of output and employment. In 1986 it accounted for approximately 6.5% of total value-added of the Community and for some 3% of total employment. An efficient financial system will obviously enhance economic welfare. The total amount of saving and investment will rise, new business formation will be encouraged and factors of production will be better allocated, increasing their productivity. That is why the Community puts heavy emphasis on the improvement of the European financial system by pursuing the establishment of a common European financial area. Distinct national banking regulation, high establishment costs for new banks, restrictions on foreign acquisitions or participations in indigenous banks, limitations in cross-frontier activities, exchange controls and other regulatory barriers have segmented the European financial markets and hence prevented their efficient operation thus far.

In line with most other Community policies, the creation of a common financial market is mainly sought via deregulation, removal of barriers and harmonisation of standards and banking licences and, last but not least, in strengthening of the Monetary System. Considerable progress has been made in the adoption by the European Council in 1988 of the Directive on the complete liberalisation of capital movements, which came into effect on 1 July 1990. From that moment on all restrictions on monetary or quasi-monetary transactions (financial loans and credits, current account, deposit account and stock market operations) were abolished. For member states facing balance of payments difficulties because of this capital liberalisation, the medium-term financial support facility (MTFS) was created, a regulation granting medium-term loans.

The free movement of capital is one of the cornerstones of the Common Market and also a prominent step in achieving the first stage of the EMU (see also Chapter 1, Section 1.2). Another important goal in this stage is the enhancement of the exchange rate stability of the Community currencies.

Notwithstanding this trend towards integration of the financial system within the Community, marked discrepancies in financial attitudes and practices can still be observed at present in Europe. Examples can be found in the field of:

(a) the financing of firms (see Section 7.5.2);
(b) monetary policies (see Section 7.5.3);
(c) stances and responsibilities of Central Banks (see Section 7.5.4).

7.5.2 *Financing of firms*

In the *financing of firms* there is a dominating role for banks (and special credit institutions) in Germany, Spain, France and Italy. Only in the UK is the stock market of major importance. Financing of companies through the stock market is also more widespread in the United States and especially in Japan. See Table 7.2.

Table 7.2 Stock market capitalisation at 29 December 1989

	Billion ECU	*% of GDP*
UK	557	74.1
FR Germany	236	21.8
France	182	21.1
Spain	62	18.1
Italy	95	12.1
Japan	2632	102.3
USA	1968	34.8

Source: European Economy Supplement A, No 8/9 1990

In both Spain and Italy, the stock market has been very underdeveloped up till now. This is less the case in Germany and France, where they are of growing importance. The method of company financing is of particular relevance in affecting management attitudes towards risk and profits. On the one hand, financing through stock markets has the advantage of spreading more widely business risks. This can encourage investment involving high risks, because banks are generally reluctant to engage in this kind of business. Another advantage of market-based financing is that financial vulnerability of companies will be reduced because equity is higher. Furthermore, public information on business will be more widely available because of legal disclosure requirements for firms issuing stocks and bonds. This will enhance transparency of the capital markets. Against this, it is recognised that security-based finance can result in a preoccupation of management with short-term profits and dividend goals as Stone explains in Chapter 6. Focusing on short-term objectives may have a negative influence on long-term development and performance. Most shareholders (including institutional investors) are not concerned with the running of companies, while banks generally supply expertise if they are financially involved in a firm.

If we apply the foregoing remarks to company financing in Europe, we reach the following conclusions. In Spain, Italy and arguably Germany stock markets should play a more prominent role. Well-developed, risk capital markets are missing in these countries, frustrating new business formation and new venture initiatives. In the UK, by contrast, the dominance of stock market financing prevents business management from achieving long-term goals and objectives, essential for survival and long-term profitability of the companies involved. The best solution may be a convergence of the two extreme positions; the UK shifting to long-term finance through banks and the other countries to a more security-based financing. There are clear signs that this is happening.

In Tables 7.3 and 7.4 some additional figures on the financial structure of enterprises in the five major EC countries are presented. Table 7.3 again highlights the prominent role of equity in the financing of British firms and the noticeable significance of short-term debt financing, for example, of French, Spanish and (especially) Italian firms.

Table 7.3 Financial structure of enterprises in the major EC countries (liabilities) – 1987

	Germany	Spain	France	Italy	UK*
1 Net capital	14.1	19.5	9.3	11.7	7.6
2 Reserves and provisions	28.3	20.2	21.4	21.4	42.7
3 Total capital and reserves (equity; = 1 + 2)	42.4	39.7	30.7	33.1	50.3
4 Medium- and long-term debt	18.3	14.1	23.1	10.2	7.2
5 Short-term debt	39.3	46.2	46.2	56.7	42.5
	100	100	100	100	100

*1986

Source: *Database of Harmonised Company Accounts* (BACH, DG II, October 1989)

Table 7.4 clearly indicates that financing through the stock market reduces financial risks. The ratio of indebtedness to equity for the UK is only a fraction of the French and Italian enterprises. Other than that, the financial soundness of enterprises in most countries has improved remarkably since the economic crisis of the early 1980s. Only France is a clear exception. Despite the vigorous improvement in profits in that country, self-financing has not been a major source of investment. Operations and the accumulation of productive resources is mainly financed by short and medium-term indebtedness and bonds. Table 7.4 also clearly demonstrates that profitability has risen enormously in each of the countries during the 1980s, with Germany and France (again) at the top of the list. Germany also confirms its solidity and relatively stable development: profitability during the economic crisis of the beginning of the decade did not fall as sharply as in the other countries.

Table 7.4 Profitability (P) and financial soundness (FS) of firms

	P^a		FS^b	
	1982	*1987*	*1982*	*1987*
FR Germany	12.7	18.7*	1.3	1.0
Spain	−2.2	4.4	1.6	1.2
France	−1.3	12.0	1.5	2.1
Italy	−12.6	7.7	2.0	1.4
UK	6.6	9.3*	0.5	0.5

*1986
$^a P$ = profits/total capital and reserves (equity)
$^b FS$ = short and medium-term indebtedness/equity
Source: European Economy Supplement A 8/9, 1990

7.5.3 *Monetary policies*

With respect to *monetary policies* there is a distinction to be made between Germany on the one hand, and Spain, Italy and the UK on the other. These differences mainly relate to the level of interest rates. Germany has a long-standing tradition for low interest rates. The Central Bank (*Bundesbank*) has needed to make relatively little use of (high) interest rates as a weapon against inflation, or as a way of attracting foreign capital. After the relative expansionary policies of the early 1980s, intended to counteract the economic crisis, monetary policy was tightened in the second half of the decade in an attempt to prevent overheating in the economy. Compared with other European countries and the USA, Germany's nominal interest rates remained very low, however, which also reflects the low inflation rate. Only recently, has there been some pressure to increase interest rates in order to reduce capital export. The situation is different for Spain and Italy. Spain, for instance, needs high interest rates to counter inflation and to attract the foreign capital required for its rapid expansion. Italy uses high interest rates to fight inflation and to attract short-term capital to support the exchange rate. The necessity to deploy the interest rate mechanism is more urgent in Italy, because this country needs to rely much more on monetary than on fiscal policy. Weak and unstable coalition governments are less able to implement consequent policies than the more independent financial institutions, as Fineschi points out in Chapter 5. The UK for some time has used manipulation of the rate of interest mainly to support an exchange rate which is inclined to drop because of the UK's persistent current account deficits. High nominal short-term interest rates are maintained to secure the inflow of short-term capital, to counterbalance the large current account deficits. Interestingly, nominal long-term interest rates are much more in line with the EC average.

Clearly, large nominal interest rate differentials will be hard to maintain, once monetary unification occurs. Expectations of high interest rates and capital yields will not then be tempered by anticipated currency depreciation or uncertainty. Again, it must be stressed that EMS and monetary policies are closely interrelated.

7.5.4 *Stance and responsibilities of Central Banks*

The *stance and responsibilities of Central Banks* vary greatly in the Community. At one extreme is the German Central Bank. The Deutsche Bundesbank is almost completely independent from the German Treasury. Its main goal is to support price stability and the value of the D-Mark. Furthermore, it is supposed to support the economic policy of the Federal Government, but only in so far as this policy *does not interfere* with its main task. This arrangement reflects the German preoccupation with inflation, originating from Germany's traumatic pre-war experiences. In general, it has proved to be very successful.

In Italy, too, the Central Bank is relatively independent of central government. Since 1982 it has no longer been obliged to act as 'buyer of last resort' of public debt bonds. This 'divorce from the Treasury' was mainly effected in order to ensure a more solid stance of monetary authorities towards inflation, government itself being too much left to the mercy of unstable political relations and interests.

The German and Italian systems are in sharp contrast to those of the British, Spanish and French. In France for example, the Banque de France is narrowly related to the centralised French state and played an even more important role in the state-induced credit distribution in the past.

In the UK, the Bank of England is a public sector body which acts under the (ultimate) authority of the Treasury, so the Bank of England can be considered a policy instrument of the British government.

In Spain too there are close links between the banking sector and government; besides the Central Bank (*Banco de España*) many banks are state-owned.

The different banking systems, and especially the position of Central Banks in these systems, constitute a major obstacle for the reaching of EMU. Germany especially is an avowed proponent of an independent federation of European Central Banks (Eurofed), which should be 'politician-proof' and, above all things, inflation-resistant. Some countries, led by the UK, however, are afraid of another loss of sovereignty. The opposite solution would be to bind the proposed Eurofed to the ultimate decision-making of ECOFIN (European Council of Finance Ministers). There are still many issues to be settled before a European Monetary and Economic Union is achieved.

7.6 National specialisation within the Community

The establishment of a large common market will almost certainly induce a reallocation of production factors and economic activities, according to each country's specific competitive advantages. This will be the case because artificial barriers, protecting inefficient industries, will be removed. This raises the question of how the distribution of industries will look in the future Europe. Obviously, nothing can be said for sure, but a tentative attempt can be made to identify some future industry patterns in Europe. A higher degree of specialisation can be expected in the field of tradeable goods and services along the lines of a country's or region's strong and weak points.

This raises the question of, first of all, by which conditions are comparative advantages of nations determined? It might be clear that this question is not simple to answer. According to Michael Porter, international successes of a particular (branch of) industry in a certain country are dependent on four determinants:

1 the costs and availability of factors of production;
2 demand conditions;
3 the presence of related and supporting industries;
4 firm strategy, industry structure and rivalry.

These determinants are strongly interrelated and form a kind of mutually reinforcing system (called a 'diamond' in Porter's terminology). Additional variables, influencing the national system, are government and chance. Without relying completely on Porter's system, one can appreciate, as he clearly demonstrates, that competitiveness is dependent on a whole range of conditions. A large and demanding domestic market, vigorous competition, sufficient scale, favourable physical conditions, a high concentration of related industries, a good infrastructure, entrepreneurship, starting positions and government support play a prominent role. With this in mind we will try to ascertain some possible fields of specialisation for the five major European countries (Table 7.5). The list, which does not pretend to be complete, is principally based on existing dominant positions and future perspectives.

Table 7.5 Possible fields of specialisation within the European Community

Germany

Manufacturing:
  electrical engineering (electric motors, generators, transformers, household appliances, telecommunications)
  mechanical and instrument engineering (machinery, machine tools and equipment, plant for mines, iron, steel)
  motor vehicles and motor vehicles parts and accessories
  metal articles
  chemicals

Spain

Services:
  tourism
Manufacturing:
  motor vehicles
  oil refinery
  electrical household appliances
  insulated wires and cables
  food and drink products
  footwear, household textiles, clothing
  rubber goods, ceramics
  wine, olive oil
Agriculture:
  fruit and vegetables

France

Services:
  tourism
  engineering
Manufacturing:
  data processing, office machinery
  motor vehicles, parts and accessories
  aerospace
  nuclear power and hydroelectricity

electrical equipment
food
drink (wine, brewing and malting, soft drinks, water)
pharmaceutical products
wool
Agriculture:
dairy, livestock produce, fruit and vegetables

Italy

Services:
tourism
design services, fashion
Manufacturing:
motor vehicle parts and accessories, motorcycles
textile and leather, footwear and clothing
furnishing
jewellery
machinery, machine tools
electrical household appliances
insulated wires and cables
food industry (manufactured pasta, wine)

United Kingdom

Services:
financial services (banking, insurance, financial intermediation)
business services (advertising, management consulting, accounting,
engineering)
trading services
Manufacturing:
chemicals (basic, industrial and agricultural)
pharmaceuticals
aircraft, aircraft parts and engines
office machinery, computers and computer parts, software
printing and publishing
telecommunications equipment
electrical plant and machinery and other equipment
brewing, soft drinks
Energy:
oil products

Specialisation within a particular country in a certain field of industry in this list does not mean that other countries will retreat from this kind of activity; it merely indicates that this country has or will possibly develop a leading position in branches of this industry. Moreover, dominant positions can be shared with other countries. Apart from these specialisations, many industries continue to exist in virtually every country, simply because these industries are hardly able to serve more than local markets (e.g. construction and most services).

The table shows that – in broad terms – it is to be expected that Germany will remain the industrial workshop of Europe, the UK the financial heart and Italy the designing and fashion centre. Similarly striking national specialisations cannot so easily be identified in France or Spain; only in tourism do these countries occupy relatively dominant positions (a position which they share with Italy). The scope of activities in both countries is fairly broad; France being engaged in industrial activities at a more advanced level and Spain still at an intermediate level. The key to the German success is a high level of productivity, quality and reliability. Maintaining and strengthening the German position will crucially depend on R&D, education and stability. German competitiveness in international services is rather weak. The UK has a leading position in this field, with the City of London the third financial centre of the world, along with New York and Tokyo. Recent technical innovations and deregulation have led to the reinforcement of the dominant position of the City. London is confronted more and more, however, by competition from its continental rivals in Frankfurt and Paris in particular. Commitment to Europe is an essential condition for London to maintain its position. The use of English as a major language of communication may be one of the explanations of the strong presence of the UK in the international business service market. Italy's powerful place in the area of design, fashion, apparel and related industries can be attributed to the sophisticated demand of the domestic market and the country's ability to develop these kind of activities also in small and medium-sized companies, which are typical of the Italian private sector. The strength of the French nuclear power and defence industry is partly due to favourable government procurement and state intervention policies and the independent attitude with regard to national defence of consecutive French governments.

A dominant position, once established, tends to reinforce itself. The removal of administrative barriers can act as a further catalyst. So, the 1992 project will have a positive effect on national specialisation.

7.7 Final conclusions

In concluding this book, we will return to the subject of the importance of national states within the emerging European Economic and Monetary Union. The completion of the EMU before the end of the millennium will mean that monetary and budgetary policies will be carried out chiefly by a central authority, backed up by centrally controlled policies in the field of infrastructure, education, R&D, environment, regional and competition. Important responsibilities left to national governments are expected to be the supply of public goods (those without cross-frontier effects), income transfers and redistribution and fiscal policies (in part).

This transfer of power from national to a supranational level means a considerable reduction of national sovereignty and will lead to a loss of significance of the national states as independent entities.

This development notwithstanding, there will remain substantial geographical differences within the Community. These differences are determined by distinct industry patterns, inequalities in economic development and performance, variations in mentalities, tastes and culture, and will even be reinforced by an eventual higher degree of local specialisation.

With the national states losing influence as economic and political entities, however, regions probably will become relatively more important. Barriers between neighbouring regions will be broken down and cross-frontier contacts intensified.

Regions within nations will possibly be of increasing importance as well. This can apply to differences between rural and urban areas, but also to differences between one agglomeration and another. New opportunities and increased competition caused by the integrated market may emphasise not only local specialisation, but also disparities and unequal developments between regions. National instruments to adjust these developments will be partly dismantled or transferred to the Community level. Size, effectiveness and degree of differentiation of the Community policy in this respect is not clear yet. But despite of this expected shift in relative importance from the national to the regional level, national differences will probably remain of great interest, even in a united Europe.

7.8 Bibliography

Commission of the European Communities, *European Economy* (4 issues per year) plus *Supplement A: Economic Trends* (11 issues per year)

OECD, *County Surveys* (annually)

The Economist Intelligence Unit, *Country Reports* (4 issues per year)

Part D

Statistical annexe

List of tables

Main economic indicators 1961–90

Population

Labour force and employment

Gross domestic product

Wages and productivity

Consumption, saving, investment

Prices

Government

D 18   Total expenditure, general government
D 19   Net lending or borrowing general government (% of GDP, market
       prices)

Finance

D 20 (A and B)   Nominal short-term (A) and long-term (B) interest
                 rates

International relations

D 21 (A and B)   Structure of EC exports (A) and imports (B) by country
                 and region, 1958/1988
D 22   Exports of goods and services at current prices (% of
                 GDP)
D 23   Balance of payments by main heading
                 Net flow in Mio ECU 1987
D 24   Exchange rates: ECUs per national currency unit, 1979
                 = 100

Figures

D 1   ECUs per national currency unit, 1979 = 100

Sources

All data are derived from official EC publications:

European Economy, nr 42, Statistical Annexe: Tables 1 − 6, 9 − 12,
     15 − 22, 24.
Eurostat, *Basic Statistics of the Community,* 27th Edition (1990): Tables
     7, 8, 13, 14, 23.

1989 and 1990 figures are estimates and forecasts made by Commission
staff using the definitions and latest figures available from national
sources.

Symbols and abbreviations used

B   Belgium
DK   Denmark

D	Federal Republic of Germany
GR	Greece
E	Spain
F	France
IRL	Ireland
L	Luxembourg
NL	The Netherlands
P	Portugal
UK	United Kingdom
EUR12	Total of Member States of the EC
–	nil
:	not available
Mio	Million
ECU	European Currency Unit
PPS	Purchasing Power Standard
GDP	Gross Domestic Product

Main economic indicators, 1961–90[1]

Main economic indicators, 1961–90

Table D 1 Federal Republic of Germany (Annual percentage change, unless otherwise stated)[1]

	1961–73	1974–81	1982	1983	1984	1985	1986	1987	1988	1989	1990
1 Gross domestic product											
At current prices	8.9	6.7	3.7	4.8	4.8	4.3	5.5	4.0	5.2	6.2	6.3
At constant prices	4.4	1.9	−0.6	1.5	2.8	2.0	2.3	1.9	3.7	3.8	3.5
Price deflator	4.3	4.7	4.4	3.3	2.0	2.2	3.1	2.0	1.4	2.4	2.7
2 Gross fixed capital formation[2]											
Total	4.0	0.1	−5.3	3.2	0.8	0.1	3.3	1.8	5.9	7.7	5.1
Construction	:	−0.9	−4.3	1.7	1.6	−5.6	2.7	0.2	4.7	4.8	3.2
Equipment	:	2.1	−7.0	5.6	−0.2	9.9	4.3	4.1	7.5	11.3	7.4
3 Share of gross fixed capital formation in GDP[3]											
Total	24.9	21.2	20.5	20.5	20.2	19.7	19.5	19.4	19.8	20.7	21.1
General government	:	3.5	2.8	2.5	2.4	2.3	2.4	2.4	2.3	2.3	2.3
Other sectors	:	17.6	17.6	18.0	17.8	17.4	17.1	17.0	17.5	18.3	18.8
4 Inflation (Price deflator private consumption)	3.6	5.0	4.7	3.2	2.4	2.1	−0.2	0.7	1.1	3.1	2.7
5 Compensation per employee											
Nominal	9.2	7.1	4.2	3.7	3.5	3.1	3.9	2.9	3.1	3.1	3.4
Real, deflator private consumption	5.4	2.0	−0.5	0.5	1.0	1.0	4.1	2.2	2.0	0.0	0.7
Real, deflator GDP	4.6	2.3	−0.2	0.4	1.5	0.8	0.7	0.9	1.7	0.7	0.7
6 Productivity[4]	4.1	2.3	1.1	3.1	2.7	1.3	1.3	1.2	3.0	2.3	2.1
7 Real unit labour costs[5]											
Index: 1961–73 = 100	100.0	103.7	102.2	99.6	98.4	97.9	97.4	97.0	95.8	94.2	92.9
Annual percentage change	0.5	0.0	−1.2	−2.5	−1.2	−0.5	−0.6	−0.3	−1.3	−1.6	−1.4
8 Relative unit labour costs in common currency Against 19 competitors											
Index: 1961–73 = 100	100.0	111.5	97.8	97.1	92.6	91.0	99.5	104.8	101.2	95.9	93.3
Annual percentage change	2.3	−2.6	−0.3	−0.7	−4.6	−1.8	9.4	5.3	−3.4	−5.2	−2.7
9 Employment	0.2	−0.4	−1.7	−1.5	0.1	0.7	1.0	0.7	0.6	1.4	1.3
10 Unemployment rate[6]	:	3.7	6.8	6.9	7.1	7.3	6.5	6.4	6.4	5.6	5.4
11 Current balance[7]	0.7	0.5	0.5	0.7	1.3	2.6	4.4	3.9	4.1	5.3	5.8
12 Net lending (+) or net borrowing (−) of general government[7]	:	−3.0	−3.3	−2.5	−1.9	−1.1	−1.3	−1.8	−2.1	0.0	−0.4
13 Gross debt of general government[7]	:	28.8	39.3	40.9	41.8	42.5	42.7	43.9	44.6	43.3	42.6
14 Interest payments by general government[7]	:	1.7	2.8	3.0	3.0	3.0	3.0	2.9	2.8	2.7	2.6
15 Money supply (end of year)[8]	10.9	8.1	7.1	5.3	4.7	5.0	6.6	5.9	6.9	5.5	:
16 Long-term interest rate[9]	7.2	8.1	9.0	7.9	7.8	6.9	5.9	5.8	6.1	7.0	8.9

Notes; see page 250

Table D 2 Spain (Annual percentage change, unless otherwise stated)

	1961–73	1974–81	1982	1983	1984	1985	1986	1987	1988	1989	1990
1 Gross domestic product											
At current prices	14.8	19.1	15.2	13.6	12.9	11.1	14.6	11.8	10.9	12.3	10.8
At constant prices	7.2	1.8	1.2	1.8	1.8	2.3	3.3	5.5	5.0	4.7	4.0
Price deflator	7.1	17.0	13.8	11.6	10.9	8.5	10.9	5.9	5.7	7.3	6.6
2 Gross fixed capital formation[2]											
Total	10.4	−1.3	0.5	−2.5	−5.8	4.1	10.0	14.6	14.0	13.9	9.9
Construction	:	−1.6	0.1	−2.0	−5.2	2.0	6.5	10.0	13.5	14.6	10.9
Equipment	:	−0.5	2.2	−4.8	−7.3	9.1	15.8	24.2	14.7	12.8	8.7
3 Share of gross fixed capital formation in GDP[3]											
Total	24.2	23.9	21.3	20.6	18.8	18.9	19.2	20.7	22.5	24.4	25.7
General government	:	2.2	3.1	2.8	3.0	3.7	3.7	3.5	3.8	4.2	4.4
Other sectors	:	21.7	18.2	17.7	15.7	15.2	15.5	17.1	18.7	20.2	21.3
4 Inflation											
(Price deflator private consumption)	6.6	17.5	14.5	12.3	11.0	8.2	8.7	5.4	5.1	6.8	6.3
5 Compensation per employee											
Nominal	14.6	21.2	13.7	13.8	10.0	9.4	9.5	6.4	6.4	7.6	7.1
Real, deflator private consumption	7.5	3.2	−0.7	1.3	−0.9	1.1	0.7	0.9	1.2	0.7	0.8
Real, deflator GDP	7.1	3.6	−0.1	1.9	−0.9	0.8	−1.2	0.4	0.7	0.3	0.5
6 Productivity[4]	6.5	3.3	2.2	2.3	4.3	3.7	1.0	0.1	2.0	1.1	1.4
7 Real unit labour costs[5]											
Index: 1961–73 = 100	100.0	104.7	102.1	101.8	96.7	94.1	92.0	92.3	91.1	90.3	89.6
Annual percentage change	0.6	0.3	−2.2	−0.3	−4.9	−2.8	−2.2	0.3	−1.3	−0.8	−0.8
8 Relative unit labour costs in common currency											
Against 19 competitors											
Index: 1961–73 = 100	100.0	120.8	117.6	103.4	102.8	102.3	105.6	109.1	114.4	122.2	124.8
Annual percentage change	1.8	1.4	−3.2	12.1	−0.5	−0.5	3.2	3.3	4.9	6.8	2.1
9 Employment	0.7	−1.5	−0.9	−0.5	−2.4	−1.3	2.3	5.4	2.9	3.5	2.5
10 Unemployment rate[6]	:	7.5	16.3	17.8	20.6	21.9	21.2	20.5	19.6	17.6	16.5
11 Current balance[7]	−0.2	−2.0	−2.5	−1.5	1.4	1.6	1.7	0.1	−1.1	−2.9	−4.0
12 Net lending (+) or net borrowing (−) of general government[7]	:	−1.3	−5.6	−4.8	−5.5	−7.0	−6.1	−3.6	−3.2	−2.6	−2.4
13 Gross debt of general government[7]	:	15.5	28.7	35.1	41.9	47.2	48.0	48.3	44.1	43.8	42.0
14 Interest payments by general government[7]	:	0.6	1.0	1.3	2.0	3.2	3.8	3.5	3.3	3.4	3.5
15 Money supply (end of year)[8]	:	18.6	16.6	16.2	13.3	12.9	12.2	13.6	10.3	12.9	:
16 Long-term interest rate[9]	:	:	16.0	16.9	16.5	13.4	11.4	12.8	11.8	13.6	14.8

Notes; see page 250

Table D 3 France (Annual percentage change, unless otherwise stated)

	1961–73	1974–81	1982	1983	1984	1985	1986	1987	1988	1989	1990
1 Gross domestic product											
At current prices	10.7	13.7	14.6	10.5	8.9	7.6	7.2	5.0	6.7	6.7	6.0
At constant prices	5.4	2.5	2.5	0.7	1.3	1.7	2.1	2.2	3.4	3.3	3.2
Price deflator	5.0	11.0	11.7	9.7	7.5	5.9	5.1	2.8	3.2	3.3	2.7
2 Gross fixed capital formation[2]											
Total	7.7	0.2	−1.4	−3.6	−2.6	2.8	2.9	3.7	7.3	5.6	5.5
Construction	:	−0.2	−2.5	−3.6	−2.9	0.6	2.5	3.3	4.3	3.8	3.4
Equipment	:	0.7	1.6	−3.5	−0.9	6.7	2.5	4.7	9.7	7.0	7.0
3 Share of gross fixed capital formation in GDP[3]											
Total	24.0	23.3	21.4	20.2	19.3	19.2	19.1	19.4	20.1	20.5	21.1
General government	:	3.3	3.4	3.3	3.0	3.2	3.2	3.0	3.3	3.2	3.2
Other sectors	:	20.0	17.9	17.0	16.2	16.0	15.8	16.3	16.8	17.3	17.9
4 Inflation (Price deflator private consumption)	4.8	11.5	11.5	9.7	7.7	5.8	2.7	3.1	2.7	3.5	2.7
5 Compensation per employee											
Nominal	9.9	14.9	14.1	10.1	8.2	6.6	4.1	3.7	3.8	4.0	4.0
Real, deflator private consumption	4.8	3.0	2.3	0.4	0.5	0.8	1.4	0.6	1.1	0.5	1.3
Real, deflator GDP	4.6	3.5	2.1	0.4	0.7	0.7	−0.9	0.9	0.6	0.7	1.3
6 Productivity[4]	4.7	2.3	2.4	1.1	2.3	2.0	1.9	2.1	2.8	1.8	2.0
7 Real unit labour costs[5]											
Index: 1961–73 = 100	100.0	106.0	108.0	107.2	105.6	104.3	101.4	100.1	98.0	96.9	96.3
Annual percentage change	−0.1	1.2	−0.3	−0.7	−1.5	−1.3	−2.8	−1.2	−2.1	−1.1	−0.6
8 Relative unit labour costs in common currency											
Against 19 competitors											
Index: 1961–73 = 100	100.0	95.6	89.9	87.1	85.1	86.8	89.2	88.7	85.3	82.4	81.1
Annual percentage change	−0.8	0.3	−4.9	−3.1	−2.3	2.0	2.8	−0.6	−3.9	−3.4	−1.5
9 Employment	0.7	0.2	0.2	−0.4	−0.9	−0.3	0.2	0.1	0.6	1.4	1.2
10 Unemployment rate[6]	:	5.2	8.3	8.2	9.9	10.3	10.4	10.5	10.2	9.5	9.1
11 Current balance[7]	0.4	−0.1	−2.1	−0.8	0.0	0.1	0.5	−0.4	−0.4	−0.5	−0.5
12 Net lending (+) or net borrowing (−) of general government[7]	:	−1.0	−2.8	−3.2	−2.8	−2.9	−2.8	−2.0	−1.4	−1.2	−1.1
13 Gross debt of general government[7]	:	23.5	27.9	29.5	31.8	33.2	33.8	35.2	35.8	35.5	35.3
14 Interest payments by general government[7]	:	1.3	2.0	2.6	2.7	2.9	2.9	2.8	2.8	2.7	2.8
15 Money supply (end of year)[8]	13.7	13.4	11.4	11.5	9.5	6.8	6.3	7.3	7.3	7.9	:
16 Long-term interest rate[9]	6.9	11.7	15.6	13.6	12.5	10.9	8.4	9.4	9.0	8.7	10.0

Notes; see page 250

Table D 4 Italy (Annual percentage change, unless otherwise stated)

	1961–73	1974–81	1982	1983	1984	1985	1986	1987	1988	1989	1990
1 Gross domestic product											
At current prices	11.0	20.8	16.5	16.2	14.9	12.1	10.6	8.9	10.1	10.1	9.8
At constant prices	5.3	2.6	0.2	1.1	3.2	2.9	2.9	3.1	3.9	3.5	3.0
Price deflator	5.4	17.7	16.2	15.0	11.3	8.9	7.5	5.6	6.0	6.3	6.6
2 Gross fixed capital formation[2]											
Total	4.3	0.5	–5.7	–0.1	5.3	2.5	1.4	5.2	4.9	5.2	4.0
Construction	:	–0.4	–6.6	1.1	0.0	–0.6	0.7	–1.3	3.7	4.0	3.0
Equipment	:	1.9	–4.4	–4.2	9.3	8.2	2.0	15.0	6.0	6.2	4.8
3 Share of gross fixed capital formation in GDP[3]											
Total	25.9	24.4	22.3	21.3	21.3	21.1	20.0	19.9	19.8	20.1	20.0
General government	:	3.0	3.7	3.7	3.6	3.7	3.5	3.5	3.4	3.4	3.4
Other sectors	:	21.4	18.6	17.6	17.7	17.3	16.4	16.4	16.3	16.6	16.6
4 Inflation											
(Price deflator private consumption)	4.8	17.6	15.9	15.0	11.7	9.3	5.8	4.8	4.9	6.3	6.0
5 Compensation per employee											
Nominal	11.6	20.5	16.2	15.9	11.8	10.3	7.4	9.0	8.8	9.2	8.0
Real, deflator private consumption	6.5	2.5	0.2	0.8	0.0	1.0	1.6	4.0	3.8	2.7	1.9
Real, deflator GDP	5.9	2.4	0.0	0.8	0.4	1.3	–0.1	3.2	2.7	2.7	1.4
6 Productivity[4]	5.7	1.9	–0.3	0.4	2.8	2.0	1.9	2.9	2.5	2.6	2.4
7 Real unit labour costs[5]											
Index: 1961–73 = 100	100.0	107.5	107.8	108.2	105.7	104.9	102.9	103.2	103.3	103.4	102.4
Annual percentage change	0.2	0.5	0.3	0.4	–2.3	–0.7	–2.0	0.3	0.2	0.1	–1.0
8 Relative unit labour costs in common currency											
Against 19 competitors											
Index: 1961–73 = 100	100.0	88.8	92.1	98.6	98.1	97.5	103.2	107.7	108.0	111.7	115.0
Annual percentage change	–0.3	–0.3	1.3	7.1	–0.5	–0.6	5.9	4.3	0.3	3.4	2.9
9 Employment	–0.4	0.7	0.6	0.6	0.4	0.8	0.9	0.2	1.4	0.9	0.6
10 Unemployment rate[6]	:	7.0	8.7	9.0	9.5	9.4	10.6	10.1	10.6	10.5	10.6
11 Current balance[7]	1.5	–0.7	–1.6	0.3	–0.7	–0.9	0.5	–0.1	–0.6	–1.3	–1.4
12 Net lending (+) or net borrowing (–) of general government[7]	:	–8.4	–11.3	–10.6	–11.6	–12.5	–11.6	–11.1	–10.6	–10.2	–9.8
13 Gross debt of general government[7]	:	58.7	66.4	72.0	77.1	83.7	88.0	92.7	95.9	98.2	100.2
14 Interest payments by general government[7]	:	4.5	7.1	7.5	8.0	8.0	8.5	8.0	8.2	9.0	9.1
15 Money supply (end of year)[8]	15.4	18.5	18.0	12.3	12.1	11.1	9.4	8.3	8.4	10.8	:
16 Long-term interest rate[9]	7.0	14.2	20.9	18.0	15.0	14.3	11.7	11.3	12.1	13.0	13.3

Notes; see page 250
[1] 1961–88: Eurostat and Commission services.
1989–90: Economic forecasts.
[2] At constant prices.
[3] At current prices.
[4] GDP at constant market prices per person employed.
[5] Deflator GDP.
[6] Percent of civilian labour force.
[7] Percent of GDP.
[8] M3.
[9] Levels.

Table D 5 United Kingdom (Annual percentage change, unless otherwise stated)

	1961–73	1974–81	1982	1983	1984	1985	1986	1987	1988	1989	1990
1 Gross domestic product											
At current prices	8.4	16.7	8.9	9.2	6.6	9.4	6.8	8.9	11.0	9.0	7.5
At constant prices	3.2	0.7	1.2	3.8	1.8	3.6	3.1	3.8	4.2	2.2	2.1
Price deflator	5.1	15.9	7.6	5.2	4.7	5.6	3.6	4.9	6.6	6.7	5.3
2 Gross fixed capital formation[2]											
Total	4.6	−1.8	5.4	5.0	8.6	3.8	0.9	5.5	13.1	4.6	1.7
Construction	:	−3.3	8.8	5.0	6.1	−2.2	3.7	3.9	6.5	−1.4	−1.0
Equipment	:	−0.1	1.3	4.8	11.4	10.1	−1.8	7.2	20.4	10.3	4.0
3 Share of gross fixed capital formation in GDP[3]											
Total	18.5	18.8	16.2	16.1	17.1	17.1	16.9	17.3	18.8	18.8	18.6
General government	:	3.4	1.6	2.0	2.1	2.0	1.8	1.6	1.2	1.5	1.5
Other sectors	:	15.4	14.6	14.1	15.0	15.1	15.1	15.7	17.6	17.3	17.1
4 Inflation											
(Price deflator private consumption)	4.8	15.1	8.8	4.8	5.1	5.3	4.4	3.9	5.0	5.3	5.5
5 Compensation per employee											
Nominal	8.3	17.1	8.4	8.6	5.3	6.7	7.4	6.9	7.4	8.3	8.7
Real, deflator private consumption	3.3	1.7	−0.3	3.6	0.2	1.4	2.8	3.0	2.3	2.9	3.0
Real, deflator GDP	3.0	1.0	0.8	3.3	0.6	1.1	3.6	1.9	0.8	1.5	3.2
6 Productivity[4]	2.9	1.1	3.1	5.1	−0.1	2.0	2.7	1.9	1.0	0.4	1.3
7 Real unit labour costs[5]											
Index: 1961–73 = 100	100.0	103.0	98.7	97.0	97.6	96.7	97.6	97.7	97.4	98.5	100.3
Annual percentage change	0.1	−0.1	−2.2	−1.7	0.7	−0.9	0.9	0.1	−0.2	1.1	1.9
8 Relative unit labour costs in common currency											
Against 19 competitors											
Index: 1961–73 = 100	100.0	89.7	104.0	95.8	93.5	94.7	88.6	89.6	98.7	100.7	102.4
Annual percentage change	−1.9	3.7	−6.7	−7.9	−2.3	1.2	−6.4	1.1	10.2	2.1	1.7
9 Employment	0.3	−0.4	−1.8	−1.2	1.9	1.6	0.4	1.9	3.1	1.7	0.7
10 Unemployment rate[6]	:	5.0	10.5	11.2	11.4	11.5	11.5	10.6	8.7	6.8	6.5
11 Current balance[7]	−0.1	−0.4	1.5	0.9	−0.2	0.7	−0.9	−1.6	−3.2	−4.1	−3.3
12 Net lending (+) or net borrowing (−)											
of general government[7]	:	−3.7	−2.5	−3.3	−3.9	−2.7	−2.4	−1.5	0.8	1.5	1.1
13 Gross debt of general government[7]	:	57.8	58.1	57.7	59.2	57.7	56.8	55.5	49.9	44.8	41.1
14 Interest payments by general government[7]	:	4.4	5.0	4.7	4.9	5.0	4.5	4.3	4.0	3.5	3.1
15 Money supply (end of year)[8]	9.5	12.1	8.9	10.4	10.0	13.4	18.9	22.4	20.3	18.4	:
16 Long-term interest rate[9]	7.6	13.9	12.7	10.8	10.7	10.6	9.8	9.5	9.3	9.5	11.2

Population

Table D 6 Population; total (1000)

	B	DK	D	GR	E	F	IRL	I	L	NL	P	UK	EUR12	USA	J
1960	9 119	4 581	55 433	8 327	30 583	45 684	2 832	50 349	314.0	11 483	8 559	52 373	279 636	180 671	94 118
1965	9 448	4 758	58 619	8 551	32 085	48 778	2 876	52 144	331.5	12 293	8 645	54 350	292 878	194 303	98 851
1970	9 638	4 929	60 651	8 793	33 876	50 772	2 950	53 822	339.2	13 032	8 565	55 632	302 999	205 052	104 674
1971	9 673	4 963	61 284	8 831	34 190	51 251	2 978	54 074	342.4	13 194	8 514	55 928	305 222	207 661	105 713
1972	9 709	4 992	61 672	8 889	34 498	51 701	3 024	54 381	346.6	13 330	8 495	56 097	307 135	209 896	107 156
1973	9 738	5 022	61 976	8 929	34 810	51 118	3 073	54 751	350.5	13 438	8 500	56 223	308 930	211 909	108 660
1974	9 768	5 045	62 054	8 962	35 147	52 460	3 124	55 111	355.1	13 543	8 594	56 236	310 399	213 854	110 160
1975	9 795	5 060	61 829	9 046	35 515	52 699	3 177	55 441	359.0	13 660	8 879	56 226	311 686	215 973	111 520
1976	9 811	5 073	61 531	9 167	35 937	52 909	3 228	55 718	360.7	13 773	9 075	56 216	312 798	218 035	112 770
1977	9 822	5 088	61 400	9 309	36 367	53 145	3 272	55 955	361.3	13 856	9 156	56 190	313 922	220 239	113 880
1978	9 830	5 104	61 327	9 430	36 778	53 376	3 314	56 155	362.0	13 939	9 196	56 178	314 989	222 585	114 920
1979	9 837	5 117	61 359	9 548	37 108	53 606	3 368	56 318	362.9	14 034	9 325	56 242	316 225	225 055	115 880
1980	9 847	5 123	61 566	9 642	37 386	53 880	3 401	56 434	364.2	14 148	9 395	56 330	317 516	227 757	116 800
1981	9 852	5 122	61 682	9 730	37 756	54 182	3 443	56 508	365.3	14 247	9 488	56 352	318 728	230 138	117 650
1982	9 856	5 118	61 638	9 790	37 980	54 480	3 480	56 640	365.6	14 312	9 540	56 306	319 506	232 520	118 450
1983	9 856	5 114	61 423	9 847	38 172	54 728	3 504	56 836	365.6	14 368	9 499	56 347	320 060	234 799	119 260
1984	9 855	5 112	61 175	9 896	38 342	54 947	3 529	57 005	365.9	14 423	9 578	56 460	320 687	237 011	120 020
1985	9 858	5 114	61 024	9 934	38 505	55 170	3 540	57 141	366.7	14 488	9 648	56 618	321 407	239 279	120 750
1986	9 862	5 121	61 066	9 966	38 668	55 394	3 541	57 246	368.4	14 567	9 716	56 763	322 278	241 613	121 490
1987	9 870	5 127	61 199	9 998	38 832	55 632	3 543	57 345	370.8	14 664	9 756	56 930	323 267	243 915	122 090
1988	9 870	5 130	61 506	10 028	38 996	55 875	3 535	57 446	371.5	14 760	9 785	57 066	324 369	246 355	122 690
1989	9 870	5 133	61 957	10 058	39 159	56 099	3 530	57 561	372.2	14 847	9 815	57 218	325 619	248 778	123 290
1990	9 870	5 135	62 358	10 088	39 316	56 323	3 525	57 676	372.6	14 934	9 844	57 376	326 818	251 176	123 890

Labour force and employment

Table D 7 Working population and employment – 1988

Country	Civilian working		Civilian employment	
	1 000	As % of total population	1 000	% of females
EUR 12				
1 Belgium	4 132	41.8	3 668	39.7
2 Denmark	2 886	56.3	2 700	45.4
3 Germany (FR)	29 156	47.5	26 841	39.5
4 Greece				
5 Spain	14 633	37.5	11 780	31.2
6 France	23 587	42.2	21 144	42.0
7 Ireland	1 297	36.7	1 078	32.5
8 Italy	23 718	41.3	20 832	34.5
9 Luxembourg	160.5	42.8	174.1	34.8
10 Netherlands	6 549	44.4	5 934	37.4
11 Portugal	4 604	44.8	4 280	41.9
12 United Kingdom	28 236	49.5	25 896	43.2
USA	121 669	50.1	114 968	45.0
Japan	61 660	50.3	60 110	40.1

Table D 8 Civilian employment by main sectors of economic activity – 1988 (%)

Country	Agriculture	Industry	Services	Total
EUR 12				
1 Belgium	2.7	28.2	69.1	100.0
2 Denmark	6.3	26.3	67.4	100.0
3 Germany (FR)	4.3	41.2	54.5	100.0
4 Greece				
5 Spain	14.4	32.5	53.1	100.0
6 France	6.8	30.4	62.9	100.0
7 Ireland	15.4	27.8	56.8	100.0
8 Italy	9.9	32.6	57.5	100.0
9 Luxembourg	3.4	31.6	65.0	100.0
10 Netherlands	4.8	26.5	68.7	100.0
11 Portugal	20.7	35.1	44.2	100.0
12 United Kingdom	2.2	29.4	68.3	100.0
USA	2.9	26.9	70.2	100.0
Japan	7.9	34.1	58.0	100.0

Table D 9 Unemployment rate 1960–90 (Percentage of civilian labour force)

	B	DK	D	GR	E	F	IRL	I	L	NL	P	UK	EUR 9	EUR12	USA	J
1960	3.1	1.6	1.0	:	:	0.7	4.7	7.2	0.1	0.7	:	1.6	2.5	:	5.4	1.7
1965	1.8	1.2	0.6	4.8	2.7	1.6	4.6	5.4	0.0	0.6	2.6	1.2	2.0	2.1	4.4	1.2
1970	1.9	0.7	0.6	4.2	2.6	2.5	5.9	5.5	0.0	1.0	2.6	2.2	2.4	2.5	4.8	1.1
1964–70	2.1	1.2	0.9	5.0	2.7	2.0	5.1	5.4	0.0	1.0	2.6	1.7	2.3	2.4	4.1	1.2
1971	1.8	1.1	0.7	3.1	3.4	2.8	5.5	5.5	0.0	1.3	2.6	2.8	2.7	2.8	5.8	1.2
1972	2.3	1.0	0.9	2.1	2.9	2.9	6.2	6.4	0.0	2.3	2.6	3.1	3.1	3.0	5.5	1.4
1973	2.4	0.9	1.0	2.0	2.6	2.8	5.7	6.4	0.0	2.3	2.7	2.2	2.8	2.8	4.8	1.3
1974	2.5	3.6	2.2	2.1	3.1	2.9	5.4	5.4	0.0	2.8	1.8	2.1	3.0	3.0	5.5	1.4
1975	4.5	4.9	4.1	2.3	4.5	4.1	7.3	5.9	0.2	5.3	4.6	3.3	4.4	4.3	8.3	1.9
1976	5.9	6.4	4.1	1.9	4.9	4.5	9.1	6.8	0.3	5.6	6.4	4.9	5.1	5.1	7.6	2.0
1977	6.7	7.4	4.0	1.7	5.3	5.1	9.0	7.2	0.5	5.5	7.5	5.2	5.4	5.4	6.9	2.0
1978	7.3	8.4	3.8	1.8	7.1	5.3	8.3	7.3	0.7	5.4	8.1	5.2	5.5	5.6	6.0	2.2
1979	7.5	6.0	3.3	1.9	8.8	6.0	7.2	7.8	0.7	5.5	8.2	4.7	5.4	5.8	5.8	2.1
1980	7.9	6.6	3.3	2.8	11.6	6.4	7.4	7.7	0.7	6.2	7.8	5.7	5.8	6.4	7.0	2.0
1971–80	4.9	4.6	2.7	2.2	5.4	4.3	7.1	6.6	0.3	4.2	5.2	3.9	4.3	4.4	6.3	1.8
1981	10.2	10.4	4.7	4.0	14.4	7.6	10.0	8.0	1.0	8.6	7.6	9.1	7.6	8.1	7.5	2.2
1982	11.9	11.1	6.8	5.8	16.3	8.3	11.6	8.7	1.3	11.6	7.5	10.5	8.9	9.5	9.5	2.4
1983	12.6	9.5	6.9	9.0	17.8	8.2	15.2	9.0	3.6	12.5	7.7	11.2	9.2	10.0	9.5	2.6
1984	12.6	9.1	7.1	9.3	20.6	9.9	17.0	9.5	3.0	12.5	8.4	11.4	9.8	10.8	7.4	2.7
1985	11.7	7.6	7.3	8.7	21.9	10.3	18.4	9.4	3.0	10.4	8.5	11.5	9.7	10.9	7.1	2.6
1986	11.9	5.8	6.5	8.2	21.2	10.4	18.3	10.6	2.7	10.3	8.3	11.5	9.8	10.8	6.9	2.8
1987	11.5	5.8	6.4	8.0	20.5	10.5	18.0	10.1	2.7	10.2	6.8	10.6	9.4	10.4	6.1	2.8
1988	10.4	6.4	6.4	8.5	19.6	10.2	17.8	10.6	2.2	10.3	5.6	8.7	9.0	10.0	5.4	2.5
1989	9.4	7.4	5.6	8.5	17.6	9.5	16.7	10.5	1.8	9.9	5.2	6.8	8.2	9.0	5.1	2.5
1990	8.8	7.6	5.4	8.5	16.5	9.1	16.2	10.6	1.7	9.6	5.2	6.5	8.0	8.7	5.2	2.6
1981–90	11.1	8.1	6.3	7.9	18.6	9.4	15.9	9.7	2.3	10.6	7.1	9.8	9.0	9.8	7.0	2.6

Gross domestic product

Table D 10 GDP at current market prices (National currency: billion)

	B	DK	D	GR	E	F	IRL	I	L	NL	P	UK	EUR12	USA	J
1960	557.1	41.15	302.7	105.2	698	300.7	0.631	26 748	26.11	44.42	71.4	25.74	270.3	513.6	16 011
1965	830.0	70.32	459.2	179.8	1 425	490.3	0.959	45 094	35.10	71.98	107.5	35.83	426.4	701.7	32 866
1970	1 262.2	118.63	675.3	298.9	2 624	793.5	1.620	72 478	55.04	121.18	177.8	51.43	665.9	1 009.2	73 345
1971	1 382.1	131.12	750.6	330.3	2 962	884.2	1.853	78 964	56.05	136.53	199.1	57.78	740.5	1 095.4	80 701
1972	1 545.5	150.73	823.7	373.7	3 476	988.0	2.238	86 587	63.21	154.26	231.8	63.97	825.4	1 203.7	92 395
1973	1 755.1	172.86	917.3	484.2	4 190	1 129.8	2.701	103 440	76.82	176.04	282.2	73.75	954.5	1 345.0	112 497
1974	2 057.0	193.63	984.6	564.2	5 131	1 303.0	2.988	127 614	93.64	199.78	339.3	84.03	1 100.5	1 456.4	134 244
1975	2 271.3	216.26	1 026.9	672.2	6 023	1 467.9	3.792	144 510	86.74	219.96	377.2	106.11	1 253.2	1 583.9	148 328
1976	2 578.9	251.22	1 121.7	824.9	7 248	1 700.6	4.653	180 561	99.60	251.93	468.9	126.47	1 468.6	1 764.8	166 573
1977	2 785.2	279.31	1 197.8	963.7	9 195	1 917.8	5.703	219 088	102.56	274.93	625.8	145.62	1 685.2	1 967.5	185 622
1978	2 987.5	311.38	1 285.3	1 161.4	11 251	2 182.6	6.757	256 168	112.22	297.01	787.3	168.07	1 917.5	2 218.9	204 405
1979	3 188.8	346.89	1 392.3	1 428.8	13 158	2 481.1	7.917	311 428	122.15	315.96	993.3	196.76	2 196.6	2 464.8	221 546
1980	3 451.2	373.79	1 478.9	1 710.9	15 209	2 808.3	9.361	390 432	132.93	336.74	1 256.1	230.70	2 516.1	2 688.5	240 177
1981	3 571.2	407.79	1 540.9	2 050.1	16 989	3 164.8	11.359	468 049	141.69	352.85	1 501.1	254.20	2 796.0	3 009.5	257 364
1982	3 885.9	464.47	1 597.9	2 574.7	19 567	3 626.0	13.381	545 124	158.79	368.86	1 850.4	276.83	3 110.3	3 121.4	269 628
1983	4 120.7	512.54	1 674.8	3 077.8	22 235	4 006.5	14.786	633 571	174.68	381.02	2 301.7	302.30	3 428.9	3 353.5	280 256
1984	4 425.6	565.28	1 755.8	3 804.7	25 111	4 361.9	16.483	727 798	193.67	400.25	2 815.7	322.34	3 748.5	3 722.3	297 947
1985	4 726.6	619.58	1 830.5	4 616.3	27 889	4 695.0	17.619	815 630	207.47	418.18	3 524.0	352.58	4 074.1	3 967.5	316 303
1986	4 982.4	667.14	1 931.2	5 543.2	31 948	5 034.9	18.543	902 238	220.54	429.88	4 403.4	376.52	4 410.4	4 191.5	330 116
1987	5 183.9	693.03	2 009.1	6 389.5	35 715	5 288.7	19.775	982 595	223.53	431.82	5 169.2	409.85	4 715.9	4 472.9	343 730
1988	5 468.8	724.09	2 113.0	7 616.8	39 618	5 644.3	21.099	1 082 075	243.02	451.86	6 000.7	455.13	5 111.2	4 824.9	365 078
1989	5 876.2	763.61	2 244.9	8 976.3	44 480	6 020.9	23.148	1 190 902	260.23	475.93	7 064.6	496.10	5 544.3	5 178.5	388 705
1990	6 290.1	800.74	2 386.4	10 581.4	49 278	6 379.2	25.200	1 307 827	278.23	501.33	8 276.7	533.24	5 980.1	5 523.4	415 923
(in ECU, billion):															
1989	138.3	95.2	1 079.8	49.3	340.6	863.0	30.5	738.5	6.1	204.0	41.0	750.9	4 382.3	4 664.7	2 553.5

Table D 11 GDP at constant market prices (National currency; annual percentage change)

	B	DK	D	GR	E	F	IRL	I	L	NL	P	UK	EUR12	USA	J
1961	5.0	6.4	4.6	11.1	11.8	5.5	4.7	8.2	3.8	3.1	5.2	3.3	5.6	2.8	12.0
1965	3.6	4.6	5.5	9.4	6.3	4.8	2.0	3.3	1.9	5.2	7.6	2.1	4.3	5.9	5.8
1970	6.4	2.0	5.1	8.0	4.1	5.7	3.5	5.3	3.3	5.7	7.6	2.3	4.7	-0.1	10.7
1961–70	4.9	4.5	4.5	7.6	7.3	5.6	4.3	5.7	3.7	5.1	6.4	2.8	4.8	3.8	10.5
1971	3.6	2.7	2.9	7.1	4.6	4.8	3.4	1.6	2.8	4.2	6.6	2.6	3.3	3.2	4.3
1972	5.3	5.3	4.2	8.9	8.0	4.4	6.4	3.2	6.5	3.3	8.0	2.3	4.2	5.1	8.4
1973	5.9	3.6	4.7	7.3	7.7	5.4	4.7	7.0	8.6	4.7	11.2	8.1	6.3	4.8	7.9
1974	4.1	-0.9	0.3	-3.6	5.3	3.1	4.3	4.1	4.2	4.0	1.1	-1.0	1.9	-0.7	-1.2
1975	-1.5	-0.7	-1.6	6.1	0.5	-0.3	3.7	-3.6	-6.2	-0.1	-4.3	-0.7	-1.1	-1.0	2.6
1976	5.6	6.5	5.4	6.4	3.3	4.2	1.4	5.9	2.4	5.1	6.9	3.7	4.8	4.9	4.8
1977	0.5	1.6	3.0	3.4	3.0	3.2	8.2	1.9	1.9	2.3	5.5	1.0	2.4	4.4	5.3
1978	2.7	1.5	2.9	6.7	1.4	3.4	7.2	2.7	3.9	2.5	3.4	3.7	3.0	5.1	5.1
1979	2.1	3.5	4.2	3.7	-0.1	3.2	3.1	4.9	2.7	2.4	6.1	2.2	3.2	2.0	5.2
1980	4.3	-0.4	1.4	1.8	1.2	1.6	3.1	3.9	1.2	0.9	4.8	-2.0	1.3	-0.1	4.4
1971–80	3.2	2.2	2.7	4.7	3.5	3.3	4.5	3.1	2.7	2.9	4.9	2.0	2.9	2.7	4.6
1981	-1.5	-0.9	0.2	0.1	-0.2	1.2	3.3	1.1	-0.2	-0.7	1.3	-1.1	0.2	2.3	3.9
1982	1.5	3.0	-0.6	0.4	1.2	2.5	2.3	0.2	1.5	-1.4	2.2	1.2	0.8	-2.6	2.8
1983	0.2	2.5	1.5	0.4	1.8	0.7	-0.2	1.1	2.9	1.4	0.0	3.8	1.6	3.9	3.2
1984	2.3	4.4	2.8	2.8	1.8	1.3	4.2	3.2	6.2	3.2	-1.4	1.8	2.3	7.2	5.0
1985	0.9	4.2	2.0	3.1	2.3	1.7	1.6	2.9	3.7	2.6	2.8	3.6	2.5	3.8	4.7
1986	1.9	3.3	2.3	1.2	3.3	2.1	-0.4	2.9	4.7	2.1	4.3	3.1	2.6	3.0	2.4
1987	2.0	-1.0	1.9	-0.4	5.5	2.2	4.1	3.1	2.5	1.3	4.7	3.8	2.8	3.6	4.3
1988	4.0	-0.4	3.7	4.0	5.0	3.4	3.7	3.9	5.2	2.8	3.9	4.2	3.8	4.4	5.8
1989	4.2	1.6	3.8	2.5	4.7	3.3	5.1	3.5	3.7	3.8	4.7	2.2	3.4	2.9	4.8
1990	3.3	2.0	3.5	2.3	4.0	3.2	4.6	3.0	3.3	3.0	4.6	2.1	3.1	2.1	4.2
1981–90	1.9	1.9	2.1	1.6	2.9	2.1	2.8	2.5	3.3	1.8	2.7	2.4	2.3	3.0	4.1

Table D 12 GDP at current market prices per head of population (PPS EUR 12; EUR 12 = 100)

	B	DK	D	GR	E	F	IRL	I	L	NL	P	UK	EUR12	USA	J
1960	95.4	118.6	117.2	38.4	59.2	104.3	61.4	91.2	134.5	117.8	37.3	127.6	100.0	188.7	55.5
1965	96.5	121.3	115.3	45.2	69.6	106.2	60.1	93.2	125.3	114.4	41.6	117.8	100.0	182.4	67.9
1970	98.6	115.4	112.5	51.2	73.3	109.1	60.7	100.4	120.8	115.0	47.1	107.1	100.0	163.6	91.1
1971	99.3	114.8	111.7	53.3	74.1	110.4	60.7	99.1	119.9	115.5	49.2	106.6	100.0	162.7	91.8
1972	100.6	116.1	111.7	55.7	76.6	110.4	61.4	98.2	121.9	114.0	51.5	105.0	100.0	163.4	94.8
1973	100.6	113.1	110.1	56.3	77.4	109.3	59.9	98.8	123.9	112.1	54.2	107.2	100.0	160.4	95.4
1974	102.9	110.0	108.7	53.3	79.5	110.4	60.5	100.8	125.6	114.0	53.4	104.6	100.0	155.6	91.7
1975	102.7	110.6	109.1	56.8	80.4	111.3	62.7	98.1	118.3	114.7	50.2	105.5	100.0	154.9	94.4
1976	103.7	112.6	110.7	57.2	78.6	110.7	59.9	99.0	115.5	114.5	50.3	104.8	100.0	154.1	93.7
1977	102.0	111.8	111.9	57.1	78.4	111.5	62.7	98.4	115.1	114.2	51.6	103.8	100.0	156.2	95.7
1978	102.0	110.1	112.3	58.5	76.6	111.8	64.6	98.1	116.3	113.3	51.7	104.9	100.0	158.2	97.1
1979	101.2	110.7	113.7	58.3	73.8	111.7	63.7	99.8	115.8	112.0	52.6	104.2	100.0	155.2	98.5
1980	104.5	109.0	113.8	58.2	73.4	111.9	64.5	102.5	115.6	111.0	54.2	101.1	100.0	151.9	101.2
1981	103.0	108.3	114.0	57.8	72.7	112.8	65.9	103.8	115.3	109.7	54.5	100.1	100.0	154.0	104.5
1982	104.0	111.0	112.7	57.4	72.7	114.4	66.3	103.2	116.3	107.0	55.1	100.8	100.0	147.7	106.2
1983	102.7	112.3	113.2	56.5	72.6	113.1	64.8	102.4	118.0	106.6	54.5	103.2	100.0	149.8	107.2
1984	102.9	114.8	114.4	56.5	72.1	111.8	65.7	103.2	122.6	107.3	52.2	102.7	100.0	155.8	109.6
1985	101.6	117.0	114.4	56.8	71.8	110.7	65.1	103.6	124.0	107.2	52.1	103.7	100.0	156.6	111.6
1986	101.1	118.0	114.4	56.0	72.2	110.0	63.4	104.0	126.3	106.4	52.8	104.2	100.0	156.1	111.0
1987	100.6	113.8	113.5	54.3	74.0	109.2	64.3	104.4	125.5	104.5	53.7	105.2	100.0	156.3	112.4
1988	101.2	109.5	113.2	54.4	74.8	108.7	64.6	104.8	127.4	103.2	53.8	105.7	100.0	156.2	114.4
1989	102.4	108.0	113.3	54.0	75.7	108.5	66.0	105.1	128.0	103.5	54.5	104.6	100.0	154.5	115.8
1990	103.0	107.2	113.4	53.6	76.3	108.6	67.3	105.2	128.7	103.1	55.4	103.7	100.0	152.1	116.9

Table D 13 Use of gross domestic product at market prices – 1988 (%)

Country	National private consumption	Collective consumption of general government	Gross fixed capital formation	Change in stocks	Balance of exports and imports of goods and services	Gross domestic product at market prices
EUR 12	**61.4**	**16.8**	**20.0**	**0.9**	**0.9**	**100.0**
1 Belgium	63.1	15.3	17.8	0.5	3.3	100.0
2 Denmark	53.7	26.0	18.0	0.7	1.6	100.0
3 Germany (FR)	61.1	13.1	19.9	0.7	5.2	100.0
4 Greece	68.6	20.6	17.4	1.0	−7.6	100.0
5 Spain	63.0	14.3	22.5	1.4	−1.2	100.0
6 France	60.4	18.6	20.1	0.8	0.1	100.0
7 Ireland	57.9	16.7	17.0	0.8	7.6	100.0
8 Italy	61.2	17.2	19.9	1.5	0.2	100.0
9 Luxembourg	57.1	17.0	24.2	0.3	1.4	100.0
10 Netherlands	59.5	15.7	21.4	0.6	2.8	100.0
11 Portugal	65.1	16.0	26.8	2.8	−10.7	100.0
12 United Kingdom	63.1	19.9	19.2	0.9	−3.1	100.0
USA	66.5	18.3	17.1	0.3	−2.2	100.0
Japan	57.3	9.3	30.5	0.3	2.6	100.0

Table D 14 Gross value-added at market prices by branch – 1987 (%)

Country	Agriculture, forestry and fishing	Industry (incl. construction)	Services and general government	Gross value-added at market prices
EUR 12	**3.1**	**36.5**	**61.4**	**100.0**
1 Belgium[1]	2.3	31.9	65.8	100.0
2 Denmark[2]	4.7	28.0	67.3	100.0
3 Germany (FR)	1.5	40.3	58.2	100.0
4 Greece[2]	15.8	28.6	55.6	100.0
5 Spain	5.2	37.3	57.5	100.0
6 France	3.7	31.5	64.8	100.0
7 Ireland	9.7	36.8	53.5	100.0
8 Italy	4.1	34.1	61.8	100.0
9 Luxembourg	2.2	30.6	67.2	100.0
10 Netherlands	4.3	32.1	63.6	100.0
11 Portugal	7.5	37.9	54.6	100.0
12 United Kingdom	1.2	36.7	62.1	100.0
USA	1.9	28.5	69.6	100.0
Japan	2.7	39.0	58.3	100.0

[1] 1985.
[2] At factor cost.

Wages and productivity

Table D 15 Nominal unit labour costs; total economy relative to 19 industrial companies; double export weights (USD: 1980=100)

	B	DK	D	GR	E	F	IRL	I	NL	P	UK	EUR12	USA	J
1960	94.4	77.6	82.4	169.2	66.2	101.8	94.5	105.4	65.7	120.6	97.9	76.1	167.5	68.5
1965	90.4	88.7	86.4	138.6	78.3	103.9	98.4	114.5	78.8	107.5	98.5	84.2	145.9	76.2
1970	85.6	95.4	96.0	122.7	75.5	91.4	97.1	106.6	86.2	116.4	86.7	80.8	157.3	72.9
1971	86.1	95.8	100.1	112.4	75.9	87.9	100.3	109.1	88.3	116.9	86.8	82.8	146.8	77.6
1972	90.0	94.5	101.3	103.6	79.4	89.5	99.4	108.4	91.1	115.8	87.0	85.3	134.7	86.1
1973	90.6	102.4	110.6	97.4	83.3	91.4	98.6	101.0	95.6	114.3	76.4	87.2	120.5	96.5
1974	93.2	107.1	110.8	106.5	86.6	86.1	94.9	95.2	98.3	130.4	77.4	85.8	115.7	100.5
1975	97.0	108.4	102.3	96.3	88.3	97.5	92.5	101.4	99.3	151.9	82.9	91.3	107.3	97.7
1976	101.0	109.0	100.3	99.0	88.9	97.0	89.7	90.5	100.3	148.9	72.1	82.8	110.6	102.1
1977	107.0	108.8	102.7	106.6	88.0	93.7	86.3	93.2	104.1	126.7	69.9	83.9	108.3	111.1
1978	107.3	110.4	104.0	105.0	89.7	94.5	88.9	93.4	105.3	106.1	72.2	86.0	99.6	130.4
1979	105.7	109.2	103.6	110.4	106.3	96.8	97.1	95.7	104.4	96.0	81.7	94.0	99.6	112.8
1980	100.0	100.0	100.0	100.0	100.0	100.0	100.0	100.0	100.0	100.0	100.0	100.0	100.0	100.0
1981	91.6	92.4	89.5	105.2	93.1	93.8	94.8	98.3	90.3	106.5	102.3	85.8	112.4	107.6
1982	81.1	90.0	89.2	113.8	90.1	89.3	97.9	99.6	92.8	100.7	95.5	80.2	127.5	96.3
1983	79.3	91.0	88.5	108.6	79.2	86.5	100.1	106.6	90.4	91.4	87.9	75.6	132.9	104.4
1984	78.4	87.3	84.5	107.5	78.8	84.5	97.1	106.1	83.5	88.5	85.9	70.0	142.4	107.0
1985	79.6	88.1	83.0	105.7	78.4	86.2	98.0	105.4	81.0	90.1	86.9	69.8	148.1	105.9
1986	83.9	93.5	90.8	90.3	81.0	88.6	103.6	111.6	85.7	89.9	81.4	76.6	119.2	132.9
1987	84.3	104.1	95.5	88.6	83.6	88.1	100.1	116.4	88.5	90.2	82.3	82.3	105.7	138.6
1988	81.4	104.0	92.3	92.5	87.7	84.7	95.5	116.7	86.1	91.2	90.6	81.1	100.7	147.4
1989	79.7	98.2	87.4	98.1	93.7	81.8	90.8	120.8	81.3	92.8	92.5	77.4	108.4	138.2

Consumption, saving, investment

Table D 16 A Gross fixed capital formation at current prices; total economy (Percentage of GDP at market prices)

	B	DK	D	GR	E	F	IRL	I	L	NL	P	UK	EUR12	USA	J
1960	19.3	21.6	24.3	19.0	20.1	20.9	14.4	27.7	20.9	24.1	23.2	16.4	21.8	18.0	29.3
1965	22.3	24.1	26.1	21.6	24.5	24.2	21.4	23.6	28.0	25.2	22.8	18.5	23.3	18.8	29.8
1970	22.7	24.7	25.5	23.6	26.1	24.3	22.7	26.2	23.1	25.9	23.2	18.9	24.0	17.7	35.5
1961–70	21.9	23.8	24.9	21.4	24.0	23.8	20.2	26.2	26.0	25.4	23.4	18.3	23.2	18.0	32.2
1975	22.5	21.1	20.4	20.8	26.4	24.1	22.7	25.2	27.7	21.1	25.9	19.8	22.6	17.2	32.5
1980	21.1	18.8	22.7	24.2	22.1	23.0	28.6	24.3	27.1	21.0	28.6	18.0	22.1	19.1	31.6
1971–80	21.7	22.5	22.3	24.2	24.5	23.9	25.6	24.6	26.1	21.9	26.5	19.1	22.7	18.8	32.7
1985	15.7	18.5	19.7	19.1	18.9	19.2	19.6	21.1	18.4	19.2	21.8	17.1	19.2	18.1	27.8
1990	19.8	17.5	21.1	19.2	25.7	21.1	18.9	20.0	22.8	22.2	30.9	18.6	20.9	16.9	32.9
1981–90	17.3	17.6	20.3	19.2	21.4	20.2	21.0	21.0	22.1	20.0	27.3	17.3	19.9	17.5	29.7

Table D 16 B Gross fixed capital formation at current prices; total economy (National currency; annual percentage change)

	B	DK	D	GR	E	F	IRL	I	L	NL	P	UK	EUR12	USA	J
1961	12.4	13.9	6.7	8.1	17.9	10.9	15.9	11.6	9.0	6.0	6.7	9.8	9.9	1.4	23.4
1965	4.1	4.7	4.7	12.8	16.6	7.0	10.0	-8.4	-13.9	5.3	10.3	5.2	3.4	9.3	4.6
1970	8.4	2.2	9.4	-1.4	3.0	4.6	0.3	3.0	10.2	7.5	11.4	2.5	5.0	-3.7	16.9
1961–70	5.8	7.0	4.4	9.3	11.2	7.8	9.8	5.1	3.7	6.7	6.9	5.2	6.0	3.8	15.7
1971	-1.9	1.9	6.1	14.0	-3.0	7.3	8.8	-3.2	10.8	1.5	10.2	1.8	2.6	5.8	4.5
1972	3.4	9.3	2.7	15.4	14.2	6.0	7.4	0.9	6.9	-2.3	14.0	-0.2	3.8	8.7	10.0
1973	7.0	3.5	-0.3	7.7	13.0	8.5	16.2	7.7	12.3	4.2	10.3	6.5	6.1	6.2	12.6
1974	6.9	-8.9	-9.6	-25.6	6.2	1.3	-11.6	3.3	-6.1	-4.0	-6.1	-2.4	-1.9	-6.0	-9.5
1975	-1.9	-12.4	-5.3	0.2	-4.5	-6.4	-2.6	-12.7	-6.9	-4.4	-10.6	-2.0	-6.4	-10.7	-1.2
1976	4.0	17.1	3.6	6.8	-0.8	3.3	13.6	2.3	-3.8	-2.2	1.3	1.7	2.5	6.9	2.7
1977	0.0	-2.4	3.6	7.8	-0.9	-1.8	4.1	-0.4	-1.1	9.7	11.5	-1.8	0.7	11.4	4.0
1978	2.8	1.1	4.7	6.0	-2.7	2.1	18.9	-0.1	1.3	2.5	7.1	3.0	2.2	9.5	8.5
1979	-2.7	-0.4	7.2	8.8	-4.4	3.1	13.6	5.8	4.1	-1.7	-2.2	2.8	3.3	2.4	5.3
1980	4.6	-12.6	2.8	-6.5	0.7	2.6	-4.7	9.4	11.8	-0.9	8.6	-5.4	2.0	-6.8	0.0
1971–80	2.2	-0.8	1.4	2.8	1.6	2.5	5.9	1.1	2.7	0.2	4.1	10.4	1.4	2.5	3.5
1981	-16.4	-19.2	-4.8	-7.5	-3.3	-1.9	9.5	-2.3	-6.7	-10.4	5.7	-9.6	-4.8	-0.1	3.1
1982	-1.7	7.1	-5.3	-1.9	0.5	-1.4	-3.4	-5.7	-0.4	-4.1	3.4	5.4	-2.0	-8.7	0.8
1983	-4.2	1.9	3.2	-1.3	-2.5	-3.6	-9.3	-0.1	-11.6	2.1	-7.6	5.0	0.1	8.8	-0.3
1984	2.1	12.9	0.8	-5.7	-5.8	-2.6	-2.0	5.3	-0.4	5.4	-17.2	8.6	1.5	15.9	4.9
1985	1.0	11.8	0.1	5.2	4.1	2.8	-6.6	2.5	-3.3	6.8	-3.4	3.8	2.5	6.9	5.8
1986	3.7	17.3	3.3	-5.7	10.0	2.9	-0.3	1.4	15.8	8.2	9.5	0.9	3.4	0.9	6.0
1987	7.6	-9.0	1.8	-3.2	14.6	3.7	0.0	5.2	5.3	1.6	19.5	5.5	4.8	3.1	10.3
1988	12.9	-6.5	5.9	9.0	14.0	7.3	-1.7	4.9	4.5	9.7	15.8	13.1	8.3	5.4	13.6
1989	12.3	0.0	7.7	6.6	13.9	5.6	8.6	5.2	4.3	6.7	11.6	4.6	6.9	2.2	9.8
1990	5.8	2.2	5.1	6.4	9.9	5.5	10.0	4.0	4.0	1.4	10.0	1.7	4.9	3.6	5.4
1981–90	2.0	1.3	1.7	0.0	5.3	1.8	0.3	2.0	0.9	2.6	4.2	3.8	2.5	3.6	5.9

Table D 17 Price deflator of private consumption (National currency; annual percentage change)

	B	DK	D	GR	E	F	IRL	I	L	NL	P	UK	EUR12	USA	J
1961	2.7	3.5	3.6	1.1	1.8	3.3	2.6	1.7	0.5	2.4	0.6	2.9	2.8	1.2	6.4
1965	4.6	6.1	3.4	4.6	9.7	2.6	4.8	3.6	3.4	4.0	4.8	4.9	4.2	1.9	6.8
1970	2.5	6.6	4.0	3.1	6.6	5.0	8.1	5.0	4.0	4.4	3.2	5.9	5.0	4.4	7.2
1961–70	3.1	5.8	2.9	2.5	5.9	4.3	4.8	3.8	2.5	4.1	2.8	3.9	3.9	2.7	5.6
1971	5.4	8.3	6.0	2.9	7.8	6.0	9.4	5.5	4.7	7.9	7.0	8.7	6.7	4.8	6.7
1972	5.4	8.2	5.7	3.3	7.6	6.3	9.7	6.4	5.2	8.3	6.3	6.6	6.4	2.9	5.6
1973	6.1	11.7	6.6	15.0	11.4	7.4	11.6	12.5	4.9	8.5	8.9	8.3	8.9	6.0	10.7
1974	12.8	15.0	7.4	23.5	17.8	14.8	15.7	20.9	10.1	9.5	23.5	17.1	14.9	10.6	21.2
1975	12.3	9.9	6.2	12.7	15.5	11.8	22.3	17.7	10.2	10.1	16.0	23.7	14.3	8.0	11.3
1976	7.8	9.9	4.2	13.4	16.5	9.9	20.0	18.1	9.5	9.0	18.1	15.7	11.9	5.8	9.2
1977	7.2	10.6	3.7	11.9	23.7	9.4	14.1	18.2	5.9	6.1	27.3	14.9	12.1	6.6	7.2
1978	4.2	9.2	2.8	12.8	19.0	9.1	7.9	12.9	3.5	4.5	21.3	9.2	9.2	7.0	4.5
1979	3.9	10.4	4.0	16.5	16.5	10.7	14.9	15.1	5.1	4.3	25.4	13.7	10.9	9.3	3.6
1980	6.4	10.7	5.8	21.6	16.5	13.3	18.6	20.2	7.5	6.9	21.4	16.2	13.5	11.0	7.1
1971–80	7.1	10.4	5.2	13.2	15.1	9.8	14.3	14.6	6.6	7.5	17.3	13.3	10.8	7.2	8.6
1981	8.0	12.0	6.0	22.7	14.3	13.0	19.6	17.9	8.7	6.3	20.0	11.3	12.1	9.3	4.4
1982	7.7	10.2	4.7	20.7	14.5	11.5	15.3	15.9	10.8	5.3	20.2	8.8	10.5	6.0	2.6
1983	6.7	6.8	3.2	18.1	12.3	9.7	9.2	15.0	8.9	2.7	25.9	4.8	8.5	3.5	1.9
1984	5.7	6.4	2.4	17.9	11.0	7.7	8.1	11.7	5.5	2.0	28.7	5.1	7.2	3.9	2.1
1985	5.8	4.7	2.1	18.3	8.2	5.8	4.5	9.3	5.2	2.1	19.8	5.3	5.9	3.1	2.2
1986	0.4	3.4	-0.2	22.0	8.7	2.7	3.9	5.8	0.8	0.6	13.5	4.4	3.8	2.2	0.5
1987	2.2	4.1	0.7	15.7	5.4	3.1	3.1	4.8	2.9	-0.3	10.2	3.9	3.4	4.2	-0.1
1988	1.2	4.9	1.1	13.9	5.1	2.7	2.5	4.9	1.5	0.8	9.6	5.0	3.6	3.9	0.0
1989	3.2	4.7	3.1	14.3	6.8	3.5	4.1	6.3	3.3	1.4	13.0	5.3	4.8	4.9	2.0
1990	3.5	3.0	2.7	15.0	6.3	2.7	4.0	6.0	3.1	2.3	11.3	5.5	4.5	4.8	2.8
1981–90	4.4	6.0	2.6	17.8	9.2	6.2	7.3	9.7	5.0	2.3	17.0	5.9	6.4	4.6	1.8

Government

Table D 18 Total expenditure; general government (Percentage of GDP at market prices)

	B	DK	D	GR	E	F	IRL	I	L	NL	P	UK	EUR9	EUR12
1960	30.3	24.8	32.5	:	:	34.6	28.0	30.1	30.5	33.7	:	32.4	32.3	:
1965	32.3	29.9	36.7	:	:	38.4	33.1	34.3	33.3	38.7	:	36.2	36.3	:
1970	36.5	40.2	38.6	:	:	38.9	39.6	34.2	33.1	46.0	:	39.2	38.4	:
1961–70	33.2	32.1	37.1	:	:	38.3	33.5	32.8	33.7	40.3	:	36.6	36.3	:
1970	38.6	42.1	38.7	:	21.7	38.9	37.5	29.7	33.1	42.3	:	36.8	36.8	:
1971	40.3	43.0	40.2	39.9	23.2	38.3	38.3	31.7	36.8	44.5	:	36.4	37.6	47.0
1972	41.3	42.6	40.9	39.7	22.8	38.3	37.0	33.5	37.2	45.0	:	37.4	38.4	48.2
1973	41.5	42.1	41.7	41.5	22.7	38.5	36.8	32.8	36.1	45.7	:	38.0	38.6	48.6
1974	41.8	45.9	44.7	44.3	22.9	39.7	42.5	32.9	35.6	47.4	:	42.7	40.8	48.8
1975	46.7	48.2	49.0	48.1	24.6	43.5	46.3	37.5	48.6	52.2	:	44.0	44.5	49.0
1976	47.2	47.8	48.0	47.5	25.9	44.0	45.5	36.6	49.2	52.4	:	43.5	44.1	48.4
1977	48.9	48.8	48.1	50.0	27.4	43.6	43.1	36.9	52.0	52.4	:	41.5	43.8	48.0
1978	50.0	50.6	47.8	50.7	29.2	44.6	44.0	40.0	51.3	53.8	:	41.2	44.6	47.0
1979	51.8	53.2	47.7	53.9	30.5	45.0	46.4	39.4	52.5	55.8	:	41.0	44.7	46.3
1980	53.2	56.2	48.3	53.8	32.8	46.1	50.4	41.6	54.8	57.5	:	42.9	46.2	45.8
1971–80	46.3	47.8	45.6	:	26.2	42.1	43.0	36.3	45.4	50.7	:	40.8	42.3	:
1981	57.6	59.8	49.2	:	35.6	48.6	51.8	45.4	58.5	59.3	41.7	44.1	48.4	47.0
1982	57.6	61.2	49.4	:	37.5	50.3	54.6	47.4	55.8	61.3	43.8	44.6	49.5	48.2
1983	57.2	61.6	48.4	:	38.8	51.4	54.2	48.6	55.1	62.0	46.1	44.7	49.7	48.6
1984	56.1	60.3	48.0	:	39.3	51.9	52.3	49.3	51.8	60.7	46.6	45.4	49.9	48.8
1985	55.8	59.3	47.5	:	42.1	52.1	53.7	50.8	51.1	59.6	43.5	44.1	49.8	49.0
1986	55.1	56.0	46.9	:	41.7	51.5	53.5	50.9	51.7	59.7	44.6	42.8	49.1	48.4
1987	53.5	58.3	47.0	:	40.9	51.3	51.7	50.7	54.3	61.2	43.0	41.2	48.7	48.0
1988	52.4	60.3	46.6	:	40.5	50.2	47.9	50.8	52.2	59.1	42.2	38.4	47.7	47.0
1989	51.2	59.9	45.1	:	40.7	49.8	44.3	51.2	51.1	56.9	41.7	37.1	46.8	46.3
1990	50.2	58.5	44.1	:	40.8	49.4	41.7	51.1	50.3	56.6	41.3	36.6	46.3	45.8
1981–90	54.7	59.5	47.2	:	39.8	50.7	50.6	49.6	53.2	59.6	43.4	41.9	48.6	47.7

Table D 19 Net lending (+) or net borrowing (–); general government (Percentage of GDP at market prices)

	B	DK	D	GR	E	F	IRL	I	L	NL	P	UK	EUR9	EUR12
1960	-2.8	3.1	3.0	:	:	0.9	-2.4	-0.9	3.1	0.8	:	-1.0	0.6	:
1965	-1.6	1.8	-0.6	:	:	0.7	-4.3	-3.8	2.9	-0.8	:	-2.0	-1.2	:
1970	-1.3	2.1	0.2	:	:	0.9	-3.7	-3.5	2.8	-0.8	:	2.5	0.1	:
1961–70	-1.5	1.3	0.4	:	:	0.4	-3.6	-2.3	1.8	-0.8	:	-0.6	-0.5	:
1970	-2.2	4.1	0.2	:	0.7	0.9	-4.3	-3.1	2.7	-1.2	:	3.0	0.2	:
1971	-3.2	3.9	-0.2	:	-0.6	0.7	-4.2	-4.5	2.3	-1.0	:	1.3	-0.6	:
1972	-3.7	3.9	-0.5	:	0.3	0.8	-4.1	-6.5	2.0	-0.4	:	-1.3	-1.6	:
1973	-3.3	5.2	1.2	:	1.1	0.9	-4.6	-6.1	3.3	0.8	:	-2.7	-1.3	:
1974	-2.6	3.1	-1.3	:	0.2	0.6	-8.2	-6.1	4.7	-0.2	:	-3.8	-2.3	:
1975	-4.7	-1.4	-5.6	:	0.0	-2.2	-12.5	-10.1	1.1	-2.9	:	-4.5	-5.3	:
1976	-5.5	-0.2	-3.4	:	-0.3	-0.5	-8.6	-7.8	1.7	-2.6	:	-4.8	-4.0	:
1977	-5.5	-0.5	-2.4	:	-0.6	-0.8	-7.6	-6.9	3.3	-1.8	:	-3.2	-3.2	:
1978	-6.0	-0.3	-2.4	:	-1.7	-2.1	-9.7	-8.5	5.3	-2.8	:	-4.3	-4.1	:
1979	-7.1	-1.7	-2.6	:	-1.7	-0.8	-11.4	-8.3	1.2	-3.7	:	-3.2	-3.8	:
1980	-9.0	-3.3	-2.9	:	-2.6	0.0	-12.7	-8.5	-0.4	-4.0	:	-3.3	-3.9	:
1971–80	-5.0	0.9	-2.0	:	-0.6	-0.3	-8.4	-7.3	2.5	-1.9	:	-3.0	-3.0	:
1981	-12.6	-6.9	-3.7	-11.0	-3.9	-1.9	-13.4	-11.3	-3.5	-5.5	-9.3	-2.6	-5.2	-5.3
1982	-10.9	-9.1	-3.3	-7.7	-5.6	-2.8	-13.8	-11.3	-1.0	-7.1	-10.4	-2.5	-5.4	-5.5
1983	-11.2	-7.2	-2.5	-8.3	-4.8	-3.2	-11.8	-10.6	2.0	-6.4	-9.0	-3.3	-5.2	-5.3
1984	-9.1	-4.1	-1.9	-10.0	-5.5	-2.8	-9.8	-11.6	3.4	-6.3	-12.0	-3.9	-5.1	-5.3
1985	-8.6	-2.0	-1.1	-13.8	-7.0	-2.9	-11.3	-12.5	5.2	-4.8	-10.1	-2.7	-4.8	-5.2
1986	-8.8	3.5	-1.3	-12.5	-6.1	-2.7	-11.1	-11.7	3.1	-6.0	-7.2	-2.4	-4.5	-4.8
1987	-7.0	1.8	-1.9	-12.3	-3.6	-2.0	-9.1	-11.2	2.5	-6.5	-6.9	-1.5	-4.2	-4.3
1988	-6.5	0.2	-2.1	-14.9	-3.2	-1.4	-3.7	-10.6	2.5	-4.9	-6.5	0.8	-3.4	-3.6
1989	-6.0	0.1	0.0	-19.9	-2.6	-1.2	-3.7	-10.3	2.4	-4.4	-6.0	1.5	-2.6	-2.9
1990	-5.7	0.7	-0.4	-20.0	-2.4	-1.1	-1.5	-9.8	2.8	-4.2	-6.1	1.1	-2.6	-2.9
1981–90	-8.6	-2.3	-1.8	-13.1	-4.5	-2.2	-8.9	-11.1	1.9	-5.6	-8.3	-1.5	-4.3	-4.5

Finance

Table D 20 A Nominal short-term interest rates (%)

	B	DK	D	GR	E	F	IRL	I	NL	P	UK	EUR10	USA	J
1961–70	5.2	6.8	5.0	::	::	5.4	::	3.7	3.8	::	6.3	5.1	4.3	::
1971	5.3	7.6	7.1	::	::	6.0	6.6	5.7	4.5	4.3	6.2	6.1	4.3	6.5
1972	4.2	7.3	5.7	::	::	5.4	7.1	5.2	2.7	4.4	6.8	5.5	4.2	5.2
1973	6.6	7.6	12.2	::	::	9.2	12.2	7.0	7.5	4.4	11.8	9.8	7.2	8.3
1974	10.6	10.0	9.8	::	::	13.0	14.5	14.9	10.4	5.3	13.4	12.3	7.9	14.7
1975	7.0	8.0	4.9	::	::	7.6	10.9	10.4	5.3	6.8	10.6	8.1	5.8	10.1
1976	10.1	8.9	4.3	::	::	8.7	11.7	16.0	7.4	8.4	11.5	9.6	5.0	7.3
1977	7.3	14.5	4.3	::	15.5	9.1	8.4	14.0	4.8	11.1	8.0	9.1	5.3	6.4
1978	7.3	15.4	3.7	::	17.6	7.8	9.9	11.5	7.0	15.5	9.4	8.9	7.4	5.1
1979	10.9	12.5	6.9	::	15.5	9.7	16.0	12.0	9.6	16.1	13.9	11.0	10.1	5.8
1980	14.2	16.9	9.5	::	16.5	12.0	16.2	16.9	10.6	16.3	16.8	13.8	11.6	10.7
1971–80	8.4	10.9	6.8	::	::	8.8	11.4	11.3	7.0	9.3	10.8	9.4	6.9	8.0
1981	15.6	14.8	12.3	16.8	16.2	15.3	16.7	19.3	11.8	16.0	14.1	15.1	14.0	7.4
1982	14.1	16.4	8.8	18.9	16.3	14.6	17.5	19.9	8.2	16.8	12.2	13.8	10.6	6.8
1983	10.5	12.0	5.8	16.6	20.1	12.5	14.0	18.3	5.7	20.9	10.1	12.1	8.7	6.5
1984	11.5	11.5	6.0	15.7	14.9	11.7	13.2	17.3	6.1	22.5	10.0	11.3	9.5	6.3
1985	9.5	10.0	5.4	17.0	12.2	9.9	12.0	15.0	6.3	21.0	12.2	10.6	7.5	6.5
1986	8.1	9.1	4.6	19.8	11.7	7.7	12.4	12.8	5.7	15.6	10.9	9.1	6.0	5.0
1987	7.0	9.9	4.0	14.9	15.8	8.3	11.0	11.4	5.4	13.9	9.7	8.9	5.9	3.9
1988	6.7	8.3	4.3	15.9	11.6	7.9	8.1	11.3	4.8	13.0	10.3	8.6	6.9	4.0
1989	8.4	8.7	6.7	19.0	14.8	8.5	9.0	13.2	7.1	14.0	13.7	10.8	8.4	4.8

Table D 20 B Nominal long-term interest rates (%)

	B	DK	D	GR	E	F	IRL	I	L	NL	P	UK	EUR12	USA	J
1961–70	6.3	8.3	6.8	:	:	6.5	:	6.7	:	5.6	:	7.0	6.7	4.8	:
1971	7.3	11.0	8.0	:	:	8.4	9.2	8.3	:	7.0	:	8.9	8.4	5.7	:
1972	7.0	11.0	7.9	:	:	8.0	9.1	7.5	:	6.7	:	9.0	8.0	5.6	6.9
1973	7.5	12.6	9.3	9.3	:	9.0	10.7	7.4	6.8	7.3	:	10.8	9.1	6.3	7.0
1974	8.8	15.9	10.4	10.5	:	11.0	14.6	9.9	7.3	10.7	:	15.0	11.5	7.0	8.1
1975	8.5	12.7	8.5	9.4	:	10.3	14.0	11.5	6.7	9.1	:	14.5	11.0	7.0	8.4
1976	9.1	14.9	7.8	10.2	:	10.5	14.6	13.1	7.2	9.2	:	14.6	11.2	6.8	8.2
1977	8.8	16.2	6.2	9.5	:	11.0	12.9	14.6	7.0	8.5	:	12.5	10.7	7.1	7.4
1978	8.5	16.8	5.7	10.0	:	10.6	12.8	13.7	6.6	8.1	:	12.6	10.4	7.9	6.3
1979	9.7	16.7	7.4	11.2	13.3	10.9	15.1	14.1	6.8	9.2	:	13.0	11.2	8.7	8.3
1980	12.2	18.7	8.5	17.1	16.0	13.1	15.4	16.1	7.4	10.7	:	13.9	13.0	10.8	8.9
1971–80	8.7	14.6	8.0	:	:	10.3	12.8	11.6	:	8.7	:	12.5	10.4	7.3	:
1981	13.8	19.3	10.4	17.6	15.8	15.8	17.3	20.6	8.7	12.2	:	14.8	15.1	12.9	8.4
1982	13.4	20.5	9.0	15.4	16.0	15.6	17.0	20.9	10.3	10.5	:	12.7	14.3	12.2	8.3
1983	11.8	14.4	7.9	18.2	16.9	13.6	13.9	18.0	9.8	8.8	:	10.8	12.7	10.8	7.8
1984	12.0	14.0	7.8	18.5	16.5	12.5	14.6	15.0	10.3	8.6	:	10.7	11.8	12.0	7.3
1985	10.6	11.6	6.9	15.8	13.4	10.9	12.7	14.3	9.5	7.3	25.4	10.6	10.9	10.8	6.5
1986	7.9	10.5	5.9	15.8	11.4	8.4	11.1	11.7	8.7	6.4	17.9	9.8	9.2	8.1	5.2
1987	7.8	11.9	5.8	17.4	12.8	9.4	11.3	11.3	8.0	6.4	15.4	9.5	9.4	8.7	4.7
1988	7.9	10.6	6.1	16.6	11.8	9.0	9.4	12.1	7.1	6.3	14.2	9.3	9.4	9.0	4.7
1989	8.5	10.0	7.0	18.0	13.6	8.7	9.0	13.0	:	7.1	14.8	9.5	9.9	8.4	5.0

International relations

Table D 21 A Structure of EC exports by country and region, 1958 and 1988 (Percentage of total exports)

Export of → / to ↓	B/L 1958	B/L 1988	DK 1958	DK 1988	D 1958	D 1988	GR 1958	GR 1987	E 1958	E 1988	F 1958	F 1988	IRL 1958	IRL 1988	I 1958	I 1988	NL 1958	NL 1988	P 1958	P 1988	UK 1958	UK 1988	EUR 12 1958	EUR 12 1987
B/L	—	—	1.2	2.0	6.6	7.4	1.0	2.8	2.1	3.1	6.3	8.7	0.8	4.4	2.2	3.4	15.0	14.9	3.7	3.1	1.9	5.2	4.8	6.5
DK	1.6	0.9	—	—	3.0	2.0	0.2	1.0	1.7	0.6	0.7	1.0	0.8	0.8	0.8	0.8	2.6	1.7	1.2	2.2	2.4	1.4	2.0	1.4
D	11.6	19.5	20.0	17.7	—	—	20.5	24.3	10.2	11.1	10.4	17.3	2.2	11.2	14.1	18.1	19.0	26.6	7.7	14.7	4.2	11.6	7.6	12.3
GR	0.8	0.5	0.3	0.8	1.3	1.0	—	—	0.1	0.6	0.6	1.2	0.1	0.4	1.9	1.6	0.6	0.9	0.6	0.3	0.7	0.6	0.8	0.8
E	0.7	2.2	0.8	1.6	1.2	3.0	0.2	1.4	—	—	1.6	4.7	0.8	1.7	0.7	4.1	0.8	1.8	0.7	11.3	0.8	3.3	1.0	2.9
F	10.6	20.0	3.0	5.7	7.6	12.5	12.8	8.6	10.1	17.2	—	—	0.8	9.1	5.3	16.6	4.9	10.6	6.6	15.3	2.4	10.1	4.7	11.0
IRL	0.3	0.3	0.3	0.5	0.3	0.4	0.4	0.2	0.3	0.4	0.2	0.4	—	—	0.1	0.3	0.4	0.5	0.3	0.5	3.5	4.9	1.1	1.0
I	2.3	6.2	5.3	4.6	5.0	9.0	6.0	16.1	2.7	0.0	3.4	12.5	0.4	3.8	—	—	2.7	6.4	4.3	4.1	2.1	5.0	3.1	7.1
NL	20.7	14.7	2.2	4.2	8.1	8.6	2.0	3.8	3.2	4.4	2.0	5.3	0.5	7.0	2.0	3.1	—	—	2.5	6.0	3.2	6.8	5.3	6.7
P	1.1	0.6	0.3	0.5	0.9	0.8	0.3	0.3	0.4	5.2	0.8	0.9	0.1	0.3	0.7	1.2	0.4	0.6	—	—	0.4	1.0	0.8	0.9
UK	5.7	9.3	25.9	12.0	3.9	9.3	7.6	8.2	15.9	8.9	4.9	9.6	76.8	35.5	6.8	8.0	11.9	10.6	11.3	14.2	—	—	5.9	8.1
Total intra-EC trade	55.4	74.2	59.3	49.8	37.9	54.1	50.9	66.8	46.8	60.5	30.9	61.6	82.4	74.1	34.5	57.1	58.3	74.7	38.9	71.5	21.7	49.8	37.2	58.7
Other European OECD countries	8.7	6.7	16.6	26.0	22.7	18.7	10.3	7.7	12.4	5.2	9.0	8.5	0.9	5.6	18.9	12.0	11.9	7.4	5.1	10.7	9.1	8.9	13.7	12.4
USA	9.4	5.0	9.3	6.0	7.3	8.1	13.6	6.8	10.1	7.3	5.9	7.3	5.7	7.7	9.9	8.9	5.6	4.2	8.3	6.0	8.8	12.9	7.9	8.7
Canada	1.1	0.5	0.7	0.7	1.2	0.9	0.3	0.7	1.3	1.1	0.8	1.2	0.7	1.0	1.2	1.1	0.8	0.6	1.1	0.9	5.8	2.5	2.3	1.1
Japan	0.6	1.2	0.2	4.2	0.9	2.3	1.4	0.9	1.7	1.7	0.3	1.7	0.0	1.9	0.3	1.9	0.4	0.9	0.5	0.8	0.6	2.2	0.6	1.6
Australia	0.5	0.3	0.3	0.6	1.0	0.7	0.1	0.6	0.3	0.3	0.5	0.4	0.1	0.8	0.8	0.8	0.7	0.4	0.6	0.3	7.2	1.7	2.4	0.7
Developing countries	18.0	9.3	9.3	10.2	20.9	9.6	7.2	10.9	18.4	21.2	46.9	16.2	1.6	6.8	26.2	13.4	17.6	9.0	42.3	6.7	33.6	17.5	27.4	12.6
of which:																								
OPEC	3.3	1.6	2.3	2.1	4.8	2.7	0.9	4.2	2.6	4.2	21.3	4.1	0.2	2.6	7.5	4.7	4.5	2.5	2.0	1.1	7.0	5.3	7.6	3.6
Other developing countries	14.7	7.7	7.0	8.1	16.1	6.9	6.3	6.7	15.8	17.0	25.6	12.1	1.4	4.2	18.7	8.7	13.1	6.5	40.3	5.6	26.6	12.2	19.8	9.0
Centrally-planned economies	4.3	1.7	3.9	2.5	5.5	4.4	16.2	4.6	4.6	2.2	4.9	2.6	0.2	0.6	5.3	4.0	2.2	1.8	1.9	1.2	3.4	2.0	4.3	3.1
Rest of the world and unspecified	2.0	1.1	0.4	0.0	2.6	1.2	0.0	1.0	4.4	1.3	0.8	0.5	8.4	1.5	2.9	0.8	2.5	1.0	1.3	1.9	9.8	2.5	4.2	1.1
World (excluding EC)	44.6	25.8	40.7	50.2	62.1	45.9	49.1	33.2	53.2	39.5	69.1	38.4	17.6	25.9	65.5	42.9	41.7	25.3	61.1	28.5	78.3	50.2	62.8	41.3
World (including EC)	100	100	100	100	100	100	100	100	100	100	100	100	100	100	100	100	100	100	100	100	100	100	100	100

Table D 21 B Structure of EC imports by country and region, 1958 and 1988 (Percentage of total exports)

Import of / to	B/L 1958	B/L 1988	DK 1958	DK 1988	D 1958	D 1988	GR 1958	GR 1987	E 1958	E 1988	F 1958	F 1988	IRL 1958	IRL 1988	I 1958	I 1988	NL 1958	NL 1988	P 1958	P 1988	UK 1958	UK 1988	EUR 12 1958	EUR 12 1987
B/L	–	–	3.8	3.5	4.5	7.7	3.3	3.4	1.8	3.0	5.4	10.8	1.8	2.3	2.0	4.9	17.8	14.0	7.3	4.1	1.6	4.3	4.4	6.9
DK	0.5	0.6	–	–	3.4	1.9	0.7	1.2	1.3	0.7	0.6	0.9	0.7	0.9	2.2	1.0	0.7	1.1	0.8	0.9	3.1	1.8	2.0	1.3
D	17.2	23.5	19.9	24.1	–	–	20.3	22.2	8.7	16.1	11.6	21.0	4.0	8.0	12.0	21.8	19.5	25.1	17.6	13.7	3.6	15.8	8.7	15.5
GR	0.1	0.3	0.0	0.3	0.7	0.7	–	–	0.2	0.2	0.2	0.5	0.2	0.1	0.4	0.9	0.2	0.2	0.1	0.2	0.2	0.3	0.4	0.5
E	0.5	1.5	0.7	0.9	1.6	1.9	0.1	1.4	–	–	1.2	4.2	0.4	1.0	0.4	2.4	0.4	1.3	0.4	13.5	1.0	2.1	0.9	2.3
F	11.6	14.8	3.4	4.7	7.6	12.1	5.4	7.8	6.8	13.6	–	–	1.6	4.0	4.8	14.8	2.8	7.5	7.7	11.5	2.7	8.5	4.4	9.3
IRL	0.1	0.7	0.0	0.5	0.1	0.8	0.0	0.5	0.6	0.5	0.0	1.0	–	–	0.0	0.6	0.0	0.9	0.1	0.3	2.9	3.5	0.9	1.2
I	2.1	4.1	1.7	3.7	5.5	9.1	8.8	12.3	1.8	9.5	2.4	11.9	0.8	2.3	–	–	1.8	3.6	3.7	9.3	2.1	5.3	2.7	6.7
NL	15.7	17.3	7.3	7.7	8.1	11.6	4.8	7.0	2.6	4.0	2.5	6.6	2.9	4.9	2.6	5.7	–	–	2.9	4.8	4.2	6.8	5.2	8.1
P	0.4	0.4	0.3	0.9	0.4	0.7	0.3	0.2	0.3	2.1	0.4	0.9	0.2	0.3	0.4	0.3	0.2	0.5	–	–	0.4	0.8	0.3	0.7
UK	7.4	7.3	22.8	7.3	4.3	6.7	9.9	4.9	7.8	6.8	3.5	7.5	56.3	47.4	5.5	5.1	7.4	7.4	12.9	8.2	–	–	5.4	6.4
Total intra-EC trade	55.5	70.4	60.0	53.7	36.3	53.3	53.7	60.9	31.8	56.5	28.3	65.1	68.9	71.2	30.2	57.5	50.7	61.6	53.4	66.4	21.8	49.2	35.2	58.8
Other European OECD countries	7.7	5.8	18.6	24.2	15.2	16.0	11.5	7.7	8.4	6.2	6.7	7.7	3.4	3.9	13.1	11.5	7.2	7.1	8.6	7.6	8.7	12.1	10.1	11.2
USA	9.9	5.4	9.1	5.1	13.6	6.1	13.7	2.8	21.6	8.9	10.0	6.9	7.0	14.5	16.4	5.6	11.3	7.8	7.0	4.4	9.4	11.0	11.4	6.8
Canada	1.4	0.7	0.2	0.5	3.1	0.8	0.8	0.3	0.5	0.5	1.0	0.7	3.0	0.7	1.5	0.7	1.4	1.0	0.5	1.0	8.2	1.8	3.6	0.8
Japan	0.6	3.3	1.5	3.4	0.6	6.1	2.0	4.2	0.7	4.7	0.2	3.1	1.1	3.9	0.4	2.5	0.8	3.6	0.0	3.5	0.9	6.1	0.7	4.2
Australia	1.7	0.4	0.0	0.3	1.2	0.5	0.3	0.1	0.8	0.4	2.4	0.5	1.2	0.1	3.0	0.7	0.2	0.4	0.9	0.3	5.4	0.7	2.6	0.5
Developing countries	19.2	9.6	5.9	8.7	23.9	11.8	9.6	17.5	32.0	18.8	45.6	12.3	9.3	3.7	29.4	14.4	24.4	15.0	27.6	15.0	34.7	11.6	29.5	13.1
of which: OPEC	5.7	2.1	0.3	1.7	6.7	2.4	1.7	9.2	17.7	6.6	19.7	3.8	0.7	0.2	13.9	5.8	11.5	5.3	6.3	5.2	11.3	1.8	10.8	4.2
Other developing countries	13.5	7.5	5.6	7.0	17.2	9.4	7.9	8.3	14.3	12.2	25.9	8.5	8.6	3.5	15.5	8.6	12.9	9.7	21.3	9.8	23.4	9.8	18.7	8.9
Centrally-planned economies	2.2	2.6	4.6	3.9	4.5	4.6	8.1	5.6	4.0	3.0	4.2	3.1	1.8	1.2	3.7	5.1	3.1	3.1	0.7	1.1	3.7	2.2	3.8	3.6
Rest of the world and unspecified	1.8	1.8	0.1	0.2	1.6	0.8	0.3	0.9	0.2	1.0	1.6	0.6	4.3	0.8	2.3	2.0	0.9	0.6	1.3	0.7	7.2	5.3	3.1	1.0
World (excluding EC)	44.5	29.6	40.0	46.3	63.7	46.7	46.3	39.1	68.2	43.5	71.7	34.9	31.1	28.8	69.8	42.5	49.3	38.4	46.6	33.6	78.2	50.8	64.8	41.2
World (including EC)	100	100	100	100	100	100	100	100	100	100	100	100	100	100	100	100	100	100	100	100	100	100	100	100

Table D 22 Exports of goods and services at current prices *(Percentage of GDP at market prices)*

	B	DK	D	GR	E	F	IRL	I	L	NL	P	UK	EUR12	USA	J
1970	51.9	27.9	21.1	10.0	13.3	15.8	37.0	15.4	88.8	44.8	24.4	23.2	21.2	5.9	10.8
1961–70	44.4	28.6	19.2	9.8	10.8	13.5	35.7	13.8	81.3	43.2	23.5	20.5	19.1	5.3	9.9
1971	50.6	27.6	20.9	10.3	14.2	16.4	36.1	15.8	88.1	45.4	25.1	23.1	21.4	5.7	11.7
1972	51.1	27.1	20.8	11.7	14.6	16.7	34.6	16.4	82.9	45.0	27.2	21.9	21.4	5.8	10.6
1973	55.6	28.5	22.0	14.2	14.6	17.6	38.0	16.3	89.3	47.4	26.7	23.8	22.5	7.0	10.0
1974	61.3	31.8	26.4	16.1	14.4	20.7	42.6	19.4	102.6	53.9	26.9	27.9	25.9	8.5	13.6
1975	53.7	30.1	24.5	16.9	13.5	19.1	42.7	19.8	92.5	49.9	20.4	25.9	24.2	8.6	12.8
1976	56.5	28.8	25.6	17.6	13.8	19.6	46.3	21.4	88.3	51.0	17.4	28.3	25.5	8.3	13.6
1977	55.4	28.8	25.3	16.8	14.5	20.5	49.4	22.8	86.9	47.6	18.4	30.1	26.0	7.9	13.1
1978	53.5	27.8	24.8	17.6	15.2	20.4	49.9	23.3	83.8	44.9	20.1	28.6	25.6	8.2	11.1
1979	58.5	29.2	24.9	17.5	15.0	21.2	49.7	24.2	90.9	49.1	27.1	28.2	26.3	9.1	11.6
1980	60.5	32.7	26.2	20.9	15.8	21.5	49.6	21.8	88.2	52.5	27.4	27.6	26.6	10.2	13.7
1971–80	55.7	29.2	24.1	16.0	14.6	19.4	43.9	20.1	89.4	48.7	23.7	26.5	24.5	7.9	12.2
1981	65.9	36.5	28.6	20.6	18.1	22.6	48.5	23.2	86.5	58.0	25.9	26.9	28.0	9.7	14.8
1982	69.8	36.4	29.6	18.4	18.8	21.8	48.1	23.0	88.9	57.6	26.4	26.6	28.1	8.7	14.6
1983	72.8	36.4	28.5	19.8	21.3	22.5	52.4	22.2	90.1	57.7	31.3	26.8	28.3	7.9	14.0
1984	77.4	36.7	30.3	21.7	23.7	24.1	59.3	22.8	101.1	62.1	37.2	28.8	30.3	7.6	15.1
1985	75.4	36.4	31.9	21.2	23.4	23.9	60.9	22.7	107.1	63.5	37.3	29.3	30.7	7.1	14.6
1986	69.2	32.1	29.7	22.2	20.3	21.3	55.8	20.2	101.7	54.1	33.1	26.3	27.6	6.9	11.5
1987	67.7	31.8	28.4	22.9	19.7	20.8	59.6	19.7	100.7	52.5	34.1	26.4	26.9	7.4	11.2
1988	71.5	32.3	29.1	22.6	19.7	21.5	64.1	19.8	104.0	54.5	34.5	24.1	27.1	8.4	11.1
1989	75.2	34.7	31.3	22.8	19.5	23.3	70.0	20.3	109.4	58.2	36.1	24.9	28.5	9.0	12.0
1990	76.7	36.1	32.7	22.8	19.1	24.1	72.1	20.3	111.4	60.1	36.3	26.1	29.4	9.4	12.6
1981–90	72.2	34.9	30.0	21.5	20.3	22.6	59.1	21.4	100.1	57.8	33.2	26.6	28.5	8.2	13.2

Table D 23 Balance of unrequited payments by main heading – 1988 net flow in million ECU

Country	A. Goods and services			B. Unrequited transfers			C. current balance (A + B)	D. Long-term capital			E. Basic balance (C + D)	Short-term capital	Reserves	Errors and omissions
	Goods (fob)	Services	Total	Private	Official	Total		Direct investment	Portfolio investment	Other long-term capital				
EUR 12	**14 018**	**17 965**	**31 983**	**–905**	**–17 805**	**–18 710**	**13 273**	**–15 222**	**–28 671**	**6 821**	**–23 799**	**14 158**	**–5 254**	**–14 886**
1 Belg./Lux.	946	3 380	4 326	39	–1 573	–1 534	2 792	1 103	–3 583	1 646	1 958	–1 142	–730	–117
2 Denmark	1 589	–2 941	–1 352	–75	–114	–189	–1 541	0	0	2 592	1 051	683	–1 171	–565
3 FR Germany	65 404	–8 890	56 514	–5 948	–9 483	–15 431	41 083	–7 420	–31 374	–2 141	148	–17 317	16 695	469
4 Greece	–5 134	1 271	–3 863	1 455	1 643	3 098	–765	768	0	451	454	508	–1 014	49
5 Spain	–15 233	8 266	–6 967	2 553	1 261	3 814	–3 153	4 896	1 945	1 215	4 903	4 161	–7 035	–2 028
6 France	–6 818	9 553	2 735	–2 056	–3 701	–5 757	–3 022	–4 687	6 410	–1 213	–2 512	809	1 085	618
7 Ireland	2 612	–3 351	–739	62	1 242	1 304	565	77	795	–1 164	–273	374	–456	–190
8 Italy	–511	–2 799	–3 310	–744	–2 361	–3 105	–6 415	1 170	288	5 176	219	4 941	–6 373	–755
10 Netherlands	6 913	–1 430	5 483	1 244	–429	815	6 298	169	2 964	–1 472	7 959	–2 192	–1 331	–2 447
11 Portugal	–4 338	175	–4 163	3 047	609	3 656	–507	693	1 510	–1 576	120	–530	–766	1 177
12 United Kingdom	–31 412	14 730	–16 682	–462	–4 898	–5 360	–22 042	–11 992	–7 627	3 306	–38 355	23 863	–4 158	18 675
USA	–107 690	12 778	–94 912	–1 512	–10 902	–12 414	–107 326	34 593	55 852	9 242	–7 639	19 303	–3 570	–8 083
Japan	80 470	–9 572	70 858	–932	–2 546	–3 478	67 380	–29 375	–44 734	–25 033	–31 762	43 369	–13 937	2 365

Table D 24 ECUs per National Currency Unit, annual average, 1979 = 100

	B/L	DK	D	GR	E	F	IRL	I	NL	P	UK	USA	J
1979	100	100	100	100	100	100	100	100	100	100	100	100	100
1980	98.9	92.1	99.5	85.6	92.2	99.3	99.0	95.7	99.5	96.4	108.0	98.4	95.4
1981	97.2	91.0	99.9	82.4	89.6	96.5	96.9	90.1	99.0	97.9	116.7	122.8	122.4
1982	89.8	88.3	105.7	77.7	85.5	90.6	97.1	86.0	105.2	85.9	115.3	139.9	123.4
1983	88.4	88.7	110.6	65.0	72.1	86.0	93.6	84.3	108.3	67.9	110.1	154.0	142.2
1984	88.4	88.5	112.2	57.5	72.7	84.8	92.2	82.4	108.9	58.0	109.4	173.7	160.6
1985	89.4	89.9	112.8	48.0	72.2	85.8	93.6	78.6	109.5	51.5	109.7	179.6	166.4
1986	91.7	90.8	118.0	36.9	66.9	85.7	91.3	77.9	114.4	45.6	96.2	139.3	182.1
1987	93.3	91.5	121.2	32.7	64.7	84.2	86.4	80.8	117.7	41.4	91.5	119.6	180.1
1988	92.4	90.7	121.0	30.4	66.9	82.9	86.4	74.2	117.6	39.5	97.0	116.6	197.9
1989	92.4	89.3	120.9	28.9	70.7	83.0	86.2	75.8	117.3	38.9	97.1	126.8	200.8

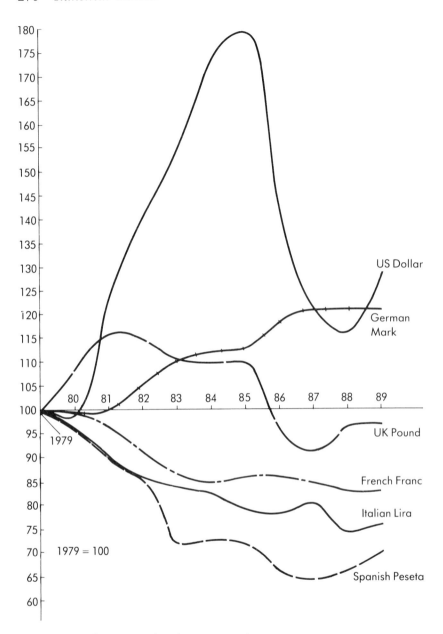

Figure D 1 ECUs per national currency unit

Glossary of abbreviations and foreign terms

Germany

AG (Aktiengesellschaft)	Joint stock company
Berufsgenossenschaften	Insurance scheme covering occupational health risks (all firms are compulsory members)
Betriebsräte	Councils of elected representatives of employees in firms
Betriebsverfassungsgesetz	Law granting employees and their elected representatives comprehensive rights of information and consultation
BDA (Bundesvereinigung der Deutschen Arbeitgeberverbände)	Umbrella organisations of German employers' associations (having their headquarters in Cologne)
BDI (Bundesverband der Deutschen Industrie)	
BMWI (Bundesministerium für Wirtschaft)	Federal Department of Commerce
Bundeskartelamt	Cartel authority (in Berlin)
Bundesländer	German states
Bundesaufsichtamt für das Kreditwesen	Regulatory authority with respect to banking activities
Bundesregierung	Central government
Bundesstaat	Federal state
Deutsche Bundesbank	Central bank in Germany
Deutsche Bundespost	Former German PTT (now split up into three separate activities: Telecommunication, Postal Services, Banking)

DGB (Deutsche Gewerkschaftsbund)	Umbrella organisations for the German labour unions
DIHT (Deutsche Industrie und Handelstag)	
Deutsche Handwerkskammertag	Regional chambers of commerce
Finanzmarktförderungsgesetz	Law to foster financial market activities
Gemeinden	Local authorities
GG (Grundgesetz)	German constitution (of 1949)
Gesetz über die Deutsche Bundesbank	Law regulating the position, tasks and instruments of the German central bank (1957)
GmbH (Gesellschaft mit beschränkter Haftung)	Limited liability company
Günstigkeitsprinzip	Principle stating that individual labour contracts may only deviate from collective agreements if such a deviation is to the advantage of the employee
GWB (Gesetz gegen Wettbewerbsbeschränkungen)	Competition law
Handwerksordnung	Craft codes
Industrie- und Handelskammer Handwerkskammer	Regional chambers of commerce
Kombinate	State enterprises in the former GDR
Landwirtschaftliche Produktionsgenossenschaften (LPG)	Agricultural co-operatives in the former GDR
Langzeitarbeitslose	Long-term unemployed (over one year)
Marktbeherrschende Unternehmen	Market dominating companies
Meisterprüfung	Formal qualification for craftsmen (second degree)
Mitbestimmungsgesetz	Law granting substantial rights of consultation, information and co-determination to employees of corporations with more than 2000 employees
Monopolkommission	Federal commission reviewing concentration processes and providing expertise in merger cases

Personalkostenzuschuss-Programm	Programme providing subsidy for employment of R&D personnel
Soziale Marktwirtschaft	Social market economy
Sozialleistungsquote	Social security expenditure as a proportion of GDP
Sozialplan	Social plan to be negotiated between management and employees in cases of mass lay-offs (of more than 10% of a firm's employees)
Statistisches Bundesamt	Central Statistics Agency
Subsidiaritätsprinzip	Principle of subsidiarity: principle whereby decision-making is delegated to the lowest possible authority
Tarifverträge	Collective labour agreements
Treuhandanstalt	Public agency concerned with the privatisation of East German state enterprises
Umbau	Restructuring (*perestrojika*)
Wellblechkonjunktur	Continuous expansion with only minor fluctuations in growth rates

Spain

ALP	The Spanish abbreviation for liquid assets
Banco de Bilbao (nowadays, Banco Bilbao-Vizcaya)	Bank of Bilbao (one of the major Spanish banks)
Banco de España	Bank of Spain (the central bank of Spain)
Bolsa de Valores	Stock exchange market
Cajas de Ahorros	Savings banks (owned by local authorities, which have evolved from their ancient savings-bank financial activity to their present fully banking business)
Comisión Nacional de Valores	National Assets Commission (the institution with the task of surveying the solvency and fair play in the stock exchange market)
Comunidades Autónomas	Autonomous communities (the official name of Spanish regions)

Consejo General de la Formación Profesional	General Council of Occupational Training (a body composed of representatives of workers, employers and the administration responsible for designing general objectives in the area of occupational training)
Cooperativas de Crédito	Credit co-operatives (private financial institutions, operating locally, and initially created for aiding regional development and presently running as banks)
Corporación Bancaria	Banking Corporation (a banking institution created in the 1980s jointly owned by the private banks and the Banco de España, which took control over some failing banks in order to sell them after re-establishing their profitability)
Dirección General de Aduanas	General Customs Direction
Disponibilidades Liquidas	The Spanish name to designate M3, a measure of the Spanish money supply
Estatuto de los Trabajadores	Workers' Statute (the legal document which sets out the workers' rights recognised by the Constitution)
Impuesto de Compensación de Gravámenes Interiores (ICGI)	Tax to compensate for home taxation (theoretically introduced in Spain in the 1960s to tax imported products as home products, but in practice meant a protection level of two or three per cent)
Instituto de Crédito Oficial (ICO)	Official Credit Institute (which comprises several (state-owned) banking institutions, each one specialised in financial transactions for specific economic activities such as industry, shipbuilding, agriculture etc.)
Instituto Español de Emigración	Spanish Institute for Emigration (the public institution responsible for emigration issues)
Mercado Continuo	Continuous market (meaning that trade of all assets in the stock exchange market can take place at any time between 09.00 and 20.00)

Mercado de Titulos de Deuda Pública Anotados en Cuenta	Treasury bill market (where there are no 'physical' transfers of titles but accounting records on books of the institutions involved)
Pagarèo and Letras del Tesoro	Short-term treasury bills
Sociedades Mediadoras en el Mercado de Dinero	Monetary market intermediary firms (non-banking monetary institutions which operate between banks and other agents selling and buying different short-term assets)
Zonas de Urgente Reindustrialización (ZUR)	Areas of urgent reindustrialisation (areas set up in the late 1980s in an attempt to counteract the effects of the industrial restructuring process)

France

ANPE (Agence Nationale pour l'Emploi)	Employment Office
Banque de France	Central bank
CAC (Cotation Assistée en Continu)	Stock exchange quotation system
CCI (Chambre de Commerce et d'Industrie)	Chamber of Commerce
CFDT (Confédération Française Démocratique du Travail)	Trade union (left-wing)
CGT (Confédération Générale du Travail)	Trade union (communist)
COFACE (Compagnie Française d'Assurance pour le Commerce Extérieur)	Foreign trade insurance company
CNPF (Confédération Nationale du Patronat Français)	Employers' federation
DATAR (Délégation à l'Aménagement du Territoire)	Industrial Development Board
EDF (Electricité de France)	National electricity company
FO (Force Ouvrière)	Trade union (socialist)
GEN (Grandes Entreprises Nationales)	Nationalised enterprises
Grande Ecole	Specialised university level educational establishments
INSEE (Institut National des Statistiques et des Etudes Economiques)	National Statistical Office

MATIF (Marché à Terme d'Instruments Financiers)	Financial futures market
OPA (Offre Public d'Achat)	Take-over bid
PME (Petites et Moyennes Entreprises)	Small and medium businesses
RMI (Revenu Minimum d'Insertion)	Basic social security income
SA (Société Anonyme)	Public limited company
SARL (Société à Responsabilité Limitée)	Private limited company
SICAV (Société d'Investisement à Capital Variable)	Unit trusts
SME (Système Monétaire Europeen)	European monetary system
SMIC (Salaire Minimum Interprofessionnel de Croissance)	Minimum salary
TGV (Train à Grande Vitesse)	High speed train
TVA (Taxe sur la Valeur Ajoutée)	Value added tax
VRP (Voyageurs, Représentant Placier)	Salaried commercial salesmen

Italy

Cassa depositi e prestiti	State institution for financing local administrations using deposits collected by the Italian Post Office
CGIL (Confederazione Generale Italiana del Lavoro)	Left-wing workers' trade union
CISL (Confederazione Italiana Sindacati Lavoratori)	Trade union whose members are, generally, supporters of the centre
Confindustria	The most relevant organisation of the Italian entrepreneurs
EFIM (Ente partecipazione e Finanziamento Industrie Manifatturiere)	State-owned industrial group
ENI (Ente Nazionale Idrocarburi)	State-owned industrial group, basically involved in chemical and oil sectors
INAIL (Istituto Nazionale di Assicurazione per gli Infortuni sul Lavoro)	State insurance institution for workers in case of accidents
INPS (Istituto Nazionale per la Previdenza Sociale)	State insurance institution for paying pensions to the workers

IRI (Istituto per la Ricostruzione Industriale)	The most relevant state-owned industrial group
ISCO (Istituto per lo Studio della Congiuntura)	Institution for studying economic cycles
Istituti speciali di credito	Finance institutions for medium and long-term loans
Montedison	The most relevant chemical group in Italy
NEC	Regions of the North-East-Centre
RAI (Radiotelevisione Italiana)	State-owned group for radio and television
SCI	Regions of the South-Centre
SME (Società Meridionale Elettrica)	State-owned industrial group of the power supply sector
SVI.MEZ (associazione per lo sviluppo dell'industria nel Mezzogiorno)	Institution for the study of the industrialisation of the south of the country
TRI	Regions of the industrial 'triangle' (Milano–Torino–Genova)
UIL (Unione Italiana del Lavoro)	Trade union of centre-left-wing workers
USL (Unità Sanitarie Locali)	Local centres of the national health service

United Kingdom

'Chunnel'	Channel Tunnel
'Big Bang'	Deregulation of the Stock Exchange (1986)
EFTA	European Free Trade Association
G7	The seven largest western industrialised economies (USA, Japan, Germany, France, Italy, United Kindgom, Canada)
GDFCF	Gross Domestic Fixed Capital Formation
RPI	Retail Price Index
MTFS	Medium-Term Financial Strategy
PSBR	Public Sector Borrowing Requirement
DA	Development Area

MMC	Mergers and Monopolies Commission
OFI	Other Financial Institutions
SE	International (formerly London) Stock Exchange
IPD	Interest, profit and dividend payments (in relation to balance of payments)

General

CAP	Common Agricultural Policy
GATT	General Agreements on Tariffs and Trade
NIC	Newly Industrialised Countries
OECD	Organisation for Economic Co-operation and Development
OPEC	Organisation of Petroleum Exporting Countries
R&D	Research and Development
USA	United States of America
VAT	Value Added Tax

Index